To my Dearest Rod,

You got me out of so many holes, I can't remember. For those that you find remain, I never asked you about. Thanks for everything - You don't know how much I have appreciated your help & friendship over the past few years.

All my love + more

Homelessness

To the memory of my mother, Anna Cowan,
sometime Barrister and Lecturer in Law
at the Universities of Southampton, Liverpool and Bristol

Homelessness
The (In-)Appropriate Applicant

DAVID COWAN
University of Bristol

DARTMOUTH
Aldershot • Brookfield USA • Singapore • Sydney

© David Cowan 1997

All rights reserved. No part of this publication may be reproduced, stored in a retrieval system, or transmitted in any form or by any means, electronic, mechanical, photocopying, recording or otherwise without the prior permission of the publisher.

Published by
Dartmouth Publishing Company Limited
Ashgate Publishing Limited
Gower House
Croft Road
Aldershot
Hants GU11 3HR
England

Ashgate Publishing Company
Old Post Road
Brookfield
Vermont 05036
USA

British Library Cataloguing in Publication Data
Cowan, David L. (David Lockhart)
  Homelessness : the (in-)appropriate applicant. -
(Socio-legal studies)
  1. Homelessness - England 2. Homelessness - England - Moral and ethical aspects 3. Homeless persons - Government policy - England 4. Homelessness - Law and legislation - England
  I. Title
  362.5'0942'09049

Library of Congress Cataloging Card Number:
Cowan, David (David S.)
    Homelessness : the (in-)appropriate applicant. / David Cowan.
        p.   cm.
    ISBN 1-85521-531-4 (hb)
    1. Homeless persons - Government policy - England. 2. Homelessness - Law and legislation - England. 3. Housing policy - England.
    I. Title
    HV4546.A4C68   1997
    362.5'8'0942-dc21
                                                                        97-24586
                                                                           CIP

ISBN 1 85521 531 4

Printed in Great Britain by Galliard (Printers) Ltd, Great Yarmouth

Contents

Figures and tables vi
Preface vii
Abbreviations ix

1 Introduction   1
2 Appropriateness   21
3 Community care   43
4 Children   69
5 Racial harassment   97
6 Violence to women   117
7 Towards *in*appropriateness   141
8 Reforming the homelessness legislation: uses of
   *in*appropriateness   163
9 Defining *in*appropriateness   187
10 Conclusion   211

Appendix 1 Study authorities' action under the homelessness
              provisions of the Housing Act 1985   217
Appendix 2 Housing tenure in study areas   221
Appendix 3 Housebuilding in study authorities   223
Appendix 4 Study authorities' acceptances issued under
              right to buy   227
Bibliography   229
General Index   247
Index of authors cited   253

Figures and tables

Figure 1.1	Local authority dwelling sales: 1980–94	4
Figure 1.2	Dwellings built nationally: 1945–94	6
Table 5.1	Ethnic composition of study areas	105
Table A1.1	Study authorities' action under the homelessness provisions of the Housing Act 1985: 1992	217
Table A1.2	Study authorities' action under the homelessness provisions of the Housing Act 1985: 1993	218
Table A1.3	Study authorities' action under the homelessness provisions of the Housing Act 1985: 1994	219
Table A2.1	Housing tenure in study areas	221
Table A3.1	Housebuilding in study authorities: 1992	223
Table A3.2	Housebuilding in study authorities: 1993	224
Table A3.3	Housebuilding in study authorities: 1994	225
Table A4.1	Study authorities' acceptances issued under right to buy	227

Preface

This book has been in the making for about the last five years of my life. Its final publication marks the most fulfilling point of my academic life to date. There is also, however, a feeling of depression. As its tale unfolds, this book tells of people trying to do their jobs to the best of their ability but hampered by the policy of a government that initially did not seem to care but subsequently cared too much. The Housing Act 1996, which reformed the homelessness legislation, is part of a movement towards the criminalization and privatization of homelessness.

Publication of this book is also a time for personal reflection. After my black letter legal education, I was introduced to socio-legal studies while a member of the Law Department at Southampton University. Julia Fionda became my tutor in this discipline, marking the beginning of a friendship which still, I am glad to say, persists despite everything. Julia was responsible with me for designing and largely conducting the fieldwork which provides the flesh of the argument in Chapters 2-6 of this book. However, Julia's influence extends far beyond this. Thus many of the ideas which appear here were mooted by us both. Further, many of the other ideas in this book have been discussed between us. For example, Chapter 8 came from discussions that we had in 1993 about the role and influence of the media at the time of the Tories' 'back to basics' conference.

Thanks are due to all those who assisted us in conducting the fieldwork for this book (particularly Jo and Rachel) as well as those who actually took part in it. There are many others who have given of their time to read segments of the text. Comments have been received from Jonathan Montgomery, Rod Edmunds, John Lowry, Martin Loughlin, Michael Gunn, Maurice Sunkin, Robin Means, David Hughes, Martin Partington, Lois Bibbings, Jenny Steele, Andrew Sanders and Ian Ward. Ian Loveland provided some valuable comments upon conducting fieldwork in local authority homeless persons units. If I can produce a text as valuable as his, I will consider this a job well done. Lee Maitland assisted with the production of the tables in the appendices. Helen Carter showed me how to organize my bibliography using Wordperfect, and Cathy Salmon was generally pestered by me. Over the past five years I have benefited enormously from discussion with colleagues at my various places of work - Southampton, Sussex, City, King's College and Bristol - as well as at the various conferences I have attended. In the latter stages, Andrew Sanders had the misfortune to occupy the office next to mine. His influence over the final text and some of the ideas in it is substantial. The usual caveats apply.

Cut from the book at a late stage were chapters on HIV and ex-offenders. This was for two reasons: first, I/we had written on these areas before and much of what I/we had written was being unnecessarily repeated (Cowan, 1995a; Cowan & Fionda, 1994c); second, I felt that the book would lose its balance were they to be included. Most of the material used in this book is therefore entirely new, although some has been published elsewhere (see, with reference to my discussion of community care in Chapter 3 and *Awua* in Chapter 8, Cowan, 1995b and 1997) and some material gained for this book, but not used, will be published later (Cowan, forthcoming). I gratefully acknowledge the *Modern Law Review* and *Journal of Law and Society*'s copyright.

Thanks should also go to Phil Thomas, who gave a chance to a very young, green academic with no particular experience. My partner has also put up with my whining and whinging.

I chose the end of January 1997 as the cut-off point for new developments. However, since that time, the Court of Appeal have upheld Collins J's judgment in *R.* v. *Hammersmith & Fulham L.B.C. ex parte M* and the High Court has held that local authorities may find a person, who has been released from prison, intentionally homeless (*R.* v. *Hounslow L.B.C. ex parte R* (unreported, 19 February 1997).

The most significant event has, however, been the election of the Labour government on May 1. They have already consulted on minimal changes to the Housing Act 1996, saying that there is insufficient time for primary legislation. Their intention appears to be to return the homelessness legislation to its 1985 Act format. Thus, the first part of this book will retain its relevance. With Jack Straw in the Home Office, and the media in full cry, the second part of this book suggests that the move towards housing exclusion will continue apace (the current example being paedophiles).

Dave Cowan
14 July 1997

Abbreviations

CJPO Criminal Justice and Public Order Act 1994
CRE   Commission for Racial Equality
DoE   Department of Environment
DoH   Department of Health
DVU   Domestic violence unit
ECHR European Court of Human Rights
HPU   Homeless Persons' Unit
HSPT Homeless Single Persons Team
IND   Immigration and Nationality Department
IoH   Institute of Housing
RSL   Registered Social Landlord
S.I. Statutory Instrument
SSD   Social Services Department

1 Introduction

In the English social welfare system, a distinction has existed for a considerable time between those who believe that recipients of welfare assistance are 'deserving' and those who believe they are 'undeserving'. This was the inheritance embraced by Michael Portillo, then chief secretary to the Treasury, who argued that

> Help from Government has become widely available with scant regard to whether the recipients have behaved reasonably, or unreasonably, responsibly or irresponsibly. As a result the penalties for fecklessness have been diminished and the rewards for personal responsibility devalued. (See Wintour, 23 April 1994)

This concept of the deserving and undeserving poor is embedded in our social welfare legislation, taking its roots from the old Poor Law (see, for example, Cranston, 1985, p.34 ff). Indeed, the social welfare battleground in the second half of the twentieth century has this as its common thread, although it is expressed slightly differently:

> The Beveridge reforms and the post-war welfare state had talked about the individual as a 'citizen', drawing on the ideas of New Liberalism about the reciprocal relationship between the state and the citizen. The citizen in this conception had both rights and obligations.... The New Right, however, focused mainly on the citizen's obligations - talking about taxpayers and ratepayers, and the need to protect their interests against exploitation (either by 'public waste' or 'scroungers'). (Clarke et al., 1987, p.141)

The thesis of this book is the rejection of the distinction between the deserving and undeserving poor. That distinction should be regarded as a deliberate obfuscation of the principles of the Thatcher/Major administrations to which this book relates. Those principles have involved reducing welfare assistance to a 'safety net'. In any event, the debate surrounding the distinction has always been sterile, for it required the creation and propagation of stereotypes and generalizations, none of which had any empirical justification. They were simply based upon prejudice and enabled the ruling classes to characterize as well as categorize the effects of poverty. This concentration on a sharp divide has also enabled the Thatcher/Major administrations to increase the scope of the 'undeserving' as part of measures designed to reduce public expenditure. In housing, that reduction since 1979 has been so significant that local authorities became unable to build new accommodation and housing associations (and other similar organizations) find their budgets cut each year. The result of this is that only the most deserving can be successful homelessness applicants, but that the construction of that category does not always require a judgment to be made about the individual. Rather, sometimes external circumstances can define that category. Thus, in Chapter 2, I have argued that we should define this category as *the appropriate applicant*.

This housing crisis has been manifested in two seemingly contradictory contexts of the homelessness legislation. The first has required a movement towards 'partnership' (different words were employed depending upon the context in which it was used) between different agencies, whether they be statutory, voluntary or quasi-public. This policy was always expressed *positively* and was one of *social inclusion*. It had a brief vogue in government policy in the late 1980s and early 1990s. Chapters 2-6 argue that the homelessness legislation provided an inadequate structure for 'partnership' to occur in the desired way. Furthermore, the homelessness legislation apparently contradicted the approach and philosophy of the new policies. The second context 'trades in images, archetypes and anxieties, rather than in careful analyses and research findings' (Garland, 1996, p.461). This process has been partly responsible for the downgrading of responsibilities to the homeless, although the effects of that downgrading are more general. Thus this concerns *negative* images and is the catalyst of *social exclusion - the inappropriate applicant*.

The direct parallel is with the discourse of criminology, with which later chapters in this book link. Garland argues that the suggested failure of the state to control crime has led to the rise of 'a new genre of criminological discourse ... that crime is a normal, commonplace, aspect of modern society' (ibid., p.450). This has caused a new method of controlling, as opposed to the eradication of, crime to develop which he terms 'the responsibilization strategy'; that is, responsibility for crime control is more actively located in the private sector, which is to work in partnership with the state agencies.

> At the same time that the administrative machinery of the state has been devising strategies to adapt to its limitations in respect of crime control, and thus come to terms with the uncomfortable realities, the political arm of the state has frequently engaged in a form of denial which appears increasingly hysterical in the clinical sense of that term. (Ibid., p.459)

Hence the recent move towards punitive, penal policies as 'an act of sovereign might, a performative action which exemplifies what absolute power is all about' (ibid., p.461). So there is also the creation of a dualist, polarized and ambivalent criminology, which Garland describes in the following terms:

> There is a *criminology of the self*, that characterizes offenders as rational consumers, just like us; and there is a *criminology of the other*, of the threatening outcast, the fearsome stranger, the excluded and the embittered. One is invoked to routinize crime, to ally disproportionate fears and to promote preventative action. The other is concerned to demonize the criminal, to excite popular fears and hostilities, and to promote support for state punishment. (Ibid., p.461; emphasis in original.)

Adapting this terminology, this book argues that precisely the same can be seen to have operated within the context of homelessness and the decision-making processes required by the homelessness legislation. The link between the two is important. There is now a *homelessness of the self*, on the one hand, represented by current policies covering, for example, community care, children, racial harassment and violence to women. On the other hand, throughout the 1990s, the Conservatives have systematically created a *homelessness of the other*, represented by specifying particular types of housing demons – squatters, travellers, 'aggressive' beggars, asylum seekers and illegal immigrants – and particular types of homelessness demons – single mothers and queue jumpers. The practical application of the policies of 'selfness' took place at the same time as 'otherness' gained dominance. It was therefore unlikely that the requisite structures, which would have facilitated that practical application, would be put in place.

The rest of this introduction first provides details of the evidence of the state's failure in the provision of housing, which is essential background information. Second, the argument in Chapters 2-6 – that 'partnership' was unlikely to be successful in practice – will be introduced and considered through its theoretical underpinnings. Third, the methodology of the fieldwork used in those chapters will be outlined. The final section provides an outline of the argument in the subsequent chapters.

The Failure of the State and the State of Failure

Thatcher's attack on state housing was based on the following premises: as a form of tenure, it was inefficient, wasteful and costly, discouraged mobility and denied consumer choice (Cole & Furbey, 1994, pp.188-94). As a result, consistently through the 1980s, the government pursued its housing

4   Homelessness

policies first and foremost through providing local authority tenants a right to buy their properties. Subsequently, when interest in the scheme began to wane, the government increased the sweeteners given to tenants in the form of massive reductions in value, depending upon how long the tenant had occupied the property. Larger sweeteners were given to those tenants occupying less desirable properties (flats and maisonettes) although sales of these properties continued to be sluggish. Nevertheless, as Figure 1.1 shows, local authority dwelling sales remained at remarkably consistent levels, despite the operation of external factors affecting other sectors of the property market.

The programme of selling was also enhanced by innovative and diverse methods of ownership creation such as the half buy–half rent and rent-to-mortgage schemes (although take-up of the latter has been negligible). By 1988, with a substantial number of the best properties sold, the government had created so many incentives to move away from local authority tenure and in favour of housing association tenure that a substantial proportion of

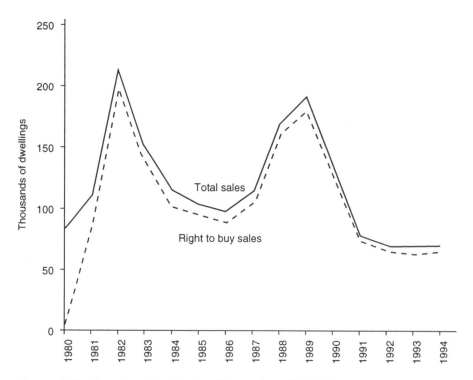

Figure 1.1   Local authority dwelling sales: 1980-94
Source: DoE 1996d

housing had been sold off *en bloc* to newly created housing associations.[1] Rumours abounded that the Conservatives' 1997 election manifesto would promise to require local authorities to transfer all their remaining stock to housing associations or the private sector. It would have been had they been elected the natural result of government policy.

Between the introduction of the 'right to buy' legislation in October 1980 and the end of June 1996, the total sales of local authority property were 1·270 million homes. Local authority tenure was therefore reduced from housing 30 per cent of the population to 22 per cent and currently stands at about 20 per cent. The authorities that assisted with the fieldwork conducted for the first part of this book have been similarly affected (for 'right to buy' statistics in our study authorities, see Appendix 4; for housebuilding in study authorities, see Appendix 3; for housing tenure in our study authorities, see Appendix 2). During the 1980s, the sale of the state's housing stock represented 43 per cent of *all* proceeds of the various privatization campaigns (Forrest & Murie, 1989). At the same time, legislatively imposed accounting practices were employed to restrict the creation of replacement dwellings (Loughlin, 1986, ch. 4; Hills, 1991, chs 6-7). Local authorities built hardly any new dwellings as Figure 1.2 shows.

The major consequences of these developments are twofold. First, local authority tenure has largely become residual because, as the better quality properties have been sold to tenants, generally poorer stock remains which nobody would buy, however great the incentive or sweetener. Second, purchasers of local authority accommodation were generally, although not exclusively, the more affluent working class who were able to afford it. The remaining rump of local authority tenants comprise the most marginalized and excluded who most commonly require state support (Forrest & Murie, 1991, pp.65-85).

Local authority *management* has also been subjected to similar processes, for authorities are required to be 'enablers' (DoE, 1987) or to facilitate the development and propagation of other forms of tenure in their areas. Management has been subjected to the supposed rigours of the private sector by authorities being required to engage in the process of offering it to the private sector through the policy of compulsory competitive tendering. Recent quasi-legislation now requires local authorities to contract out their housing allocations and homelessness services. 'Tenants' choice', a heavily publicized policy after its introduction in Part IV of the Housing Act 1988, enabled local authority tenants to vote to transfer the management of their properties to alternative bodies. Its abolition in the Housing Act 1996 was explained by the then housing minister who said that the policy itself was 'silly, ineffective, adversarial, lengthy and costly' (H.C. Standing Committee G, Twenty Sixth Sitting, col. 1041 *per* David Curry).

6 *Homelessness*

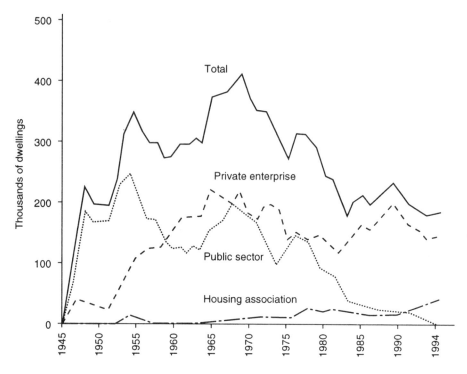

Figure 1.2 Dwellings built nationally: 1945-94
Source: DoE 1996d

The systematic destruction of the state's provision of housing was therefore a lynchpin of Conservative housing policy. However, it left a gaping hole in the provision of low-income housing. The Conservatives preferred to fill that gap through the vehicle of housing associations, which are (largely) non-profit-making organizations. Housing associations are currently funded partly by government and partly through private finance, but are regulated indirectly through the government's quango, the Housing Corporation, which is also responsible for handing out public money to housing associations. Housing association tenure has only increased slightly (to around 10 per cent). Successive budgets have reduced the level of available grant and so greater reliance has been forced upon the private sector which, in turn, requires greater risk taking (see, for example, Harrison, 1992; Randolph, 1993; Stewart, 1996, ch. 5). If housing associations are unable to pay their interest payments, the ultimate threat is insolvency. The result of this has been that housing associations are unable to 'take the strain' of providing the numbers of homes required (on current estimates, anything between 40 000 and 100 000 units of accommodation). It has been suggested that the effects of the 1996 budget will be that the number of homes produced over the next year will miss the government's target 'by a wide margin' (Coulter, 4 December 1996).

Reliance has also been placed on reinvigorating the private sector rental market (see, for example, Crook & Kemp, 1996). However, significant problems exist with this tenure. There has been a historic decline in the rental market, for a number of reasons (see Kemp, 1993) which the Conservative's policies of deregulation and decontrol have only stemmed (Crook & Kemp, 1996). It appears that a further factor responsible for this stemming – recession – had been ignored by the government in the drive to deregulate the market further (Crook & Kemp, 1996). Two crucial repercussions require consideration: first, when the market improves, many of these properties will be sold back to owner-occupation; second, even given the increase in the rental market, many landlords do not wish to rent to those in receipt of housing benefit (Bevan *et al.*, 1995). Thus this market is often too expensive for those with low or no income.

Initial success of owner-occupation has been superseded by its apparent failure, symbolized by the judicial acceptance of a new phrase: 'negative equity' (see *Palk v. Mortgage Services Funding Ltd* [1993] Ch. 330). Mortgage repossessions and negative equity have created a market in themselves. In the 1990s, in a survey of 31 lenders, repossessions leapt to an all-time high of 68 600 in 1992, falling to 45 800 in 1995, and then increasing slightly to 46 290 in 1996 (Ford, 1996, p.24). In addition, more than 211 000 households owed more than six months' mortgage payments and 85 000 owed more than 12 months' (ibid., p.26). It is hardly surprising that, apparently, 61 per cent of home owners 'strongly agree' that 'the government should expand council housing' (Denny & Ryle, 10 December 1996).

The homelessness statistics suggest a deep-rooted crisis. In England in the 1990s, the homelessness statistics have not fallen below 120 000, reaching a peak in 1992 at 142 890. That the numbers of households accepted as homeless appear to have declined from the peak of 1992 unfortunately tells us nothing. As is pointed out in Chapter 2, the definitions of homelessness are related to the availability of accommodation in the area. If there is no accommodation available in the area, it is likely that few people (if any) will be found homeless. In other words, if local authorities find fewer people to be homeless that is a more potent sign of crisis than an increase in numbers of homeless (because in the latter case the assumption is that there will be more available accommodation). Furthermore, each local authority interprets the legislation and collates its homelessness statistics *differently*. As will become apparent, some local authorities even take an estimate for the purpose of central data collection. So the homelessness statistics only *suggest* a housing crisis. They can do no more.

Creating 'the Appropriate Applicant'

Chapters 2 to 6 use the findings of a fieldwork study in 15 local authorities to sketch a context of the implementation of the homelessness legislation as it was in 1993-4 (Housing Act 1985, Part III). This context was the increasing need for homelessness officers to work in partnership or together with other organizations. The thesis running through these chapters is that the homelessness legislation provided an inadequate basis for these relationships to be fostered (Chapter 2) and that this resulted in successful applicants being defined by reference to these relationships rather than on the basis of the legislation.

The implementation of community care and the Children Act 1989 seemed to require homelessness officers to work closely with social services departments (hereafter SSDs) in planning, assessing and providing housing to those categories of persons (Chapters 3 and 4, respectively). Each of these chapters is structured so that the first substantive section outlines the housing obligations and powers created by the new legislation upon local authority homeless persons units (hereafter HPUs), the effect that the new legislation had on SSDs, and the effect each has had on HPUs.

Next, other non-legislative developments, such as guidance or research reports, have encouraged agencies (including HPUs) to work together. Two significant developments have occurred in the field of racial harassment and violence to women (Chapters 5 and 6, respectively). These chapters are structured so that prominence is initially given to the formulation of government policy and the way government believed this should affect HPU policy (if at all). Consideration is then given to whether HPU policy has been affected by these exhortations.

Throughout each chapter, our purpose is to consider the practical effect these relationships had upon the planning and assessment practices of 15 local authority HPUs. Here, the scene is set by providing a more theoretical discussion of what is meant by the word 'partnership' and considering the general problems inherent in implementing 'partnership'. The central point is a simple one: because the homelessness legislation did not provide an appropriate context for these relationships to prosper this had a dramatic effect on homelessness decision-making practices.

'Partnership' and the Limits to this Study

It should be stressed at the outset that the current endorsements of partnership are not new. There is a considerable history of exhortations, statutory and non-statutory, towards partnership (see Challis *et al.*, 1988; Hague *et al.*, 1996, ch. 2). Partly because of this long history, no concrete definition of partnership can be provided. It must be moulded in its particular context (see Kaganas, 1995). This is compounded by the different phrases used to describe the type of partnership required. The Children Act Guidance discussed 'partnership' but also 'inter-agency co-operation'; community care guidance required a 'seamless service' and 'joint assessments'; the response to racial harassment and violence to women was framed in terms of 'inter-agency co-operation' or 'multi-agency working'. These different terms generate two further organizational problems: first, it becomes clear that we are not discussing relationships between two organizations only – the term 'multi-agency' explicitly suggests many different agencies are involved; second, different partners may be appropriate at different times – hence the need for a 'seamless service'.

It is perhaps invidious to define a concept by reference to its possible effects on a sample. However, our fieldwork provided the context within which our understanding of 'partnership' begins and, to a certain extent, ends. For all the many uses of the concept in government legislation and policy, none provides any definition or any structure of the way 'partnership' is to be put into practice. Thus the HPUs in our study struggled in their own individual ways to come to terms with their decreased remit and other agencies' increased remit. It follows that each HPU put 'partnership' into practice in its own way, making any definition practically impossible. At one end of the spectrum this might have involved joint assessments by individuals from different agencies sitting as a panel. At the other end of the spectrum it might have involved a bloody-minded refusal to enter into any form of communication with other agencies. Arrangements may fall within a spectrum ranging from formal partnership to informal partnership. Kaganas notes that 'defining partnership is beset by difficulties. Not suprisingly, this uncertainty makes its implementation problematic. And even to the extent that we understand what is required, working in partnership is no simple matter' (Kaganas, 1995, p.4).[2]

This study is, however, delimited by a number of factors. In designing our research and compiling our research data, we were concerned to find out how, if at all, 'partnership' affected the process of assessing whether particular applicants fell within the necessary criteria in order to be accepted for permanent accommodation under the homelessness legislation. One might have postulated that the effect of the battery of new legislation and guidance would be reflected in the way(s) in which decisions were reached, the formulation of policy and/or actual decisions, even though much of it was not included in the homelessness Code of Guidance. For example, an

HPU might have had a policy of accepting few people under the age of 18 prior to the Children Act. Implementation of the Children Act might have had a number of different effects on that policy: the HPU might have sought more advice or guidance from the SSD, possibly involving the latter in the homelessness decision making at appropriate moments; the HPU policy might have been altered to reflect the scope of the Children Act; decisions made in individual cases might be affected because of that Act; or there might have been no change.

The more limited sense in which the term 'partnership' is used actually involves an implicit or explicit move away from privatization. Indeed, our use of the term involves a move towards increased bureaucratization, with more state agencies and other bodies involved in an assessment which is required to be made by the HPU itself. Partnership therefore involves an increase in the State's powers but this is precisely because of the failure of the market economy: 'A single-minded pursuit of narrow or personal interests may be compatible with a market economy, but its limits are the fundamental reason for espousing collective action in the first place and for valuing responsive and responsible governance' (Webb, 1991, p.233). Even though these are government policies, one might therefore anticipate that the Thatcher/Major governments would not have approached them favourably.

The second limitation on this study is that we were concerned at the outset to limit the scope of our fieldwork to a discussion of the homelessness decision-making process. We did not extend our consideration to the provision of accommodation to successful applicants. Our fieldwork was designed to ignore the partnership that is required once a person has been housed by the authority or some other body. The general availability of accommodation, or rather the HPU's own perception of the availability of accommodation, remains a crucial context of the decision-making process (see Loveland, 1995, and Chapter 2 of the present volume). However, our concern about this was reflected only in the general considerations that affect the decision-making process.

Why is 'Partnership' so Hard to do?

General themes There is little doubt that, as Chapters 2–6 testify, partnership is extremely hard to bring about. Often our interviewees argued that their resources (that is, units of accommodation and their time) and the limited resources available to their partner organizations stifled any attempts that they made at partnership. While that context provided an important and undeniable foundation, we should also bear in mind that HPU resources can usually be found if necessary (see, for example, Chapter 4). Thus other analyses must be considered.

The first point that must be made is that what partnership (in the sense in which this volume uses that term, in any event) requires is an acceptance of another's discipline and, as such, 'is so very hard to do' (see Fish, 1994). Fish argues:

> the question is, does the practice of importing into one's practice the machinery of other practices operate to relax the constraints of one's practice? And the answer I would give is no, because the imported product will always have the form of its appropriation rather than the form it exhibits 'at home'; therefore, at the very moment of its introduction, it will already be marked by the discourse it supposedly 'opens'. When something is brought into a practice, it is brought in in terms the practice recognizes; the practice cannot 'say' the Other but can only say itself, even when it is in the act of modifying itself by incorporating material hitherto alien to it. (Fish, 1994, p.239).

Fish is arguing that the term 'interdisciplinarity' conceals the fact that our own disciplines dictate the way we receive information and knowledge. The same can be suggested of the HPUs in this study, which have their own methods of seeking information and sifting out the relevant from the irrelevant. This is particularly so when they have to work with related, but alien, disciplines such as SSDs (see the distinction between 'people processing' and 'people changing' below).

For the purposes of this study, a further general consequence of the move to partnership is that forcing or exhorting different organizations to engage in partnership involves suggesting that these organizations do not have supremacy within their own areas. This is particularly important within the context of the homelessness legislation because for some time there had been no great pressure on HPUs to work with other agencies in their decision-making practices and policies. Consequently, HPUs had operated independently. The introduction of partnership in the context of the topics covered by this part of the book, as well as other areas such as asylum and immigration policy, therefore could be seen as a threat to that independence. A move from independence implied a further threat to this supremacy because no one agency could be regarded as the 'sole posssesor of necessary expertise in the area' (Langan, 1993).

Chapter 2 suggests that the reason why this independence arose in the first place was that HPUs and housing departments had the stock of housing. It was therefore natural to give them the housing obligations and powers. However, when it came to bargaining with other organizations, their retention of the resource (that is, housing) was critical because that resource could only be allocated by them. The introduction of community care and the Children Act 1989 subtly altered that position of bargaining supremacy but, as Chapters 3 and 4 point out, this was done in such a way as to obfuscate the criteria governing allocation. It was simply presumed, on the face of the various pieces of legislation and guidance, that different allocation criteria could be subsumed within one overall structure. As Webb suggests, 'Complex and multifaceted problems cry out for systematic and well ordered responses, yet the reality is all too often a jumble of services fractionalised by professional, cultural and organizational boundaries and by tiers of governance' (Webb, 1991, p.229).

It will be argued below that these 'complex and multifaceted problems' were 'fractionalized', not by the institutional boundaries or by the tiers of governance, but because of the inadequacy of the homelessness legislation and Code of Guidance. I will therefore be trying to change the focus of attack from the agencies themselves to the methods employed by the government to implement their policies. The creation of policies after the homelessness legislation made that legislation seem anachronistic. In other words, *the government provided an inadequate structure within which partnership was supposed to work.* It was hardly surprising that the agencies chosen to fulfil the policy aims were 'fractionalized'.

Theoretical models The above represents what has been termed the 'benevolent' model of partnership, described by Sampson *et al.* as 'paternalistic corporatism' (1988, p.481). However, I do not subscribe to the view that there was 'an unproblematic consensus on aims and objectives' (ibid.). The precise point of this study was to show that no such consensus existed. Nor could it have existed given the state of the guiding legislation, quasi-legislation and guidance. The benevolent analysis has usually been contrasted with the 'conspiratorial' model which views partnership as 'potentially having social control and civil liberties implications in terms of greater surveillance of service users and others, and the possible domination of community agencies by the police in particular' (Hague *et al.*, 1996, p.7). Such potential exists within the bounds of this study. For some time, the government's conceptualization of homelessness had been betrayed by its notion of partnership. In other words, homelessness is not a product of social and structural (in)justice, but a product of individual dysfunctionalism requiring the curative effect of agencies such as the SSD and also the private sector. This also required a movement away from the perception that homelessness particularly affected certain groups of people, such as women (see, for example, Gilroy & Woods, 1994), children (see, for example, Thornton, 1990) and other more marginal groups, such as those with physical difficulties (see, for example, Morris, 1990; Oliver, 1995) or ethnic minorities (see, for example, MacEwan, 1991), who are all particularly adversely affected by the housing market. Carlen refers to these as 'precipitating causes' of homelessness (Carlen, 1994, p.18). These, or some of them, are the people for whom the market has failed and for whom the state should provide.

However, the failure of the state to provide housing has led to these groups becoming further marginalized because of the influence of the caring – and therefore paternalistic (see Oliver, 1995) – professions. On this view, the government has engineered a move to view homelessness as dysfunctionalism caused by its own failure to provide. Such has been this ideological shift that the bargaining power has shifted with it, with SSDs being given duties to provide accommodation which overlap with and possibly also overcome the (limited) obligations imposed on HPUs and housing departments. This *ideological* element to the thesis therefore becomes central and provides a link between the chapters of this book.

If other agencies' involvement in individual assessments became a prerequisite of a 'good' assessment, this also implied a 'greater surveillance' by those other agencies because of their increased involvement.[3] However, this only raises the critical issue: if the HPU does not want to involve those other agencies then it will not do so. The 'conspiracy theory' will only operate when partnership occurs. However, even when partnership cannot be avoided, the process is fraught with tension.

Hudson suggests that, given some scope for collaboration exists, there are three foci which explain how partnership might develop: the environmental context, the comparative properties approach and the collaborative links themselves. The *first* suggests that the environment 'may create the necessary preconditions for inter-organisational relations by affecting the ability of organisations to function independently' (Hudson, 1987, p.176). Thus the environment of welfare organizations has been significantly altered by successive government legislation and media pressure, so that they are now guided by a management ethos. The environmental (or legislative, quasi-legislative and exhortational) landscape also changed so as apparently to enhance partnership but in an atmosphere where there was an uncertainty as to the structure of the relationships which were being created. Organizations were being told that they should not operate independently, but without being told how to facilitate partnership.

The *comparative properties approach* is split into five separate compartments: interorganizational homogeneity, domain consensus, network awareness, organizational exchange and alternative resource sources. Each of these raises particular issues for this study, because each of these suggests both 'structural' and 'organizational' conflict (Molnar & Rogers, 1979) between the various organizations involved in the partnerships we consider. Homogeneity refers to 'functional and structural similarity' although 'one obstacle to more fruitful collaboration is the difference in value systems and goals among the participants' (Hudson, 1987, p.177). Further, Hudson suggests a distinction between 'people processing' agencies, which control access to resources, such as housing, and 'people changing' agencies, 'whose explicit function has been to change client behaviour' (ibid.). This study suggests that the legislation affecting the former was the primary cause of the 'differences in value systems and goals' in relationships with the latter.

With reference to domain consensus, 'First, it requires agreement on specific organisational goals. Second, it assumes a compatibility of organisational goals, philosophies and reference orientations. Finally, it requires some agreement amongst kindred professionals upon their position in a hierarchy of professionals' (ibid.). In Chapters 2-6, it becomes more apparent that domain consensus is lacking because of the structural and organizational conflict that existed as a result of the government's inadequate and incoherent framework for partnership. The same criticism can be made within the next two aspects of the 'comparative properties' approach. Hudson asserts that network awareness can only exist if the agencies 'perceive a possible matching of goals and resources that would result in more effective goal achievement' and that organizational exchange requires reciprocity. Furthermore, the existence of alternative resource sources (such as private sector accommodation) enabled HPUs and other organizations within our study occasionally to evade partnership (see especially Chapter 4, which indicates that each agency apparently used the private sector as an evasionary measure).

The third model requires a focus on *the collaborative links themselves*. Hudson identifies four 'key dimensions' used to analyse these links: their degree of formalization, degree of intensity, degree of reciprocity and degree of standardization. In Chapters 2-6, different degrees of formalization can be seen not only (*supposedly*) guiding the relationships themselves but also (*supposedly*) governing the HPUs' assessment criteria. It is necessary to juxtapose the word 'supposedly' with these because often such formalized policies were routinely avoided. Indeed, one of the general findings of our fieldwork was that policies imposed on HPUs were avoided or evaded (if they were known by officers) whereas administrative practices which the officers themselves had built up became standardized without necessarily being written down. Furthermore, partnership often was not facilitated by formality; rather, it was stimulated by informality. Thus degrees of formalization appeared to have the opposite effect of their intentions. The same therefore also applies to the degree of intensity, reciprocity and standardization, although here too the legislative, quasi-legislative and exhortatory mechanisms stand in the way of coordinated strategies.

It will be apparent from the above that I am committed to showing how these mechanisms have made participation in the current climate practically impossible, despite the best intentions of the agencies involved. However, I am also committed to the less easily established view that this was entirely intended by government, which is desperately trying to discredit local government at every juncture.

Methodology[4]

Over the period of December 1993 to August 1994, 15 English local authority HPUs were visited. Authorities were chosen on the basis of geographical location, political affiliation, size, housing tenure and numbers of homelessness applicants. The appendixes contain the relevant information in tabular format, for the years 1992-4 where available. Additionally, they were split between 'unitary' authorities (where the various departments, such as the HPU and SSD, fell within the same administrative structure) and non-unitary authorities (where the HPU was located at borough, city or district council level and the SSD at county council level).

Each factor was crucially relevant because different policies or problems might be expected in different areas on the basis of any of these factors. Initially, we chose 15 authorities on consideration of these variables. However, if one authority pulled out of our fieldwork, it was replaced by a similar authority. The key number for us was 15 because we believed that this was a sufficient number from which we could draw some strands.

Our 10 non-unitary authorities are referred to as LA1-LA10. Of these authorities, three were Labour-controlled (LA1, LA2, LA3). LA1 and LA2 were both large city authorities in central England. They had a larger than average stock of accommodation, although LA2's was mainly one-bedroom accommodation. LA3 was a northern former mining town which also had a significant public housing stock. Three authorities were Conservative-controlled (LA4, LA6, LA8). Of these, LA4 was a small, largely rural authority in the south of England. LA6 was an eastern authority which had three large towns in its catchment area. LA8, on the other hand, was a middle to northern authority set in a largely rural area but with three towns on its border. Two authorities were controlled by the Liberal Democrats (LA5, LA7) and both comprised coastal areas. Thus the private sector was well developed and there was a significant private sector (holiday) rental market. In the other two authorities (LA9 and LA10), no political party had overall control. LA9 was in the middle of England and LA10 was in the east, but both were based in and around large towns.

Our unitary authorities, which were all situated in London, are referred to in the text as LB1-LB5. Of these, LB1 and LB2 were Conservative-controlled, while LB3 was in the hands of the Liberal Democrats; these were outer London boroughs. Both LB4 and LB5 were inner city areas where there were more significant levels of deprivation, partly shown by the housing tenure. These were the only areas in the study where there were fewer households as owner-occupiers than there were in other tenures (see Table A2.1).

The relevance of having a balance between unitary and non-unitary authorities lay in the apparent belief that partnership might have been easier in unitary authorities. One reason for reorganization of local government in the English shires was the apparent non-relationship between housing departments and SSDs. At the time of our fieldwork, the shire authorities were two-tier: SSDs formed part of the administrative make-up of county councils, whereas HPUs formed part of borough, city or district councils. As a result these two bodies often had non-coterminous boundaries and politics. The situation was different in London and metropolitan boroughs because HPUs and SSDs formed part of the administrative structure of the same authority. One of the prime aims of the Local Government Commission in its review of local government throughout the shire areas was said to be that unitary authorities 'offer the opportunity for improved coordination, quality and cost-effectiveness in the delivery of local government services' (DoE, 1991b).[5] Our interest in unitary authorities was, therefore, whether they would indeed provide better coordination. If they did not, then one might postulate that the failure lay not in the structure of local government but elsewhere, possibly in the legislation itself. Our London authorities therefore provided a crucial test of our thesis in Chapters 2-6.

The fieldwork was based on a series of taped semi-structured, informal interviews with officers in the HPU. All interviewees were informed that their identities would be kept anonymous and, furthermore, that we would not quote directly from them.[6] Only three HPUs had reasonably close professional relations with the SSD (LA3, LA5, LB5) and so we interviewed the relevant SSD liaison personnel there as well. Our practice in larger authorities was to interview a representative sample of interviewing and assessing officers as well as the principal and senior officers. In medium-sized authorities, our practice was to interview as many of the members of the HPU as was possible. In smaller authorities, such as LA4 and LA5, where there were fewer than four members of the HPU, all were interviewed. Altogether, approximately 90 interviews were conducted and then transcribed. Further details of the organization of HPUs and other matters are brought out at appropriate moments in each chapter.

A key criticism which might have been made of this fieldwork design is that, if this part of the book is about partnership, then surely it should have been necessary to interview a more balanced sample, including (for example) members of the SSD, Women's Aid, groups representing ethnic minorities, and so on. However, had we designed our fieldwork in that way, we would have set ourselves a potentially endless task. Furthermore, access to HPUs proved to be difficult enough, let alone access to these different organizations. Such justifications were purely practical and therefore pale into insignificance against the substantive justifications for our design. The primary purpose of this project always concerned the factors which influenced and assisted homelessness officers in their criteria and decision-making practice under the homelessness legislation. In other words, our key concern was access to housing. Access to housing was essentially (in this context) governed by the homelessness legislation under which homelessness officers assessed individual applicants through the homelessness criteria. This project therefore was intended to supplement the literature that discusses the thought processes of homelessness officers (see, for example, Loveland, 1995). The secondary purpose relied upon a more general belief which was inherent in my notion of partnership: adequate housing is the essence of a successful after-care programme. Thus, for example, housing had been spoken of as being the 'foundation' of community care, a 'critical element' in the programme of protection of persons subjected to violence, and essential to the well-being of children. Access to housing was therefore the key issue.

Creating 'the Inappropriate Applicant'

Having considered the problems faced by those who might have been supposed to have been included within the scope of the homelessness legislation, the second part of this book turns to an explicit discussion of the processes which have, in the 1990s, been responsible for the creation of housing *exclusion*. It is argued that exclusion has been primarily the result of the deficiency in the supply of available accommodation. Hence the need to reduce demand. The method used to reduce demand has been to scapegoat certain supposed groups of people who are then regarded as so inappropriate as not to require housing and/or other welfare services. It is noticeable that this context has been absent from the relevant debates. Rather, the focus has been upon the inappropriateness of the supposed groups themselves. In other words, *the move towards penalization has covered up the failure of the state to provide housing.*

Classic examples of this trend in the 1990s can be seen occurring in relation to squatters and travellers, 'aggressive' beggars, asylum seekers and others coming from abroad (see Chapter 7). Each of these supposed groups at one time or another may have fallen within the ambit of the homelessness legislation. Each is similarly regarded as 'taking advantage' of the system. Thus, for example, travellers with no pitch are (still) regarded as homeless but excessively penalized through criminal law, as exemplified by the Criminal Justice and Public Order Act. The recent debate about begging has resulted in a call for the return of the workhouse. Asylum seekers and certain persons from abroad, whether or not they have any form of financial assistance, are now not entitled to any form of financial assistance or state housing. In the context of this general movement towards penalization, judicial decisions in these areas have often been portrayed as being anti-government' and this has further fuelled the belief in appropriateness. In fact, the judiciary have hardly made radical decisions but the subsequent negative publicity has marginalized them.

Chapter 8 concentrates on the arguments used by the Conservative government to undermine the homelessness legislation itself. It is suggested that there were three such arguments. First, the wrong people or the 'non-genuine' were being allocated accommodation through the homelessness legislation. This group was implicitly and explicitly single mothers. Second, the homelessness legislation created a 'perverse incentive' to be found homeless because homeless people were able to jump the housing queue. Third, implicitly, there was too much demand for an insufficient supply of accommodation which had to be rationed. Concentration on the first two meant that the third critical reason could be ignored. The public discourse only ever concerned the first two rationales. In fact, there was no evidence to justify the first assertion and the available evidence suggested that the second assertion was incorrect. Furthermore, the proposals which the government came up with in 1994 actually only addressed the third rationale. The judiciary, that supposed radical body, accepted the second assertion as gospel truth, which led to a decision which was broadly in line with the government's own policy.

The final substantive chapter considers whether and how far the legislation which has brought into effect many of the last government's policies reflects any of the three rationales. It is argued that the new legislation solely concerns reducing demand for accommodation through *denial*, *deterrence* and *privatization*. There is, however, also evidence of a policy preference in favour of 'married couples'. The discussion then proceeds to consider the effect on 'partnership' and the specific issues covered in Chapters 2-6. It is argued that, if HPUs found it hard to come to terms with central government policies before, they will find it all but impossible to do so in the new political climate of attrition, retribution and elimination.

Notes

1 Early research suggests that, ironically, this was a subversion of central government

policy because properties were being transferred from one large monopoly provider to another. Further, the latter were usually staffed by the former. So, in other words, these transfers, known as large-scale voluntary transfers, were methods used by local authorities to keep control of their properties while at the same time benefiting their funding arrangements (see generally Mullins *et al.*, 1993).

2 Kaganas cites Tunnard's confident definition of partnership as 'sharing. It is marked by respect for one another, role divisions, rights to information, accountability, competence and value accorded to individual input. In short, each partner is seen as having something to contribute, power is shared, decisions are made jointly, and roles are not only respected but are also backed up by legal and moral rights' (Tunnard, 1991, p.1). Such a definition also defines partnership through a model of implementation, although this is best described as utopian.

3 A particularly good example of this has been the changed role of HPU officers when dealing with applicants seeking asylum or whose immigration status is dubious.

In these cases, a combination of the Asylum and Immigration Appeals Act 1993, *R. v. Secretary of State for the Environment ex parte Tower Hamlets L.B.C.* (1993) 25 H.L.R. 524, Asylum and Immigration Act 1996, Housing Act 1996, Parts VI & VII has resulted in homelessness officers being forced to adopt surveillance approaches. These are considered briefly in Chapters 8 and 9. Their implementation came after our fieldwork had been designed and commenced and therefore is not included in the earlier chapters of this book. However, it involves the Immigration and Nationality Department (IND) in receiving information about all potential asylum seekers and illegal immigrants who apply for housing. Thus the IND is able to control the assessment of the application as well as pursue its own objectives 'rather than engaging in inter-agency work in the spirit of mutual consultation and shared agreement of goals and objectives' (Sampson *et al.*, 1988, p.480).

4 The fieldwork for this book was designed and largely completed by myself and Julia Fionda.

5 There is some doubt as to the precise reasons why the government pursued, and continued to pursue, the course of creating more unitary authorities: see Pycroft (1995); Leach (1994). However, such was the strength of the aim to create more unitary authorities that, when John Banham (the Commission's chairman) suggested that many areas should remain as they were, he was dismissed, or resigned (McHardy, 3 March 1995). The other members of the Commission were said to be 'near mutiny' by Professor Malcolm Grant (Simmons, 25 March 1995). On 21 March 1995, 15 new unitary authorities were announced and Grant was made the new chairman of the Commission (McHardy, 22 March 1995).

6 It was believed that this would enable officers to speak more freely to us, using terminology and metaphors that they might not have otherwise used.

2 Appropriateness

The homelessness legislation does not and no doubt will never provide the relevant criteria which determine an individual's housing need. Even if adequate housing were not regarded as an absolute need (cf. Doyal & Gough, 1991, pp.22–47, 196–9) and one therefore adopted a relativist form of need, the homelessness legislation and its antecedents never concerned need. Legislation has always required us to oppress the homeless by making *moral judgments*, not about their housing need, but about *why* the homeless become homeless in the first place. Furthermore, the relationship between the criteria through which local authorities made (and make) these moral judgments have, since 1977, also explicitly been related to the *supply* of available units of accommodation.

Thus a successful homeless applicant is defined by reference to our perceptions of their deservingness as well as our perceptions of supply. Successful homeless applicants are not defined by reference to their need for accommodation. After all, if they were, the government in power (particularly the Thatcher/Major governments) would have had to revise its housing policies and ideology. The only distinction between the current system and that which obtained before 1977 is that, arguably, the type and quality of accommodation provided to the successful homeless applicant has improved (although this has occasionally been open to doubt: see for example, Watchman, 1988). Whereas in times gone by recipients of Poor Law 'relief' had to wear a P on their shoulder (Cranston, 1985, p.35), homeless people do not at present have a similar punishment imposed on them. Nevertheless, the metaphorical effect can be similar.

We should not be surprised by this. The inheritance embraced by the homelessness legislation, from the various Poor Laws to the National Assistance Act, 1948 (which supposedly abolished the Poor Laws) to the various interdepartmental circulars about the implementation of the 1948 Act and the way in which that Act was administered, was difficult to shake off, as hard as some people tried. For example, the BBC television play *Cathy Come Home* was in many ways the pivotal moment in the modern development of the homelessness legislation (see Loveland, 1991a). The play provided a vivid portrayal of a blameless two-parent family which became homeless, separated, had their children taken into care and received dormitory-type accommodation from administrators more concerned about Cathy's spiritual and moral well-being than about her housing need. When efforts were made to redress the outrages perpetuated by that scheme in the Housing (Homeless Persons) Act 1977, the emphasis of the new scheme retained much of the old despite the initial beliefs of Stephen Ross MP, who brought forward the original bill.

This chapter's basic premise is that defining the 'appropriate applicant' involves a consideration of two related themes: first, the applicant must be, in the opinion of the person(s) administering the legislation, morally deserving; second, 'deservingness' is given a further statutory overlay, which relates it to the supply of available accommodation. Thus to describe a successful homeless applicant as simply deserving is incorrect. Rather, that person is *more* deserving, or less blameworthy (however you wish to conceptualize it), than (many) others. My point here, then, is that the deserving/undeserving distinction does not adequately demarcate the debate – hence the use of the term 'appropriate'. Furthermore, if we move away from the misconceived deserving/undeserving debate (and use a more neutral term, such as 'appropriate') the true nature of the housing crisis, deliberately obfuscated by central government, becomes more apparent. The first part of this chapter seeks to draw this notion of appropriateness from the debates leading to, and effect of, legislation and quasi-legislation since 1948.

Use of this more neutral terminology also allows us to provide our own overlay and the basis for a discussion about the factors outside the legislation that nevertheless might affect the decision-making process and thus the notion of appropriateness. One example of that is Ian Loveland's work (which is heavily drawn upon in this chapter: Loveland, 1991a), which has sought to show the types of factors that might influence the decision-making process (for example, Loveland, 1987, 1988, 1991b, 1995). This has been important and in many ways pathbreaking research, particularly as it shows the effect of judicial review on decision-making practices. However, my main point is somewhat different: even where an applicant should be regarded as appropriate or more deserving, there are other factors which may affect the decision. Chapters 3-6 will discuss the way relationships between different organs of local government affect the homelessness decision-making process. Thus concentration in the second part of this chapter is on the way the homelessness legislation has constructed the parameters of these relationships.

The third section of this chapter concerns the way the judiciary have constructed the (in)appropriate applicant. This is not particularly innovative material and I do not want to spend too much time on it. However, the judicial interpretation of the homelessness legislation to 1995 (case law after this date is considered in Chapters 7 and 8) was largely so negative that, in these times of the supposed 'radical judiciary', we still need to dissect carefully some of the judgments.

Having crafted the material into this structure, there is still an important jump, which we take in the fourth section of this chapter. Martin Partington has suggested that 'there are some who regard it as surprising that any of the prescribed objectives of legislation are ever actually achieved' (Partington, 1990, p.71). Thus we need to consider the ways in which the ideology of the homelessness legislation was translated into the practice of the authorities in our study. At this stage, this is only on a general level. This involves 'unpacking' the terminology used by the officers we interviewed to describe their role. Further light is therefore shed on the notion of 'appropriateness'.

Defining Appropriateness: 1948–94

Breaking Tradition: the National Assistance Act 1948

The National Assistance Act 1948 was part of the 'new' social welfare legislation produced by the Labour government which came to power at the end of the Second World War. Provision had been dogged by an outmoded administrative structure, which reflected the Poor Laws and their traditions. Thus section 1 of the 1948 Act pronounced that the existing Poor Law was to be repealed. Part III of the 1948 Act provided the criteria governing the provision of residential accommodation as well as temporary accommodation. Interpretation of those criteria and the duties to provide the appropriate type of accommodation were placed on the National Assistance Board and local authorities (SSDs took over under the Local Authority Social Services Act 1970). Section 21 of the 1948 Act made it a duty on those bodies to provide

> (a) residential accommodation for persons who by reason of age, infirmity or any other circumstances are in need of care and attention which is not otherwise available to them;
> (b) temporary accommodation for persons who are in urgent need thereof, being need arising in circumstances which could not reasonably have been foreseen or in such other circumstances as the authority may in any particular case determine.

Whilst paragraph (a) related to the provision of residential accommodation (see Chapter 3), paragraph (b) can fairly be described as the first modern homelessness legislation. The juxtaposition of one paragraph dealing with types of physical disability and another dealing with homelessness might lead one to believe that the latter was regarded as part of the former. Even so, the criteria in paragraph (b) reflect both moral blameworthiness and supply. Thus the section was supposed to provide for the 'unforeseen and unforeseeable misfortune' (for example, fire razing a home to the ground) and not for 'negligent' or 'foolish' action (the foreseeable eviction): H.C. Debs, Vol. 448, cols 690-92 (5 March 1948). Robson and Poustie draw attention to those

> Members of Parliament [who] forcibly argued that the effect of the foreseeability test would be to call upon local authorities to exercise an unacceptable degree of moral censorship in determining applications for assistance under the Act and, therefore, should be omitted. The Ministry of Health, however [successfully argued] that the foreseeability test would cause little practical difficulty. That view was not borne out. (Robson & Poustie, 1996, p.39)

Even though subsequent ministerial circulars suggested that the duty did extend to evictions, judicial opinion did not go this far (see Hoath, 1983, p.3; *Southwark L.B.C. v. Williams* [1971] 2 All E.R. 175). The supply element is reflected by the fact that only temporary accommodation was to be provided (cf. Housing Act 1996, Part VII) as well as by the apparently limited number of people who would fit within the criteria.[1] Such a 'permissive duty' could be defined so narrowly as to avoid any obligation.

These two elements were also the central reason for the failure of the Act when implemented. As *Cathy Come Home* visibly showed, both elements represented part of the misery of homelessness. The 1948 Act was really just an extension of the old Poor Law (see, for example, Greve *et al.*, 1971; Bailey & Ruddock, 1972; Bailey, 1973). Families were separated; people were afraid to apply in case their children were taken into care; the accommodation provided was sometimes in the form of a dormitory.

Yet in 1948, the measure was heralded by politicians on all sides. It was part of a powerful body of law 'which, by its all-embracing scope and its boldness of conception, is a tribute to the faith which the people of this country have in their future' (H.C. Debs, Vol. 448, col. 711 (5 March 1948) *per* Mr Steele). The Act remains as a tribute, in one sense, not only to the positive central/local relations at this time (see Griffith, 1966; compare the current position: Loughlin, 1994) but also to the wave of optimism that occurred at the end of the Second World War. However, even at that time, there were voices, albeit few, that cast a shadow over the self-congratulation. William Shepherd MP argued:

> It may well be that 50 years hence the then House of Commons will refer to this measure as being small, and will regard the present Minister of National Insurance as hardhearted and despotic ... Indeed, a mere change of form is not, in

itself, significant, and I share the anxiety of other members who believe that this mere change of administrative form may not result in the abolition of the Poor Law spirit. (H.C. Debs, Vol. 448, cols 745-6 (5 March 1948))

Equally, expressing a view which sums up the opinion of the disaffected, Somerville Hastings MP warned: 'Whether or not a new Poor Law arises on the ashes of the old will depend entirely on the spirit of the administration. In the past, people have been more upset over the way in which relief has been administered than by its inadequacy; people do not mind being starved so much, if it is done in a nice spirit' (Ibid., col. 744).

These views demonstrate that the 1948 Act was not as radical as may initially have appeared (and was subsequently mistakenly viewed). The Act was neither a 'long-stop' nor was it part of a cogent social welfare policy granting people 'rights' to council housing stock. It was a mere change of form designed to intimate the caring face of society (only in relation to those who deserved to see that side of the face) without adequate provision. Local authorities carried on, in the most part, using the same housing stock as they had done under the old Poor Law (Robson & Poustie, 1996, pp.40-42).

Ambivalence: 1968-77

The year 1968 heralded the publication of the influential report of the Seebohm Committee on Social Services. For the first time, this report questioned whether homelessness was a subject which fell within social work's sphere of operation, as opposed to being a housing function. The justification for this view seems to have been that it would remove the 'degrading stigmas and social distinctions' (Seebohm, 1968, para. 401). Seebohm was followed by a further government committee report, by the Central Housing Advisory Committee (CHAC, known as the Cullingworth Committee Report), on local authority housing, published in 1969. This report suggested that indicators of housing need should also include social need (CHAC, 1969, paras 56-62) and thus also homelessness, although the Committee recognized that there were insufficient data available upon which to draw such a policy (ibid., paras 328-51). To the argument that allocation on the basis of social need would lead to queue jumping, the report made the following observations:

We are convinced that these fears are greatly exaggerated. The fear of 'queue jumping' can paralyse effective action in the very areas where it is most needed. So far as discouraging some from improving their [housing] conditions is concerned, we suspect that this is also exaggerated; and *to the extent that it is true it constitutes a sad commentary on our housing policies. Policy should be directed towards helping people to improve their housing situation.* (Ibid., para. 62; emphasis added)

As well as these pivotal reports, there were others written by academics, all making the same points (see Greve *et al.*, 1971; Glastonbury, 1971).[2]

The point to which these reports were generally moving was simple. Homelessness was not a symptom of personal inadequacy. Nor was homelessness something for which (at that time) traditional methods of social work could or should largely assist. Rather, homelessness could also be seen as a symptom of the failure of the housing market (see CHAC, 1969, para. 332, where this point was mooted). Both Seebohm and Cullingworth also pointed to the fact that welfare was a function of county councils, county borough councils and, in London, the London borough councils, whereas housing was a responsibility of them all except county councils:

> From our visits and from the evidence we received, it became clear that the separation of personal social service functions from housing functions in the administrative counties creates many difficulties. ... Any successful policy for the homeless therefore depends entirely upon good co-operation being established between a county and perhaps as many as twenty or thirty district housing authorities in its area. (Seebohm, 1968, para. 388)[3]

The confusion between social need, on the one hand, and housing need, on the other, tends to characterize this period and was exacerbated by a subsequent government circular issued by the DoE and the DHSS (DoE, Circular 18/74). This circular probably represents the only government action under which the morality of the applicant's actions played no part in local authority decisions as to their appropriateness. For example: 'The government believes that all those who have no roof, or who appear likely to lose their shelter within a month, should be helped to secure accommodation by advice, preventive action or, if these are not enough, the provision, permanently or temporarily, of local authority accommodation' (para. 8). The circular accepted that some areas suffered from more acute housing stress than others and thus directed housing authorities, who became the responsible agency, in these areas to give 'first claim ... to the most vulnerable', defined as 'families with dependent children living with them or in care; and adult families or people living alone who either became homeless in an emergency such as fire or flooding or are vulnerable as a result of old age, disability, pregnancy or other special reasons' (para. 10).

Implementation of the circular, however, was a disaster. A DoE review suggested that only 60 per cent of housing authorities had accepted responsibility and, furthermore, that the principles enunciated by the circular were not being followed (DoE, Press Notice 15/12/75, No 1232; see Carnwath, 1978, p.21). The legal problem was that the Act's duties remained on SSDs, whereas Circular 18/74 placed responsibilities upon housing departments and went beyond the 1948 Act. Acts are enforceable; circulars, without the authority of acts of parliament, are only exhortatory. The practical problem was that neither agency wished to accept responsibility. Homeless people were often therefore treated as 'shuttlecocks' between the different agencies, neither of which wished to accept responsibility (see Bailey, 1976).

Appropriateness Defined: Housing (Homeless Persons) Bill 1977[4]

The Housing (Homeless Persons) Bill was introduced by Stephen Ross MP as a private Member's Bill, although it had the support of DoE,[5] and was closely modelled on Circular 18/74. Homelessness was defined as having no accommodation; the priority groups were retained under the term 'priority need'; the principle of not separating families remained an important part of the ideology;[6] and responsibility for homelessness was 'clearly in the sphere of housing' (H.C. Debs, Vol. 926, col. 899 (18 February 1977) *per* Stephen Ross) and thus was to be the responsibility of the housing department.

Nevertheless, the bill was substantially amended before being enacted, partly because of, as Loveland suggests, 'a peculiar juxtaposition of political forces' (Loveland, 1995, p.69). Some less well-meaning concepts were required to be translated into statutory form. The two initial enquiries required of local authorities - whether a particular applicant was homeless as well as being in a priority group (referred to as priority need) - were overlaid with a third and fourth enquiry - whether an applicant was 'intentionally' homeless and whether the applicant had a local connection with the authority to which application was made.

These additional enquiries are central to the argument around appropriateness. Their drafting reflected some of the more abhorrent remarks of parliamentarians. It seems to have become clear from an early stage of the parliamentary procedure that two central issues would dominate the debates. The first was the belief that some people would make themselves homeless in order to take advantage of the beneficial effects of the Act. This was variously expressed as 'self-induced' homelessness, 'self-inflicted' homelessness or 'intentional' homelessness. Second, it was believed that such people would make themselves homeless to 'jump the housing queue' (see, for example, H.C. Debs, Vol. 926, col. 914 (18 February 1977) *per* Paul Channon; ibid., cols 929-30, *per* Toby Jessel; ibid., cols 943-4 *per* Julius Silverman; ibid., cols 957-8, *per* Hugh Rossi). Nicholas Scott MP suggested: 'Scrounging has been talked about so much that people outside who read our debates may gain the impression that we think that the vast majority of the homeless are scroungers, whereas in fact they are homeless through no fault of their own' (ibid., col. 983).

The most virulent opponent to the bill, William Rees-Davies, used four examples of the types of person whom he believed exemplified the intentional scrounger and queue jumper: first, there were the rent dodgers (who were 'people who are not meeting their rent obligations, many of them quite deliberately'); second were those who 'come off the beach' during high season in a resort such as Margate (in his constituency) and require the local authority to help them; third, 'strangers to an area [who] should [not] be treated in the same way as those who are resident in the area'; the fourth category was divided into two, 'what I call the in-laws and ... the winter lettings case'. The 'in-laws' case encapsulated those who went to stay with their in-laws, caused friction and were then 'kicked out. ... They are then homeless and go to the local authority and try to crash the queue ...' The 'winter lettings' case encapsulated those people who took on a winter letting and then approached the local authority when it came to its natural conclusion (see, generally, H.C. Debs, Vol. 926, cols 972-5).

This 'indictment' was framed in terms of moral blameworthiness. This was the key to each of the examples and was expressed in terms of the reasons why the subject of each example had left their previous accommodation. It was not framed in terms of the deservingness or need of homeless persons as homeless persons. For example, earlier in the debate Rees-Davies and others had referred to homeless people, who potentially would use the legislation, as scroungers and scrimshankers, explicitly referring to the in-laws example (ibid., col. 921).[7] The queue jumping image is directly related to the availability or supply of accommodation. The Act was not allowing for more accommodation to be built – it was supposed to be cost-neutral - rather it was concerned with reordering priorities and the administration. Thus the concern of Rees-Davies and others was that this reordering would mean that homeless people would infiltrate their (apparently beautiful) areas and take housing away from their residents.

There were, of course, opposing views but political reality meant that the Bill had to be palatable across the parties. Applicants were therefore not entitled to indefinite accommodation under the Act if they were found to be intentionally homeless, whether or not they had a priority need. The intentional homelessness provision in the new Act, after several attempts at drafting it, read(s) as follows:

> a person becomes homeless intentionally if he deliberately does or fails to do anything in consequence of which he ceases to occupy accommodation which is

available for his occupation and which it would have been reasonable for him to continue to occupy (s.17(1)).

Authorities were explicitly permitted by the legislation to interpret the reasonableness criterion by reference 'to the general circumstances prevailing in relation to housing in the[ir] area' (s.17(4)). This meant that moral blameworthiness, defined as intentional homelessness, also depended upon the state of the housing market in the area. Indeed, the morality of the applicant's actions was directly linked with the issue of supply.

If an applicant was homeless, in priority need, and was not morally blameworthy in this way, such an applicant would be entitled to 'reasonable preference' on the local authority's housing waiting list. However, this would only occur if the applicant had a local connection with the authority to which the application had been made or had no local connection with any authority (s.5(1)). Where the applicant had no local connection with that authority, but did have this connection with another authority, the former could refer the applicant to the latter (s.5(3)-(6)).[8] This again was framed in the parliamentary debates along the principles of blameworthiness and supply. Rees-Davies argued in this way so that his authority would be able to say to the applicant, 'No - a pox on you. Go back to where you come from. We will not be the local authority responsible for looking after you' (H.C. Debs, Vol. 934, col. 1659 (8 July 1977)). So local connection was defined by reference to residence, economic activity in the area, family associations or 'any special circumstances' (s.18(1)).

More Statutory Appropriateness: the Puhlhofer *Amendments*

The 1977 Act was subsequently tightened up and included in the Housing Act 1985, Part III. The definition of homelessness, now in section 58, was simply having 'no accommodation'. The accommodation to be provided to the successful applicant was similarly described without any additional qualification. In *R.* v *Hillingdon L.B.C. ex parte Puhlhofer* [1986] 1 A.C. 484, the House of Lords took advantage of this by holding that a family with two children living in one room in short-term accommodation were not homeless. Lord Brightman argued: 'In this situation, Parliament plainly, and wisely, placed no qualifying adjective before the word "accommodation" in section 1 or section 4 [of the 1977 Act], and none is to be implied ... Nor is accommodation not accommodation because it might in certain circumstances be unfit for human habitation ... or might involve over-crowding' (p.517).

The Housing and Planning Act 1986 introduced two amendments to the legislation in order to combat this judicial approach. First, the definition of homelessness was amended so that the accommodation previously occupied had to have been 'reasonable for [the applicant] to continue to occupy'; reasonableness was also related to the area's housing circumstances (see the definition of intentional homelessness above). Second, the accommodation to be offered to the applicant would have to be 'suitable'.

The government initially opposed the amendments on the basis that *Puhlhofer* reflected their view, but they were subsequently persuaded by two propositions: first, the amendments would simply reverse the effect of *Puhlhofer* and reinstate earlier case law; second, the amendments did not open out the legislation because the test would remain stringent (H.L. Debs, Vol. 481, cols 739-46 (3 November 1986) *per* Baroness David). The first justification was undoubtedly open to question (Hoath, 1988). Indeed, the introduction of the reasonableness criterion and its relationship with the area's housing circumstances arguably brought the definition of homelessness within the notion of appropriateness. While this, I suggest, would not be a correct interpretation of parliamentary intention, the drafting left much to be desired because it left the correlation between homelessness and intentional homelessness unclear (see the discussion of *R. v. Brent L.B.C. ex parte Awua* in Chapter 8).

Appropriateness and the Obstacle Race[9]

In order to be successful under the 1985 Act, the local authority was required to find the applicant (a) homeless, (b) in priority need, and (c) not intentionally homeless. If the applicant was able to jump over these obstacles, the appropriate local authority (depending upon where the local connection lay) was required to provide the applicant with suitable accommodation. Much attention is (rightly) given to the notion of intentional homelessness (see, for example, Loveland, 1993). However, appropriateness was also evident, albeit less clearly, in the priority need categories (s.59). These essentially were not about need itself but which homeless people were *most* needy or *most* deserving. This section was not about prioritization either because those who did not fall within its purview, mostly single people, fell by the wayside and were not owed any duties by the local authority (other than advice and assistance). Some were in, the rest were out. Single people would generally only be in priority need if they were 'vulnerable as a result of old age, mental illness or handicap or physical disability or other special reason' (s.59(1)(c)). Thus, somewhat ironically, the priority need categories were neither about prioritization, nor about absolute or relative need.

Even if applicants were decided to be homeless and in priority need, they still were required to cross the obstacle of intentionality before they could be regarded as successful. The notion of the homelessness legislation as an obstacle race was therefore most apposite. At every stage, the questions which the applicant was required to answer were designed to catch the applicant out. Furthermore, these questions were generally related to the housing circumstances of the area, whatever that meant. So moral blameworthiness is related to (a) the type of accommodation which the applicant had left or was currently living in, (b) the reason(s) why the applicant left or was having to leave their last accommodation, (c) the supply of accommodation in the area, and (d) the reason(s) why the applicant was applying to this particular authority.

All of these have been emphasized throughout successive editions of the Code of Guidance, written by the DoE, and to which authorities were required to have regard (s.71). The Code was in its third edition at the time of our fieldwork and was revised during it (DoE, 1991a; revised 1994c) and by this time it had become a more sophisticated document. Not only did it advise authorities on the implementation of the legislation, it went further in advising them which considerations might be relevant (for example, in defining reasonableness) and also whether certain people should be accepted. It nevertheless had dubious legal status because it was purely advisory and local authorities could ignore its advice if they so wished. Succeeding chapters refer to it wherever necessary.

A 'Corporate Approach'

Much of the rest of this book relates appropriateness to the way in which HPUs interact with other organizations, in particular the SSD. It is argued that the nature, quality and extent of these relationships were reflected in the type of person who was successful and unsuccessful. So, for example, the crucial determinant when it came to assessing a person who required community care services was not so much whether that person met the homelessness criteria but whether those services would, in the opinion of the decision maker, be provided. So the extent to which the HPU was able to work in partnership with other organizations affected their acceptance rate in that particular category and thus the applicant's appropriateness. Often the emphasis of the other pieces of legislation considered in other chapters or the guidance given on the particular subject usually operated on a completely different wavelength to the homelessness legislation. Having analysed the homelessness legislation as a negative approach based on moral blameworthiness, it provides a neat contrast with the generally more positive, empowering elements of the community care legislation and the Children Act 1989. This section seeks to show how the statutory requirement to work together or adopt a 'corporate approach' (Robson & Poustie, 1996, p.42) similarly affects such interaction.

Stephen Ross recognized that a corporate approach to homelessness was required, even though the SSD had been relieved of their general responsibilities:

> That does not mean that social services authorities no longer have a role to play. That cannot be the case. Homelessness is in some cases symptomatic of a deeper complex of problems with which housing authorities are not equipped to deal. Social services authorities must be involved with these problems, just as they would be if the people had not become homeless. (H.C. Debs, Vol. 926, col. 899 (18 February 1977))

Others believed the same; for example, Ernest Armstrong, a DoE minister, argued that 'it must not be assumed that the Bill is writing out or writing off the role of [SSDs]' (ibid. col. 965; see also col. 948, *per* Charles Irving). Nevertheless, the way the section was drafted suggested that the SSD would have a back-seat role:

> Where a housing authority-
> ...
> (b) request a social services authority or a social work authority to exercise any of their functions in relation to a case with which the housing authority are dealing under section 3, 4 or 5 above,[10]
> they shall co-operate with the housing authority in rendering such assistance in the discharge of the functions to which the request relates as is reasonable in the circumstances. (Section 9, 1977 Act; s.72, 1985 Act)

Any such cooperation, according to this section, was *not* to affect the HPU's interpretation of the criteria in individual cases or generally, other than through the SSD by providing information or accommodation. Rather, the duty is only to cooperate with the HPU to the extent that the HPU requests it and as is reasonable for the SSD in the circumstances. So, as was suggested, the SSD retained 'only residual responsibilities under the [Act]' (H.L. Debs, Vol. 934, col. 1017 (27 July 1977), *per* Baroness Young). Indeed, social workers were said to have 'breathed a sigh of relief' that the unpopular homelessness responsibilities had been transferred to the housing department (Stewart & Stewart, 1993, p.77). In other words, partnership was severely constricted in the new act.

Indeed, officers in our study HPUs suggested that this section was only used *negatively* by the HPUs in this study to refer applicants to the SSD, when the HPU believed that the SSD had failed to act appropriately. Thus the effect of this section enabled the HPU to avoid their responsibilities and added a further gloss to this notion of appropriateness. The practical effect of this section therefore appeared to be almost exactly the same as Circular 18/74.

Refining Appropriateness: Judicial Interpretations[11]

Whether the courts would be able to provide a relevant response to homelessness was always doubted (see James, 1974) and, as many have shown, subsequent judicial responses to the homelessness legislation have largely adopted a negative perspective of it (see Birkinshaw, 1982; Loveland, 1995, ch. 3, 1996; Hoath, 1986, 1990b; more generally, Griffith, 1991). Consequently, the judiciary appear to have narrowed the scope of the Act and so refined the notion of appropriateness. This has usually been rationalized by reference to the other competing claims for local authority accommodation, through the assertion that the homeless are queue jumping (see, for example, Cowan & Fionda, 1993; Cowan, 1997). So, for example, in *R. v. Eastleigh B.C. ex parte Betts*, Lord Brightman suggested that 'The Act is one which enables a homeless person in certain circumstances to jump over the heads of all other persons on a housing authority's waiting list, to jump the queue' ([1983] 2 A.C. 614, 627).

Lord Brightman's comments in *Puhlhofer*, parts of which have been recited like a mantra in many subsequent judicial decisions, were further classic examples of this trend:

> although the Act bears the word 'housing' in its short title, it is not an Act which imposes any duty upon a local authority to house the homeless. It is an Act to assist persons who are homeless, not an Act to provide them with homes ... It is intended to provide for the homeless a lifeline of last resort; not to enable them to make inroads into the local authority's waiting list of applicants for housing. ([1986] A.C. 484, 517)

However, earlier cases had already set about refining appropriateness, two strands of which are considered here. The first example was the judicial overlay of the doctrine of 'last settled accommodation' onto the intentional homelessness criterion. The issue arose in *Dyson v. Kerrier D.C.* [1980] 1 W.L.R. 1205 and related to Rees-Davies' example of the person who gave up their accommodation and then took a property on a winter let. When that winter let terminated, and the person applied to the HPU, what was the appropriate response? The HPU found Ms Dyson intentionally homeless. Before the Court of Appeal, the question of interpretation was whether the intentional homelessness clause should be read in the present tense (as it appeared to have been framed) or the past tense. If the former, then the clause 'relate[d] only to the existing home, if one exists, or to the last home if none exists' (p.1214), and on this basis Ms Dyson could not be intentionally homeless as the winter let had run its course. Brightman LJ *rewrote* the section in his judgement so that it referred to the past tense. His (somewhat bizarre) reasoning was that the clause 'is dealing with cause and effect. The subsection states the effect first. The specified effect is the state of being homeless. The subsection specifies that effect and then describes a particular cause which, if it exists, requires the effect to be treated as intentional' (at p.1214). The only answer to this reasoning was 'so what?' Nevertheless, Ms Dyson was held to be intentionally homeless, even though the reason why she had become homeless was that her winter let had terminated through no fault of her own. The clause may have been intended to catch such a situation but it was only through an illogical leap of faith that, in the form in which it passed into law, it could have had this effect. Subsequent cases until late 1995 applied this 'last settled accommodation' test rigorously.

The second example, less obvious perhaps than the first, has been the construction put upon the single person's priority need clause relating to vulnerability for a particular or other special reason (s.59(1)(c)). The courts have held that this involved the HPU asking themselves two questions in relation to the particular applicant: first, was the applicant vulnerable, and, second, was that vulnerability due to one of the reasons included in the subsection? Vulnerability, in this way, could be construed in a relativist sense, as opposed to an absolute sense deriving directly from the catalogue of persons who fell within this paragraph (or, as Brightman LJ might have put it, cause and effect: old age, for example, causes the vulnerability to arise in the first place). Thus, in *R. v. Waveney D.C. ex parte Bowers* [1983] Q.B. 238, the Court of Appeal suggested that vulnerability did not bear its ordinary dictionary meaning. Rather, applicants would need to satisfy the following test: the applicant must be 'less able to fend for [themselves] so that injury or detriment would result when a less vulnerable [person] will be able to cope without harmful effects' (p.244). Subsequently, this was specifically related to housing so that the fending had to be considered in relation to finding and keeping accommodation (*R. v. Bath C.C. ex parte Sangermano* (1984) 17 H.L.R. 94). Furthermore, as Robson and Poustie point out, *Bowers* also suggested that vulnerability should be related to what 'may be broadly described as involuntary and voluntary vulnerability' (p.143). So, if you caused your own vulnerability, you were not vulnerable – a sort of intentional vulnerability bar. While, as the authors also point out, this test was rarely if ever used, it showed that the judiciary always seem to bear in mind the morality of the applicant's behaviour.

Appropriateness and the Administrative Process: the Study Authorities

The previous sections have argued that the homelessness legislation required the decision makers to make their judgments on the basis not of the applicant's deservingness or need but on the basis of moral judgments about the applicant's conduct and the supply of accommodation. The further issue of the effect on the decision-making process of poor relationships with other organizations has also been mooted. This section develops these ideas further through a consideration in two parts of the language used by officers to describe their roles. The first was that officers were 'gatekeepers' and the second was the way other officers interpreted the legislation as 'needs-based'. It is argued that the difference between these two can be exaggerated and that needs-based decision-making (in the context of the homelessness legislation) seemed closely linked to gatekeeping, no doubt because the notion of 'needs' was being defined by reference to the homelessness legislation itself. The section ends with a broad appraisal of policy-making practices and their implementation. These sections are illustrated with examples from Chapters 3–6.

Gatekeeping

A significant number of officers in our study described themselves explicitly as gatekeepers. With two exceptions, the others described themselves in this way without explicitly using this terminology. This description is most commonly associated with front-line workers who, for example, decide whether a person has approached the correct department (for the ways in which such people manipulate and stereotype in the homelessness context, see Lidstone, 1994). However, in this context, gatekeeping described in one word several fundamental, but underlying, aspects of the decision-making process which broadly approximate to the notion of appropriateness as suggested above.

First, officers explicitly accepted that the background to the decision-making process was the rationing of resources. The gate should only be opened for those people who were the most deserving. Those who were not considered to be the most deserving had the gate shut in their face. For example, if it was believed that people under 18 should not leave home unless they could show either a breakdown in their relationships at home or that they would act responsibly by, for example, being employed, that person would not be housed by the authority. Or if it was believed that owner-occupiers should be more willing to seek alternative remedies rather than leaving their accommodation as a result of harassment or violence, that would be the policy.

Second, and closely related to that point, the gate would only be opened for those whom the decision maker believed would best use, or be able to use, the opportunity. Thus there was an explicit relationship between the acceptance criteria and estate management. For example, the officer might consider whether the applicant was capable of maintaining an independent tenancy. If this could only be done with appropriate support, the next issue was whether the officer believed that support would be provided. If the officer did not believe this would happen, they would not assign permanent accommodation to the applicant. If they did in these circumstances, they believed that it would be unfair on the applicant who had been 'set up to fail' and who would probably come back to the HPU (the 'revolving door syndrome'). Or, if the applicant might not occupy the property for a long time, in the case of a person who has fled from a violent situation but who nevertheless might return to that situation, this might not be considered to be an appropriate use of resources. There was also a group of people who were regarded as 'unhouseable' (often those with high-care needs) and officers would do their best to avoid providing permanent accommodation to such people. Temporary accommodation would often be provided but it would be their poorest quality because officers believed they would otherwise lose the good quality temporary accommodation. Landlords would simply withdraw their accommodation from the HPU's use.

Third, as some form of rationing was required, it was therefore necessary to seek to avoid opening the 'floodgates'. Barriers might therefore be constructed, within and outside the legislative concepts, to make it more difficult generally as well as for certain other specific groups to be successful applicants. In addition to these barriers, interpretation of the criteria in the homelessness legislation would be narrowed wherever possible. So, whilst there was limited discretion available to HPUs in defining the priority need concepts of pregnancy or dependent children, the vulnerability category was also delimited. In an earlier study considering the HPU response to HIV, it became apparent that HPUs had begun to alter their definition of vulnerability in relation to those who were HIV-positive precisely for this reason (Cowan, 1995a). Additionally, few HPUs would extend their definitions of vulnerability to all under-18s, except for LA2, which (somewhat bizarrely) accepted all single people under 25 as in priority need.

Officers in some authorities would be less likely to make decisions which involved complex inquiries, reflecting the lack of administrative resources available to the HPUs. This was particularly true of decisions on intentional homelessness. This was justified on one or more of three explicit and one implicit bases. Some argued that the time required was not justified by the result in some cases, although in others it was true that enquiries would be pursued. Some appreciated that the case law was so complicated that they might fall foul of it. Many realized that some intentional decisions might be unacceptable on the facts of a particular case. Implicitly also, the decision-making process would sometimes be skewed where there was an internal appeals mechanism in operation and it was believed that the applicant would use it (see also Baldwin *et al.*, 1992, for similar data). Sometimes HPUs would be more willing to consider intentional homelessness where, for example, the quality of the applicant's behaviour, in the officers' view, demanded it. In this sense, intentional homelessness was used as the *ultimate punishment*. Also some HPUs would 'buy themselves out' of potential challenges to their intentional homelessness decisions by offering accommodation even when such a decision had been made.

Fourth, the assumption so far has been that authorities were forced to ration because of a general deficit in the supply of accommodation. This was not necessarily true. The Conservative's privatization initiatives had disproportionate effects on some areas compared to others (see Forrest & Murie, 1991, ch. 8). Some HPUs were also beginning to find innovative solutions to the deficit, although this was certainly most difficult in LB4 and LB5, our hardest-pressed London authorities, where accommodation was most scarce. However, in LA4, our rural authority, after a period when single people had been automatically told that the authority would not be able to provide accommodation for them, at the time of our visit they were able to be fairly flexible. This was a product of significant housing association activity in the area, which in turn was a foretaste of a probable large-scale transfer of LA4's stock of accommodation to the local housing association. LA1 was sometimes able to offer accommodation to those it had found intentionally homeless. LA2 had a sufficient, albeit dwindling, supply of one-bedroom accommodation which no doubt enabled it to keep its 'generous' policy to under-25s. LB2 had a burgeoning relationship with local estate agents, which meant that it was able to use private sector leasing arrangements as short-term temporary accommodation. It was able to use this partly to avoid applicants challenging their (ab)use of the Children Act. In general, if authorities required accommodation to house a single person, it may well have been possible to find it even if only temporarily. Permanent accommodation in these areas, as with most of our other study authorities, was more difficult to find, particularly within their own stock. The more appropriate the applicant, the more possible it was to find accommodation.

We explicitly asked officers during interviews whether they considered the amount of available accommodation in their area when making their decisions. Few explicitly admitted that they did. However, it was apparent that specific decisions would be made on the basis of resourcing implications. Much of what has been suggested already certainly suggests this. In addition, policies which were implemented would usually reflect the rationing requirement.

The term 'resources' is being used here to mean not only the supply of accommodation but also the ratio of officers to cases they handled. The more cases an officer handled, the less likely that enquiries would be conducted completely. Every officer we interviewed was aware that they were operating within a resource-stretched environment. Thus, while not initially apparent, resources would play a part in the type of decisions made. Each of the succeeding chapters bears considerable testament to the effect of resources in this broader sense on the decision-making process.

Need: a Contrasting Approach?

In LA5, the senior homelessness officer described his approach to the homelessness legislation as always having been needs-based. In LB4, the principal homelessness officer described her approach in similar terms, but believed that this involved a significant change in emphases. She felt that any alternative approach, in a culture which had been significantly reshaped by the implications of the Children Act and community care, would be moribund. The officers used 'need' in a different way. LA5's officer used it in more absolute terms. So, for example, he argued that all homeless people were vulnerable and thus in priority need. Even though LA5 was a seaside resort, he also criticized the view that homeless people flocked to the area because 'it's a nice place to be homeless' (inherent in the media notion of the *Costa del Dole*). His past undisclosed experiences informed this approach to the legislation. He was also aware that the quality of accommodation available in LA5 was poorer and applicants would have to spend considerable time in temporary accommodation.[12] He suggested that his interpretations were not well-known in the area, although they were approved by most senior officers in the authority. He also believed that, even if a person was 'trying it on', this did not matter because the majority did not.[13] This ideological position had a significant and positive effect on his relationships with other agencies, such as the SSD or the local branch of Shelter, which is detailed in subsequent chapters. However, it did not stop him from considering intentional homelessness in certain cases. As he therefore had to look back to consider the reasons why the applicant left their last settled accommodation, as opposed to the current needs of the applicant, it would appear that his approach could not subvert the malevolent influence of the notion of appropriateness. Indeed, it may be argued that to avoid this influence, one would need to step outside the parameters of the homelessness legislation.

Certainly, of all the HPUs in this study, LB4 was the most alegal and so it already operated outside the legislation. The decision-making systems in place reinforced this operationalization. All decisions were made by an interviewing officer in consultation with one of four senior homelessness officers. The latter, with one exception, had limited knowledge of the legislation, let alone case law. The principal homelessness officer, who was responsible for the functioning of the HPU as well as its administration, had worked in the housing sector since the early 1970s. She characterized the homelessness legislation in negative terms as meaning that they had to reject as many people as possible. However, she suggested that in the 1990s this was anachronistic and, through a merger with the SSD, she believed that the HPU would become totally needs-based. Nevertheless, once again it must be doubted whether the principal homelessness officer was describing a completely needs-led basis for homelessness assessments. First, she assumed that the supply of accommodation would always be the key within the homelessness assessment. In LB4, this was a natural concomitant of the general housing shortage. Their heavy dependency on bed and breakfast accommodation long after most other authorities had sought to avoid its use combined with a limited private sector market suggested that the needs-based terminology would be extremely difficult to apply in practice. Second, as is described in subsequent chapters, the applicant's appropriateness would be tested in a number of ways. Third, the way in which the reorganization was being implemented was, as is suggested in Chapter 3, bound to cause structural problems which would give rise to the appropriateness considerations outside the applicant's deservingness.

Policy Making and Implementation

It became apparent at an early stage of our fieldwork, not really to our surprise, that the ways in which staff implemented the HPUs' policy depended upon a number of different variables. Policy manuals might have caused the decisions of individual officers within this study's larger HPUs to be consistent (that academic lawyer's touchstone). However, where there was a policy manual, it was generally the case that officers would not be familiar with it. It might only be cited on rare occasions when an officer required some guidance on a case. In other authorities, while officers might have been required to read it initially, they may well have forgotten its contents.

The quality of such manuals was also diverse. For example, some, such as that used in LA9, simply repeated the Code of Guidance. Others contained more information on the HPU's supposed policies. LB4's manual, an example of this, had been collated at different times when various information, such as the approach councillors or principal officers desired the HPU to take, became available. Officers rarely referred to it. LB5's policy manual was so complicated that few people actually understood it and so it was usually discarded. At the time of our visit, it was in the process of being updated and simplified. The most significant policy manual was that used in LB2, which not only defined the authority's policy fairly closely but also was the most legally proficient. The framing of the policy manual was partly caused by the way in which decisions had been taken (see Chapter 3) and partly by the senior homelessness officer, who had drafted it. He had a law degree, was interested in homelessness law and was thus particularly aware that the quality of decision making in the HPU required consistency as well as a legal basis.

Where there was no policy manual, officers often suggested that they had the Code to fill any gaps. Where the many gaps in the Code surfaced, administrative solutions would replace any of its provisions so that the often heard refrain 'we go by the law here', in relation to the Code, appeared erroneous (see Burkeman, 1976). Furthermore, the Code has no legal status and sometimes the courts find that its provisions are themselves unlawful.

Perhaps more important than policy manuals, though, were the discussions between individual officers, within and between teams of officers if they existed, and general discussions with senior and principal officers. These were often fora in which policies might be developed or individual decisions discussed. Sometimes an afternoon each week would be set aside for this purpose.

Whether policies would be applied in practice depended, to a large extent, upon whether the HPU officers agreed with, or believed in, the policy. Policies imposed upon HPUs particularly required their support for successful implementation. This was not 'radicalism' but a conscious decision often taken jointly by several or all of the members of the HPU after discussion as to the appropriate priority to be afforded to particular cases. Thus, in LA1, officers generally did not implement the policy prescribed by councillors of granting priority in cases of racial harassment. Exactly the same occured in relation to LB4's similar policy on racial harassment which had been prescribed by senior managers, as opposed to councillors. On the other hand, 'bottom-up' policies would be implemented precisely because the people responsible for them were also responsible for their implementation. Thus there was a contrast between the implementation of LA1's racial harassment policy (failure) and their violence policy (success).

Conclusion

This chapter has sought to discard the historical and ideological baggage that has led some people to describe the homelessness legislation as 'needs-based' or as observing the distinction between the deserving and the undeserving. Both of these are outlandish myths, as subsequent chapters show. What appears to be the crucial emphasis is upon whether the applicant is appropriate or not. That, in turn, requires consideration of the applicant's moral blameworthiness, the supply of accommodation, and the use the applicant will make of an independent tenancy.

This chapter has outlined the way appropriateness has been defined by three separate bodies: parliament, the judiciary and the HPUs in this study. Each had their own particular definition and, indeed, within each there were differences. Parliament was guided by two contrasting philosophies: on the one hand, homelessness was caused largely by imbalances in the housing market, a view reflecting most of the research, government and academic, into the causes of homelessness; on the other hand, homelessness was caused by fecklessness, scrounging and welfare dependency. The proponents of the latter view also believed that the homelessness legislation would cause people to become homeless to take advantage of the preference they would be afforded in the allocation of housing. The latter view is one which now permeates discussions about homelessness, also influenced by neo-conservative New Right theories such as Murray's notion of the British 'underclass' (Murray, 1990, 1994).

The judiciary have consistently appeared to adopt the belief that the homeless are encouraged to 'queue jump'. They have thus attempted to narrow the scope of the legislation in order to avoid this unfortunate result. In doing so, they have ignored the other philosophy which, since the Conservative government reached its majority, is more prevalent than ever before.

HPUs in our study appeared to have largely adopted a 'gatekeeper' ideology which required them to balance a number of different considerations, which related not only to moral blameworthiness and supply, but also to other apparently legally irrelevant considerations such as the use that the applicant might make of accommodation. The succeeding chapters provide further examples of all of these considerations to which administrative solutions have been sought.

Notes

1 The duty to provide only temporary accommodation may well also have reflected the fact that, at this time, local authority housing was allocated only to those who appeared to be 'suitable' or appropriate. Those who allowed themselves to require temporary accommodation no doubt did not fit within that notion of appropriateness.
2 Robson and Poustie note that, while it is relatively easy to avoid the messages of academic reports, 'it [is] more difficult to do so when demands for a radical reappraisal of policy [comes] from committees set up by government itself' (1996, p.42).
3 This is the subject of discussion in the next two chapters.
4 Concentration in this section is upon the language and ideological bents which dominated the parliamentary proceedings. For those wishing to gain further insights into the legislative process, see the following texts: Loveland (1991a, 1995, ch. 3).
5 The original bill used was, in fact, the DoE's. For a full account of the genesis of the Bill,

see H.C. Debs, Vol. 926, cols. 896-7 (18 February 1977) *per* Stephen Ross MP.
6 The definition of 'applicant' throughout the Act was sufficiently wide to encompass 'other person[s] who normally reside with him as a member of his family or in circumstances in which the housing authority consider it reasonable for that person to reside with him' (s.1(1)(a)).
7 Although it is no doubt true that Rees-Davies himself did believe that homeless people were as a group undeserving.
8 This could only occur if the applicant did not run the risk of domestic violence in that other area (s.5(1)(c)).
9 This analogy was used by Watchman and Robson when describing the way the act worked in practice (Watchman & Robson, 1981).
10 Respectively, the duties to inquire and accommodate pending enquiry; duties to those threatened with homelessness; and local connection provisions.
11 It is certainly not my intention to discuss the (huge amount of) case law that exists on homelessness. This is more than adequately dealt with in Hunter & McGrath (1992, supp. 1995), as well as Robson & Poustie (1996).
12 He believed that 40 per cent of the local population lived in temporary accommodation, which was usually bed and breakfast hotels.
13 He was, in this sense, closely aligned to Loveland's notion of the subversive employee (particularly true when the authority had been Conservative-controlled): Loveland (1989).

3 Community care

The role of housing was largely ignored in the development of central government's policy on community care. The White Paper devoted one page out of 106 to housing and this mostly concerned home ownership (DoH, 1989). No mention was made of the possible implications of community care for HPUs, even though it had been argued for some time that housing was the foundation of community care (see Oldman, 1988; Association of Local Authorities, 1989; NFHA/Mind, 1989; Hoyes & Means, 1991). It is thus not surprising that research has consistently shown that, in the community care process, housing had been marginalized by social workers (who are responsible for the assessment of clients and the purchasing of the necessary care) and that community care had itself been marginalized by housing professionals (see Morris, 1990; Arnold & Page, 1992; Arnold *et al.*, 1993; Spicker, 1993; Ball, 1994). As a DoH study suggested, 'Institutional and cultural barriers between departments still worked against integrating housing and community care assessment ... Common or collaborative approaches to eligibility criteria were seldom evident, and existing assessment systems failed to identify vulnerable people with low level multiple needs' (DoH, 1994, pp.23-4).

Central government's conversion to the importance of housing allocation to community care appeared first in a joint circular issued by the DoE and the DoH in 1992 (DoH/DoE, 1992). It became apparent from this circular as well as the initial community care guidance that one of the (many) aims of community care was to provide a 'seamless service' between the various assessing and providing agencies so that the client (or 'user') and their carer were effectively empowered (ibid., DoH, 1990a; see also the report of the government's Mental Health Task Force 1994, para. 15). Thus community care requires a high degree of corporatism amongst all these agencies, which in turn requires an ability and willingness to work with each other. Smith *et al.* argued that 'effective community care can be achieved only through effective working together by a range of people from a variety of organisations, whether the focus is on community care planning, assessment of need or delivering a flexible package of care and support' (1993, p.1; see also, generally, Means & Smith, 1994). The apparent lack of corporatism between local authority departments and between local authorities appears to have been partly responsible for several of the *causes célèbres* (see, for example, Ritchie *et al.*, 1994; Blom-Cooper *et al.*, 1995, pp.135 ff). Our fieldwork data suggested that in many areas relationships between HPUs and SSDs had effectively broken down at the time of our visit.

There are thus two interrelated purposes of this chapter. First, an attempt is made to suggest reasons why, while not being inevitable, good relationships between SSD and HPU were hard to achieve in the first place. The argument is that the purpose and structure of the community care and homelessness legislation were in conflict with each other.[1] This was not surprising bearing in mind that the government's interpretation of the phrase 'community care' effectively disowned the importance of giving access to housing. Furthermore, this tension was exacerbated by the often conflicting aims of community care itself.

Second, and central to the structure of this book, it is necessary to examine closely how the failure of the SSD and the HPU to cooperate and collaborate affected our study HPUs' assessment process. In doing so, this chapter seeks to add a further layer to the notion of the 'appropriate applicant'. Often 'appropriateness' is related to, or treated as being directly concurrent with, each applicant's individual 'deservingness'. This chapter suggests that this is simplistic, or one-dimensional, and that even some of the most deserving applicants may nonetheless be regarded as *inappropriate* applicants. Commmunity care was the apotheosis of this idea because the result of the relationship breakdown between HPU and SSD was often that applicants who would normally fall within the criteria in the homelessness legislation do not. This relationship breakdown might have affected the 'deserving' applicant adversely in a number of ways. For example, necessary information might not be provided or required; inadequate referral procedures between the two organizations might operate; or, and this is the crux of the chapter, the obligations to successful homelessness applicants would simply be avoided until the conflict could be resolved in relation to each individual case. The paradox was that community care might have been the reason why an applicant fulfilled the homelessness criteria but it was also the reason why the obligations were not carried out.

In mapping out these effects, the structure of the discussion of the fieldwork data is divided between the non-unitary authorities (LA1-LA10) and unitary authorities (LB1-LB5). There are a number of reasons for this split (which is also made in the next chapter). First, some provisions of the community care legislation do not apply in unitary authorities and thus the expectation might be that this will affect actual practice. Second, it might have been anticipated that community care would be better organized and work better in unitary authorities because the agencies are closer together and work within the same administrative structure (see, for example, Smith, 1992; Warner, 1992, 1994; Seebohm, 1994; Wistow, 1994). One reason given for the Local Government Commission's consideration of whether English local government should become unitary was that such authorities 'offer the opportunity for improved coordination, quality and cost effectiveness in the delivery of local government services' (DoE, 1991b). However, if the lack of departmental interaction in our study was not related to the structure of local government but to other reasons, local government reform will at best have nil effect.

Access to Housing and the National Health Service and Community Care Act 1990

Defining Community Care

While community care has been a touchstone of policy for many years (the first use of the phrase can be traced back to 1957), attempts to define it have apparently proved 'rather sterile' (Social Services Committee, 1985, paras 8-11). Nevertheless, definitions are important because they tell us much about where access to housing fits into the process. Thus the traditional approach has been to seek to define the concept in terms of the carer involved and has two different uses. On one level, the phrase harks back to earlier times when it is supposed that there was a community of people looking out for each other – this is care *by* the community. On another level, it reflects care by professionals *in* the community (see Bayley, 1973; Walker, 1982).

In these senses, housing is being used differently. If the policy ideal is care by the community, then the *provision* of housing can be ignored because the *sub silentio* assumption is that the client already has housing. The community, in that case, has already been defined. On the other hand, care in the community requires housing for its fulfilment because without it one cannot define the make-up of the community. The provision of housing has played an important part also in movements which have placed the client's wants at their forefront (see Arnold & Page, 1992; NFHA/Mind, 1989). Community care is seen as the battleground in these movements because it is prescriptive of, and not reactive to, needs (see Morris, 1993, 1994; Oliver, 1995). Thus the 'Independent Living' group's philosophy includes giving the user 'the ability to decide and to choose what [that] person wants, where to live and how, what to do, and how to set about doing it' (see Laurie, 1991). On this and other similar models, 'special needs' housing is ghettoization (Morris, 1990); what is required is ordinary housing.

Consideration of housing provision plays an important part in each of these definitions except for care by the community, but the government's position significantly adopted the latter. In 1981, the government suggested that 'Care *in* the community should increasingly become care *by* the community' (DHSS, 1981; see also Audit Commission, 1986). When the government asked Sir Roy Griffiths to consider the future for community care, he used the definition of community care provided in the DHSS's evidence to the Social Services Committee. The first strand was that it should 'enable an individual to remain in his own home wherever possible, rather than being cared for in a hospital or residential home' (Social Services Committee, 1985, paras 3.6-3.7). This definition predicated itself on initial ownership or at least occupation of accommodation and did not touch its reprovision. Crucially, this led Griffiths to the conclusion that housing departments should only be responsible for the 'bricks and mortar' of housing provision, without saying how this was to be done. Little else was made of the role of social accommodation (Griffiths, 1988, para. 4.9).

When the government's White Paper came, it was also a disappointment. Its much-quoted foreword argued that 'Helping people to lead, as far as possible, full and independent lives is at the heart of the Government's approach to community care.' It then went on to define community care as 'providing the services and support which people ... need to be able to live as independently as possible in their own homes, or in "homely" settings in the community' (DoH, 1989, para. 1.1). This message was crystal-clear: either own or occupy your own home or be provided with residential care, but do not expect us to provide you with your own independent accommodation. It then went on to use familiar homilies such as 'Suitable good quality housing is essential' in a paragraph about social care (ibid., para. 2.4). Further, it asserted that 'housing needs should form a part of the assessment of care needs', without offering any suggestion of how these housing needs were to be satisfied (ibid., para. 3.5.4). None of this should surprise us if care in the community were to mean care *by* the community. Thus updating the existing methods of housing allocation to reflect the changing structures in the 1990 Act was effectively avoided.

The Administrative Structure

The 1990 Act built a new administrative structure, devised by Griffiths and the DoH, around pre-existing statutes which defined the various types of services which might be provided to a client. Thus the types of services available remained the same but the way they were arranged (and provided) was fundamentally altered.

The structure of community care involves a three-stage process with the SSD as the lead, or organizing, agency. *Stage 1* requires SSDs to produce a plan concerning the provision of community care services in their area, and to update it each year. SSDs are under a duty to consult

> in so far as any proposed plan, review or modifications of a plan may affect or be affected by the provision or availability of housing and the local authority is not itself a housing authority, within the meaning of the Housing Act 1985, every such local housing authority whose area is within the area of the local authority. (Section 46, 1990 Act)

There are at least three limitations on this duty to consult housing authorities: (a) the duty is only to consult, not to take any notice of, their views; (b) the duty only bites if the plan affects the housing department; and (c) where the authority is unitary, no such duty exists.

Stage 2 requires an SSD to make an individual assessment of need of each person 'where it appears to a local authority that any person for whom they may provide or arrange for the provision of community care services may be in need of such services' (s. 46(1), 1990 Act). If the person urgently requires the provision of community care services, nothing shall prevent their provision. As part of this assessment procedure, if it appears to an SSD

> that there may be a need for the provision to him of any services which fall within the functions of a local housing authority (within the meaning of the Housing Act 1985 [including the homelessness legislation]) which is not the local authority carrying out the assessment, the [SSD] shall notify that ... local housing authority and invite them to assist, *to such extent as is reasonable in the circumstances*, in the making of an assessment. (Emphasis added)

Once again there are limitations on this duty: (a) this would not apply in a unitary authority because of the phrase 'which is not the local authority carrying out the assessment'; (b) the housing department can refuse the invitation if it is not reasonable; (c) it is only an assessment and does not trespass on the criteria within the homelessness legislation; and (d) it does not provide any housing duties.

Stage 3 requires the purchase and provision of the services commensurate with the assessed need in stage 2 and also in accordance with available resources. At this stage, SSDs shall take account of any services likely to be made available by the housing department (s.47(1)(b), 1990 Act).

Some Threats to Social Work

The 1990 Act not only refined the administrative structure of community care. Together with the Policy Guidance and other documents, it also effected a change to the nature of the assessments which were to be made as well as the role of the social worker. These changes were not always expressed consistently. One example of this was the notion in both the White Paper and the Policy Guidance of empowering the client, in terms of assessment, but nevertheless ensuring that the local authority would define needs:

> The 1990 Act made it clear that local authorities and not users were to identify needs. Nevertheless, authorities were expected to involve users and carers in the process of assessment and to pay attention to their perceptions of their needs, although the Department of Health found itself in some difficulty on this point. (Lewis & Glennerster, 1996, p.153)

Furthermore, the relevance of resources to the way in which authorities defined need in individual cases was unclear. This was 'a cultural shift [which] required [social workers] to think first about needs and then openly about the services that might be offered, rather than in terms of services that were known to exist' (ibid., p.152). As Lewis suggested, 'The process of assessing need ... encapsulates the tension between choice and rationing' (Lewis, 1994, p.156). This difficult divorce between stage 2 and stage 3 of the process was ultimately designed to enhance the Thatcherite notion of the 'mixed economy of care', which meant that care services should be provided as much from the private sector as possible along a 'level playing field' with the public sector – not surprisingly, as much privatization as possible was therefore to be encouraged (Griffiths, 1988, paras 3.2-3.5; DoH, 1989, paras 3.1.3-3.1.4). Operationally, however, it appeared that the government was manipulating the shape of the playing field through its control of the purse strings (Walker, 1989; Evandrou, *et al.*, 1990; Hoyes *et al.*, 1994).

The role of the social worker has also changed, reflecting these new ideological principles. The movement has been towards a North American scheme:

> Without always being stated explicitly, community care ... implies a clear and unequivocal move away from approaches to social work which are based on medical and psychiatric or therapeutic models and stress the importance of case work. Instead social workers – *possibly renamed care managers* – are intended to act as coordinators putting together packages of care ... In this model, a clear distinction is made between 'purchaser' and 'provider'. (Cochrane, 1993, p.80, emphasis added; see also Audit Commission, 1992)

The operationalization of care management involved a clear threat to the traditional role of the social worker. Thus Lewis and Glennerster's fieldwork in SSDs suggested that care managers spent far more time with 'heavily dependent' clients and 'more time is devoted to the more practical tasks that were arguably always done by social workers, but that were accorded less prestige' (Lewis & Glennerster, 1996, p.139). This fieldwork also suggested that the 'high risk strategy' of using resources according to definitions of need raised questions to which the answers remain unknown (ibid., p.163).[2]

Apart from these points, the more explicit requirement to collaborate with other organizations, at every stage of the community care process, involved an implicit threat to the expertise and professionalism of the social worker because it was recognized that the individual social worker was not 'the sole possessor of necessary expertise in the area' (Langan, 1993). It was also assumed that the individual social worker was able to be aware of the objects, policies and practices of those other agencies with which that person had to collaborate.

Likely Effect on Working Together

With such difficult and no doubt painful processes of change operating during the course of our fieldwork, it was not surprising that we found that our interviewees from HPUs felt that their relationships with the SSD in their area had broken down. However, the changes heralded by the 1990 Act were bound to lead to sharp divisions between HPUs and SSDs. Rather than bringing them together, as had apparently been intended, the changes were, it is submitted, almost inevitably bound to lead to problems of interaction. Client empowerment was clearly not an object of the homelessness legislation.

The assessment required by the homelessness legislation cannot be separated from the service to be provided to those who are successful (that is, the provision of accommodation). The availability of that service defined, to a large extent, the way the criteria in the homelessness legislation were generally interpreted. If the government was truly committed to appropriate community care, it should surely have updated these criteria in line with the 1990 Act. It did not. At the very least, when it redrafted the homelessness Code of Guidance in 1991 and subsequently revised it in 1994, it perhaps might have referred to these changing priorities and the importance of collaboration with the SSD. It did not.

In 1992, the DoE and DoH issued a joint circular in response to concern expressed by the Association of District Councils over the legal duties in community care on housing departments. With both departments' resources stretched, it was important for each to be aware of their bargaining position. Other than suggest, somewhat unhelpfully, that 'community care in itself creates no new category of entitlement to housing', all the circular did was set out the requirements, without guidance on how they were to be carried out (DoH/DoE, 1992, para. 15). A cynic might suggest that this was deliberate obfuscation designed to ensure that any failures could be blamed on local government.

In addition to these divergences, there was a further lack of coordination because the homelessness legislation required HPUs to adopt an explicit moral perspective on the behaviour of the applicant. This was entirely different from the 1990 Act and Policy Guidance with its albeit limited notion of user empowerment. The explicit moral blameworthiness element to the homelessness legislation had no equivalent in the 1990 Act. It was therefore no surprise that the disagreements between our study HPUs and the SSD were caused first and foremost by the HPUs' interpretation of the homelessness criteria.

Community Care: Policy and Practice in LA1–LA10

This section sets out and considers the response to community care policy of the non-London HPUs in our study. Each of the areas had non-coterminous boundaries with the SSD and sometimes, for example in LA1 and LA2, SSDs had been organized so that within the catchment area of the HPU there were at least two decentralized offices of the SSD. The general experience for the HPUs had been negative at all stages of the community care administrative process. All other studies conducted before or at the same time as ours produced broadly similar data (for example, Social Services Inspectorate, 1990; Arnold & Page, 1992; Hoyes & Means, 1991).

This section first outlines the common problems encountered by the HPUs in our study. Consideration is then given to the planning and inter-agency arrangements. Finally, it considers the effect community care had on the HPUs' assessment process. Throughout each of these stages, it was clear that the way in which relationships between HPU and SSD were constructed influenced the policies of the HPU. Thus the notion of the 'appropriate applicant' became defined not by reference to the homelessness legislation but by reference to the nature and quality of that relationship.

Five Common Problems

First, there were the many issues that derived from the conflict caused by the legislation.[3] The SSDs' expectations, in terms of housing, were felt to be excessive by our interviewees. All HPUs reported conversations which had begun with the social worker saying, 'We want a house.' In one or two authorities, social workers had apparently said, 'We want a place in supported accommodation.' Reflecting on these demands, HPU officers frequently suggested that SSDs should appreciate the HPU resource limitations and legislative boundaries. No HPU was prepared to respond to such a demand and some even refused to see the client because of the way the demand/request had been framed.

Many HPU officers also reflected on the fact that the SSD definition of vulnerability was likely to be different from their own. Vulnerability is the central criterion that a single person must satisfy before being in 'priority need' under the homelessness legislation. Most HPUs usually had a written list of those regarded as vulnerable, or at least some working practices. Most also recited the legal definition of vulnerability for the homelessness legislation. SSDs, on the other hand, seemed to believe that any person who needed accommodation was vulnerable. Thus friction ensued.

Furthermore, HPUs also felt that there was a completely different ethos in the two departments. They felt that social workers would act as an advocate for their client and, therefore, regard the HPU as their opponent. This usually resulted in confrontation and an adversarial stance being adopted. If an HPU officer refused to give ground, this would cause further animosity.

On the other hand, some SSDs would simply send a client to the HPU with no information and no warning. If any warning was given, it was likely to be short. If the HPU thought that the client had mental health problems, they might contact the particular social worker. Often the response was 'It's not our problem, it's yours.' Sometimes the buck-passing went further, with the SSD denying responsibility altogether or passing the client to another social worker. For example, where a client had not mental health problems, but a drug problem, a particular social worker might say that they therefore could not help. This, in the eyes of the HPU, usually seemed to happen with difficult clients. Sometimes the social worker would refuse to give any information to the HPU about a particular client because of the stigma attached to particular illnesses. HPU officers usually appreciated this reasoning, but felt that they were being required to make decisions without the most relevant facts, so that it was the client who suffered.

A second common problem was more practical in nature but equally critical to the make-up of the 'appropriate applicant'. Once a community care user had been housed, all HPUs reported that difficulties had emerged. For example, other residents had complained because of nuisances caused by such people, or there were fears (which sometimes became reality) that some applicants might become violent or harass other residents. Thus HPU officers believed that applicants within what they believed to be the community care client group were simply not ready to be housed in independent accommodation.

The third common problem was that staff training of HPU officers in community care was lacking. Most HPU officers had little appreciation of the depth of the community care legislation. They believed that it simply catered for the discharge of people from institutions and the subsequent closure of institutions. The only exception to this was the senior officer in LA3 who had read widely on community care and was aware, for example, of the independent living debate. He also recognized the potentially serious housing implications of community care. Otherwise, the general lack of appreciation of the extent of the web of community care makes responding to the issues it raises virtually impossible or, at best, limited. Furthermore, it must be (and was) a clear cause of inter-agency conflict.

Similarly, HPU officers keenly felt that social workers had a limited appreciation of the homelessness legislation. They believed this was partly responsible for the social workers' generally high expectations because they did not appreciate the HPU's legislation, definitions, interpretations and, in most cases, the basic case law. One or two HPUs were also concerned that individual social workers did not have an understanding of the 1990 Act. Applicants would therefore be affected by this mutual lack of knowledge.

Fourth, there was the issue of hospital closures affecting all our study areas except LA4. All the HPUs (except LA4) had experience of clients being discharged from hospital at 4 o'clock on a Friday afternoon and being sent directly to the HPU. This was understandably a cause for much concern, particularly because in some areas clients would arrive in dressing gown and slippers. In LA1, for example, a large hospital was in the process of being wound down. It was a fairly regular occurrence for a client to arrive at the HPU having been put in a taxi by the hospital with a letter. All HPUs had made attempts to stop this happening, by informing medical staff that, in many cases, they would be unable to help and suggesting that it would be better to give advance warning so that enquiries could be made before the person's discharge. The response to this seemed piecemeal, depending on the particular medical officer.

The fifth common problem, related to the first three above, was that HPUs felt unable to assess how many of the applicants required community care services because the 1985 Act and 1990 Act used such different concepts. This meant that many HPUs felt unable to respond to community care. Nevertheless, all our interviewees felt that they had assessed more people as being vulnerable under the 1985 Act. It would be unreliable to place too much reliance on such statistics as an indicator of the community care case load. For example, this might also reflect an increase in other client groups, such as those under 18, who do not fall within the ambit of the 1990 Act.

Much of the evidence, therefore, tends to be anecdotal and possibly reactive. Almost every interviewee questioned about community care suggested that they had experienced a large increase in the volume of (what they considered to be) the community care case load. They had also found themselves negotiating with social workers more often than a year before.

We found that problems given weight in the literature, such as the lack of boundary coterminosity between county and district councils, were of little relevance to the breakdown of relationships between the HPU and SSD (see, for example, Arnold & Page, 1992). While this was an annoyance in some of our study areas, particularly where the SSD had decentralized, so that an HPU might have a number of different SSDs within its catchment area, it was never anything other than an administrative inconvenience. Greater annoyance was caused because, in some of our study areas, the SSD was continually restructuring itself. LA1 had begun to think that there was no purpose to this restructuring other than to create administrative confusion. The real problems arose from the legislation and the impact of the case load stretching resources even further. This was particularly suggested by the fact that responsibility for many of these difficulties may not have lain principally with the SSD itself, but nonetheless the blame was placed first and foremost at its door.

Planning and Inter-agency Collaboration

Planning The degree of mistrust and mutual enmity that seemed to exist between these two agencies was reflected throughout the planning and assessment phases of the community care process. The key seemed to lie in the planning process. With only one exception,[4] the HPUs in our study had felt *marginalized* when the SSD was engaged in this process. Common errors were that housing departments had not seen the plan until it was practically completed. If they had been involved in the process, they had felt that their views were not taken into consideration. Most plans paid lip service to housing being at the centre of community care but this, in fact, only exacerbated the feeling of marginalization because their voice had not been heard. Indeed, all felt that unreasonable expectations had been encouraged by such lip service. Equally, though, the expectations of our HPUs had been raised by community care. They had felt that community care was the key to the problems faced by a large sector of their applicants who, if the HPU housed them, would be 'set up to fail'. This expression was used to mean that a substantial number of successful applicants often returned to the HPU at a later time, when the likelihood was that they would be found intentionally homeless (for example, as the result of rent arrears caused in the main by a failure to appreciate the burdens of living independently: the revolving door syndrome). By the time of our visits, most HPUs had corrected their initial expectations because nothing seemed to have changed.

LA3 and LA8 were typical examples, although from opposite ends of the political spectrum. LA3's intentions were completely frustrated at the planning stage of community care. They were sent a draft community care plan along with every other statutory and non-statutory agency. Within the county council area, they were one of the few districts to respond to this draft showing a willingness and an interest in the issue. The final care plan contained the statement that 'Housing is the cornerstone of care in the community for all age groups.' However, the plan effectively marginalized housing by arguing that eight key tasks were to be tackled through community care. Housing, or its imaginative use, was not one of those tasks. The HPU was engaged in joint working groups and joint training, including social workers, but it was felt that this was no use. When it came to the formal care plan, they were ignored. They wholeheartedly laid the blame for this failure at the door of the SSD.

This frustration was all the more evident because they had been involved in the consultation process but their representations had not been noticed. It became apparent that this frustration would feed into the assessment process. We suggested to them that since, as they had remarked, they were one of the few districts in the county taking community care seriously, they would be in receipt of far more referrals or requests from SSDs for help because the SSD would see them as willing collaborators. They replied that they would not accept a referral from the SSD until the SSD had involved them in the planning and the assessment process.

While it was unusual for a housing department to be consulted at this stage of the planning process, it was a salutary lesson that, even when consultation did occur, the implementation of community care could cause problems. In LA8, the principal homelessness officer was involved in the planning process at the third tier, a liaison group, whose views fed into the final plan. They had developed a protocol governing liaison between the SSD and HPU, although this was usually ignored as liaison was achieved informally anyway. The HPU had been sent a copy of the draft plan but it showed that the SSD had no appreciation of their resources. The HPU thus felt that the SSD were using them as a dumping ground. The housing department went 'on record', saying that they had been inadequately consulted and that there was inadequate provision in the district for that portion of the client group which did not need institutional care but could not cope with independent living. Nevertheless, in a public document, the opening paragraph ironically acknowledged that 'there has been good, useful cooperation between the two agencies for a number of years'.

While these examples encapsulated the general experience of community care planning, there was one exception. LA5 had a positive experience of the planning and collaboration side of community care. They had been involved at an early stage by the SSD, and the senior homelessness officer had a positive impression of organizations moving in the same direction. LA5 should not, however, be regarded as an enigma, for two reasons. First, this officer interpreted his responsibilities to be needs-led, without any reference to resources. Consequently, his impression of the role of the homelessness legislation counteracted the common problems observed above. Second, before the 1990 Act, some (published) research had already been completed on community care provision in the HPU's area which undoubtedly would have had an effect on the SSD.

Nevertheless, in many areas the widespread frustration and disillusionment had been channelled into positive action by HPUs, usually ignoring the SSD. For example, LA2 was in the process of setting up a community care team. Applicants under the 1985 Act, who formed part of the community care case load, would be channelled to this specialist team. At the time of our visit, applicants for these posts were in the process of being interviewed. LA1, having experienced continual frustration from its relationship with the SSD, had decided to set up its own supported lodgings, with 24 spaces. LA4 had realized that their 'move-on' accommodation was effectively becoming permanent (or 'silted up') because their housing stock was insufficient to meet the needs of the clients. They believed that, if they sold their housing stock to a housing association, this situation might improve. Although this was also politically motivated, the homelessness officer saw this as a possible method of alleviating their current problems. Members were in the process of considering this large-scale transfer. All these projects were begun without the involvement of the SSD and were usually bred out of frustration with the planning process as well as a perceived lack of suitable and innovative housing.

Inter-agency collaboration Inter-agency collaboration must be considered both at a managerial level and at the level of assessment because of the effect that one had on the other. At the managerial level, it was apparent that many principal homelessness officers viewed joint structures as a talking shop, providing nothing useful. In this sense, they were viewed as providing organizational and constituent participation but little input into policy making. Homelessness officers believed that, if they were invited to meetings, it would only be an afterthought. LA1 aimed to be more proactive and arranged for a series of meetings and workshops at the city council offices on issues of housing and community care. Although the SSD were invited, they failed to attend. The principal homelessness officer felt that this was symptomatic of their poor working relationship.

In general, HPUs felt marginalized and isolated at managerial level, and this tended to be repeated at assessment officer level. Managerial arrangements usually gave rise to forms having to be completed by assessing officers. As was remarked in LA8 and LA9, these were usually incorrectly completed and few HPU officers were invited to case conferences. This caused exasperation because housing requirements which they might not be able to meet would be decided without their input. If HPU officers were asked to attend, they felt that their views would usually be ignored (except in LA5). In LA7, for example, one officer had been to a case conference where she was given an estimation of the requirements of the client. She was asked in the meeting whether the client met the criteria employed by LA7 under the homelessness legislation. When she suggested that this was unlikely (because the client would not have a priority need) she was told that she *had* to help even though there was no suitable accommodation available for this client.

In large HPUs, most communication between the two departments was by telephone. Generally, this was acrimonious. In smaller HPUs, such as LA4, LA5, and to a certain extent in LA7, some communication was done personally. This usually led to a good social relationship developing between them, which in turn had an impact on their work relationship. In LA4, which received few applications generally, the homelessness officer was able to take time to consider possible solutions to any problem, liaising with social workers and attempting to evaluate the needs of the local community. It should, however, be stressed that LA4 was not under any particular housing stress. In all the other areas except LA5, particularly where the HPU's resources were stretched, there was limited time to engage in this proactive work and relationships were consequently particularly poor. Homelessness officers often commented that they were talking to a faceless bureaucrat.

This found its most evocative example in LA1. In 1989, the SSD had put in place a special officer whose sole task was to liaise with the HPU. The principal homelessness officer reported that the SSD was then offered any number of units by the HPU for medium-term accommodation and support. However, apparently somewhat suddenly, the funding for this specialist worker was withdrawn during the SSD's restructuring. Since that time, inter-agency relations in LA1 had vanished.

Assessment and the 'Appropriate Applicant'

Many HPUs in our study expressed a commitment to community care, but only LB5 was close to such an assessment (see below). Other than a few case conferences that had taken place in one or two of our study areas, HPUs' assessments were very much their own, with only occasional input from the SSD. No HPU reported that, in making their 1985 Act assessment, they took into account community care needs. However, they were all aware that part of their client group had such needs.

A widespread dilemma became apparent from the very beginning of our fieldwork, relating to the common problem (noted above) that, while the HPU might have been able to house a particular client, officers believed that limited support and aftercare were actually provided. All HPUs except LA5 reported that, when they had housed a person who (in their view) required community care services, it had often been unsuccessful because the applicant either could not cope or had caused neighbourhood problems. In some cases, even though they felt it was an unsatisfactory short-term solution, arrangements would be made for the eviction of these clients. These cases seemed to stick in the minds of the officers, who felt a different solution was demanded at the assessment stage because otherwise they viewed it as a waste of their resources in terms of both assessment and provision.

Most of our HPUs, irrespective of their housing supply, had found an alternative solution. Rather than considering the standard criteria in the 1985 Act or policy questions, the assessing officer would always attempt to appraise whether, in the officer's view, the applicant was capable of living independently. The SSD would then be contacted and told that permanent accommodation would not be provided until an appropriate commitment – sometimes almost a binding contract or an undertaking was required in LA6, LA8, LA9 and LA10 – was given by the SSD to provide the necessary care that would allow the client to prepare for and remain in the accommodation. Without that commitment, and this was the implicit threat, the client would remain in poor-quality temporary accommodation and eventually end up on the street. From the perspective of the HPU, this approach enabled them to force activity out of the SSD and, they hoped, provided the best solution for their client. It also meant that, if the client should fail in that accommodation, the HPU would be able to divert the blame. This commitment would therefore place the client in the appropriate applicant category and was a solution to the problems of wasted resources, potentially explosive relationships with other tenants in the area, and sometimes explicitly to a huge increase in applicants within this client group.

No officer suggested that this was ideal. For example, many homelessness officers felt that they were making doctors' decisions for them and they were ill-equipped to make such decisions. Furthermore, it was an explicit net-narrowing approach similar to Carlen's notion of agency-maintained homelessness (Carlen, 1994, pp.18–20). The rationale was that it avoided a perceived waste of resources as well as forcing action out of the SSD. Where the applicant was evicted from accommodation provided by the HPU or returned to the HPU for some other reason, it was likely that the HPU would consider making a finding of intentional homelessness. The HPU recognized that this would be more harmful to the applicant, and its resources, than their current process.

Community Care: Policy and Practice in LB1-LB5

With one exception (LB5), community care in the London HPUs in our study suffered from exactly the same problems as in our non-London HPUs. All our London HPUs had adopted the same type of administrative solutions that we heard about in LA1-LA10. As a response to the perceived problems created by community care, organizational change was, or was in the process of being, effected. Organizational change is certainly easier to coordinate in unitary authorities but it seemed only to mask the central defects.

The first part of this section takes a deeper look at the organizational level employed in the authorities visited, with particular emphasis on LB2 and LB4. The second part considers the problems and solutions adopted by each borough to community care, with particular emphasis on LB1, which operated a 'mental assessment panel'. There were particular difficulties associated with this panel which mirrored those experienced more generally. The last part considers the approach adopted by LB5, which was a potential model arrangement even though there were some fundamental flaws in its bureaucracy.

The notion of appropriateness was used in the same ways by these authorities and for the same reasons as LA1-LA10. So, for example, all of the five key problems found in LA1-LA10 were equally evident in LB1-LB5. Many were exacerbated by the larger numbers of applicants experienced in LB1-LB5, by way of contrast to LA3-LA10. However, LB5's assessment process had been designed to mitigate such issues and we test its success in these terms.

Organization

One of the implicit suggestions behind the further creation of unitary authorities is that there will be better collaboration, leading to a more efficient service, if SSDs and housing departments are housed within the same administrative structure (DoE, 1991b; cf. Pycroft, 1995; Leach, 1994). This tends to deny the inherent paradox in welfare organizations that, while 'ostensibly devoted to the public interest', they act in a manner contrary to it (Cranston, 1985, p.194). The paradox remains the same when considering the relationship between statutory agencies. HPUs continually found that SSDs were remote. Often they were not located in the same building.

Cooperation and collaboration did not seem to occur. In fact, on a day-to-day basis, organizationally and practically, the mutual enmity between the two departments mirrored that of the non-London authorities. Once again, these problems cut across political boundaries. The only real distinction between unitary and non-unitary authorities appeared to be that the former were in a better position to reorganize as they were not shackled by two separate, impenetrable bureaucracies.

However, reorganization was not the answer to the problems faced in LB2. Indeed, it exacerbated them, inducing professional jealousies and cultural and communication problems. In 1990, the housing section (including the HPU), the SSD, welfare benefits and trading standards sections of LB2 were reorganized into three generic advice centres in the north, south and west of the borough. The idea for these centres came from a high managerial level. Officers were expected to be involved in all areas of work and, in so doing, to have a better grasp of the overall picture. In turn, it was thought that this would benefit the consideration of individual cases.

Several problems emerged to thwart these good intentions. Homeless persons officers felt that administrative support was inadequate. There was no central collation of statistics (often this was not even performed in the individual centres). There were no central policy guidelines or manual. In practice, statistics sent to the DoE were usually made up. A wide disparity in the workloads of the centres developed and many casework decisions were not made. Staff had felt insufficiently trained to meet the demands of the centre.

Decentralization ultimately and almost inevitably ended in failure. However, these 'systems reasons', while partially responsible for the failure of the centres, were not the only cause. According to homelessness officers who worked in the centres, all officers were reluctant to become involved in other cases or to liaise effectively with the work of other departments in the centre. For example, if a social worker interviewed a person with housing problems, the social worker would terminate the interview and hand it over to a housing officer, and vice versa. Effectively, then, the advice centres operated mini-HPUs and mini-SSDs, which was precisely what the organization had sought to avoid. Eventually, the centres were disbanded and recentralized. The HPU was then completely separated from the SSD although the bitterness and tension was reflected in the assessment process during which liaison was practically non-existent (see below).

This past experience had confirmed the poor rating of SSD officers in the minds of HPU officers. While one of the officers bemoaned the fact that she could not picture the social worker to whom she was talking on the telephone, all the HPU officers were happy to have been separated from the loveless marriage. Their experience reinforced the view that the legislation, together with the language and culture that form part of each, cannot be happily married. More than administrative or organizational change was required. Recognizing this, a senior homelessness officer, appointed in 1992, had begun to make radical changes by encouraging assessing officers to adopt an area of specialization. Three specializations are relevant for this chapter: general hospital referrals, sheltered housing for the elderly, and mental health referrals (the latter two were run by part-time staff, being their only responsibility). Officers were encouraged to specialize in what they felt strongly about, thus circumventing a general departmental notion of appropriateness.

Three reasons caused this change in emphasis. First, there was a possibility of surplus staff capacity for, as the workload from the centres decreased, there was less for officers to do. Second, some officers had wanted to take on specialist areas which arose; this would help their career development as well as the senior officer's goal of providing an efficient, quality service for their clients. Third, although never explicitly stated, it seemed to be recognized that individual personalities could transcend bureaucratic mechanisms. If the SSD had a particular contact point within the HPU, this might improve their work and inter-agency collaboration. Personal relationships could be developed with people from other specialities.

The failure of the management-inspired reorganization should be contrasted with the potential success of the officer-inspired internal organization. It seemed to be an almost general rule in our study authorities that ideas or policies imposed on HPU officers were rarely given their full effect. On the other hand, those that came from officers usually worked because their commitment was assured. As Means and Smith noted: 'strategic discussions between housing managers and social services managers about the need for joint working will only take root within their organisations if field level staff are encouraged and supported to work together' (Means and Smith, 1994, p.194).

The HPU in LB4 had been housed in a 'one stop shop' (a misnomer) for two years. The HPU had its own entrance to the building and was to all intents and purposes entirely separated from the other departments in the same building. Indeed, the SSD had only moved into the building six months before the visit. A management-led, community care-inspired reorganization was about to take place when we visited, through which the HPU and the SSD would be integrated. At the time of our visit, the restructuring had reached the third-tier management level. The two directorates – housing and the SSD – had been linked together by coupling resources and personnel.

The principal homelessness officer was positive about this reorganization, feeling that the traditional enmity between the two departments was outmoded. For her, the way forward was to provide a service to meet the needs of the client, which often required the provision of services other than housing. She welcomed the move away from the 'gatekeeper' mentality, which she saw as trying to avoid obligations to as many people as possible. Nevertheless, she recognized the inherent tension between the HPU, which treated clients as 'guilty until proven innocent', and the SSD's advocacy approach. She believed that so far the restructuring had gone smoothly and that, at management level, the SSD had a sound knowledge of the legislative requirements.

A different perception was held amongst the officers of the HPU: relationships were uniformly poor between the HPU and the SSD; HPU officers felt that unrealistic demands were made upon them by the SSD. A number of interviewees also suggested that at least 40 per cent of the people referred to them by the SSD were not homeless. As part of the process of reorganization, four HPU officers had visited the SSD for a week (although they also had to be present in the HPU during that period). The purpose of the visit was to build relationships between the two departments. During our visit, we spoke to two officers about their reactions to the exercise. Both had said that, while appreciating it was a start, they had gained no real experience of the work of the SSD during their visit. They had simply shadowed a duty officer and had been fairly bored. They believed that it would have been of far more use to have had some intensive experience for a day, or perhaps longer, because they felt that they had not gained anything from the experience. Indeed, it appeared to have reinforced various prejudices, such as the lack of work load within the SSD.

As a result of this approaching reorganization, morale was lower than usual amongst the HPU officers, who realized that their jobs were at risk, although no one knew which officers would lose their jobs. Officers did not believe the restructuring would ameliorate their relationship with the SSD and, instead, felt that their poor interrelationship would be exacerbated. It remained to be seen how successful it would be, but inadequate training and the secrecy attached to the process did not bode well. The principal homelessness officer tended to shrug off these negative feelings. She believed that this was the predictable reaction of those living in the present but such reactions were rapidly becoming anachronistic.

Planning and Inter-agency Collaboration: LB1-LB4

In general terms, every HPU visited replicated the same concerns and the same problems as those HPUs outside London. In LB2, this had been exacerbated by past experience and, in LB4, by the assessing officers' fears about the future reorganization. Further, in LB3 there was at least a suggestion that the SSD would refuse to consider anybody who was not registered with a doctor.[5] So the belief that unitary authorities make community care work better was not being realized. Indeed, none of the officers, not even principal officers, had been consulted about the community care plan. However, the fact that each HPU had sought to respond to community care, either organizationally or otherwise, shows that community care was considered to be a live issue.

Joint Assessment and the Appropriate Applicant: LB1-LB4

The only London HPU in our study operating a form of joint assessment was in LB1, which had operated a mental health review panel since 1988. There was some doubt as to why it had been set up. It was suggested by one senior homelessness officer that it had been a response to a particular *cause célèbre*. Other officers believed that initially it had been set up to provide a forum for the SSD and HPU to liaise about individual cases. A member of the panel suggested that the inadequacies of the previous system were responsible because the authority's psychiatrist would always say that if someone had mental health problems they were vulnerable. An internal document suggested that 'The importance of the social as well as medical factors in psychiatric illness has been recognised in the setting up of this panel.' All officers believed the panel worked exceptionally well and took out of their hands decisions which they did not believe they were capable of making.

On approach by a person with mental health problems, that person would be housed in a bed and breakfast hostel awaiting assessment from a social worker and medical reports. When these had been collated, they would be sent to the members of the panel. Those members would then meet and discuss the case with the social worker, considering whether the applicant was homeless and in priority need because of vulnerability. Intentional homelessness was not considered by the panel as it was believed that none of these applicants would have the capacity to form 'intention'. If the applicant was considered by the panel to be homeless and in priority need, the most suitable form of housing would be discussed.

The panel comprised members of the SSD mental health team, a principal homelessness officer (who was also responsible for bed and breakfast allocation), the senior accommodation officer, the acting head of housing needs and a team manager from the housing department. The client was not present at panel meetings but was represented by the person who wrote their report, usually their social worker. Thus 'user empowerment' was subverted in the decision-making process.

Ostensibly, therefore, this was a positive system of arranging and allocating responsibility, taking decisions away from those who did not feel that they had the requisite qualifications and giving the decision-making power to those that do. However, it was breaking down at the time of our visit. The HPU was becoming frustrated because it usually took the SSD about one year before it managed to find the time to visit a client and write its report. Sometimes the social worker had only been able to visit the client once before presenting the case to the panel and the principal homelessness officer felt that she usually knew the client far better than the social worker.

The panel were only able to hear six cases in an afternoon. Consequently, there was a backlog. At the time of our visit, there were 17 single people in bed and breakfast, some of whom had waited over a year for their panel hearing. Behavioural problems could develop, brought on by boredom and interminable waiting. The availability of other types of suitable accommodation for this client group was negligible, primarily because planning permission was often refused for hostels in residential areas. Until an assessment had been made and support provided, bed and breakfast was considered to be the most appropriate form of accommodation for this client group.

These two problems were considered to be the most pressing. However, it also became apparent that there was a deeper issue at stake: the lack of a definition of mental health. Whose case would be referred to the panel depended on the HPU and SSD ground-level officers' interpretation of the phrase 'mental health'. For example, cases of phobias were often, although not always, referred. The same went for clients who had suffered a nervous breakdown. One panel member believed the rule was, if in doubt, refer to the panel, the only requirement being that there must be some vulnerability in housing terms (citing the judicial definition of vulnerability). Another panel member suggested that the qualifying definition was whether the applicant had sought, or was seeking, medical treatment, not necessarily psychiatric. Questions on the standard homelessness application form were meant to elicit this information but there was a suspicion amongst officers that this was inadequate and referral depended to a large extent on the gut feeling of the assessing officer. While no officer believed it was a 'vulnerability' panel, it is hard to resist the impression that this was precisely what it was – a panel to decide whether a particular client was vulnerable and what support would be required. Thus there were two stages where the appropriateness of the applicant was considered.

Panel members also suggested that many cases referred from the SSD did not have housing problems per se but more general problems of coping with independent living. However, on the panel, relations with the SSD were good. Law was rarely an issue and there was a high level of agreement that the problems of the panel were not induced by the SSD but by their lack of resources. The positive benefit of the panel was that many people were housed and would receive a comprehensive care programme. Decisions were also taken about whether a client was capable of independent living, which was not considered to be within the client's jurisdiction – it was believed that whether or not they were vulnerable was an issue for the authority. This was a decision, one panel member suggested, that professionals had to make on the basis of the 1985 Act because there seemed no point in accommodating people who could not cope with independent living, ultimately causing their eviction.

Other than LB1's panel, all HPUs made their own assessments. There were uniformly poor relations with the SSD because they often did not seem to appreciate the HPU's role. LB1's 'mental health review panel' tended to avoid the problem experienced in the non-London boroughs of refusing to provide permanent housing until a care package had been organized. However, all the other HPUs adopted this as their standard practice. For example, in LB2, there was no communication between the HPU and the community care advice centre, which created frustration and the belief that the latter were letting the HPU's clients down. In turn, this led the senior homelessness officer into refusing to provide permanent accommodation until an appropriate written care package had been received.

All HPUs, on the other hand, admitted to having good liaison with hospitals. This mostly prevented clients arriving directly from hospital, although there were still some reported cases of clients turning up late on Friday afternoons. In LB2, the local hospital had heard of and been impressed by the individual links that were being forged, and had developed the practice of specifically asking for a particular individual HPU officer to deal with their referrals. This was working well, avoiding many of the earlier problems. One HPU officer suggested that this had made the social worker attached to the hospital jealous.

Even so, all HPUs believed that many of their clients were discharged too early from hospital without adequate consideration of the client's accommodation or support requirements, or even whether the client was suitable for independent living. Some authorities had taken steps to combat this perception. For example, in LB4, when front-line officers were faced with a client exhibiting symptoms of mental illness, they referred the client to the local hospital so that their capacity for independent living could be assessed. This should be contrasted with this authority's more general approach of not accepting single people who showed no visible signs of vulnerability. If the hospital's assessment was that the client was capable and vulnerable, there would be an automatic priority need and no question of intentionality. The assessment was initially supposed to take six weeks but at the time of our visit it was taking much longer.

Other than these responses, it became apparent that a number of HPUs, as a result of the differing legislative approaches, had made a conscious attempt to balance the needs of the client against their resources. LB2's new policy manual was specifically drawn up to include such balances. However, this commonly gave rise to underlying tensions, particularly when the stark balance of comparing different clients' needs and their own resources had to be made. The reality for all the HPUs was that resources ruled their assessment.

LB5: a Potential Model?

The preceding paragraphs have not considered the policy and practice of LB5, partly because its organizational structure potentially provided a model. LB5's approach had been in existence since 1987, although further impetus had been provided by the introduction of the 1990 Act.

The HPU was split into three teams: families, elderly (over 55) and special needs. Internal memoranda suggest that the reasons for this split were financial. In addition, the assistant director of housing had realized that this would be an opportunity to streamline services to make them more compatible with the new legislation. The senior officer in the elderly section was the HPU representative on joint committees. Importantly, she also had responsibility for writing the single homelessness section of the community care plan for the authority. Initially, that officer experienced difficulty in being heard on the committees, but it was soon appreciated that the HPU held the purse strings for housing. She felt that her input had also been accepted because the SSD had underestimated the numbers of assessments that were required. However, she struggled to maintain the importance of her role in the face of SSD opposition.

The special needs (which dealt with all single homeless under 55) and elderly teams had the most direct contact with community care and they both had an extra section in the already lengthy application form which catered directly for assessing care needs.[6]

The SSD had a team of officers that dealt with generic homelessness issues, known as the Homeless Single Persons Team (HSPT). Set up in 1986 as a response to the homelessness provisions of the Housing Act 1985, until the 1990 Act the HSPT had been in danger of being restructured out of existence. It was appreciated that the 1990 Act required a specialist homelessness team in the SSD and, in fact, most of the officers were upgraded in 1990. As the name suggested, the HSPT dealt only with single people; it also only covered those single people with some form of disability (a word which was interpreted loosely). The HSPT worked closely with the special needs team of the HPU and all special needs clients initially found in priority need were referred to the HSPT.

The working relationship between these two teams had made a virtue out of the strains that we observed in our other study authorities. Other HPUs had been forced to require a care plan before they housed any client requiring community care services. LB5 had an arrangement where the HSPT would enter into a form of contract to provide the necessary care for any vulnerable client. Both agencies recognized that this would be the ideal way forward and would enhance mutual collaboration and a certain amount of harmony.

However, many problems did exist. The family team rarely had any contact with the SSD or the HSPT and, when it did, relationships were extremely strained. The elderly team also had little contact with the HSPT although, as the senior officer was responsible for community care in the HPU, better relationships had been established with the SSD. The part of the homelessness assessment form that required assessment of care needs was rarely filled in because officers believed that they could not make such an assessment. In this sense, their lack of expertise caused applicants to lose their appropriateness. However, the HSPT never saw this assessment form because they had their own referral form and, equally, did not believe that housing officers had the necessary expertise to make any assessment of care needs.

There were few arguments about local connection or ordinary residence, but there was plenty of discussion on the question of priority need. This was partly due to differing definitions of vulnerability. The HSPT took the line that all homeless people were vulnerable, which raised the problems experienced in all our other authorities. Furthermore, while case conferences were often called between the two departments, and the HSPT believed they were vital, usually it was impractical for the special needs officer to attend.

Other problems seemed equally detrimental. While HPU officers had to make decisions fairly quickly, the HSPT could not (except in serious cases) make immediate assessments. Some special needs officers, therefore, believed that the SSD was more keen to let somebody move into temporary accommodation and see whether they were able to cope with independent living. Clients that did not fit within the statutory definition of vulnerability were not referred to the HSPT even though many might well have required some form of community care services. Finally, the assistant director (who had been responsible for the reorganization of the HPU) resigned just before our visit. With the departure of the person who had initiated the changes, there was a suspicion amongst special needs officers that they would be reorganized back into a generic HPU. This was confirmed by senior staff and so the whole edifice of providing a corporate response was about to fall down.

Conclusion

This chapter has added a further layer to the notion of the appropriate applicant. No matter how deserving or needy the applicant is, external factors may redefine the criteria for their acceptance under the homelessness legislation. The external factor here was partly the relationship between HPU and SSD. That this relationship had largely broken down, I have argued, was due to the mismatch between the legislation, in terms of both culture and ideology. HPU officers' views reflect the frustration they felt (and possibly also media perceptions of the SSD) about this relationship which was largely not a personality issue but a definitional one. Where that relationship was close to breaking down or there was mistrust between the two agencies, administrative solutions to perceived problems would be sought by the HPU. In this case, that solution was to refuse to house applicants whom the HPU believed to fall within the community care client load until an appropriate care plan had been devised and would be implemented. Furthermore, the construction of the relationship, perhaps reflected in the way in which requests or demands were made by the SSD, also affected the assessment of the client.

Finally, this relationship breakdown was evident in all authorities, whether they were unitary or non-unitary. This is important because if, contrary to what is suggested here, the poor relationships were a product of the organization of local government in the shires – the SSD being the responsibility of the county councils and housing the responsibility of the district and city councils – then one would expect the relationships to be better in unitary authorities. That they were not suggests that the argument that the breakdown in relationships was caused by the legislation deserves some credence. Furthermore, the increased move to unitary status for some areas of local government in England, and for all in Wales and Scotland, may well result in no improvement in service provision.

Notes

1 Such an argument represents a slight modification from the view taken in an earlier published work (Cowan, 1995b) where it was suggested that the needs-based approach of community care could not be reconciled with the resource-based approach of the homelessness legislation.
2 For discussion of the legal relevance of resources in community care, see Schwehr (1995),

Preston-Shoot (1996) and the important Court of Appeal decision in *R.* v. *Gloucestershire C.C. ex parte Barry* (unreported, 27 June 1996).

3 The only exception to this was LA5, which had adopted a perspective broadly equivalent to the SSD's.
4 LA5 had positive feelings about their role in community care (see Chapter 2). The senior officer felt that this was due to his needs-based approach. Other factors may well have been earlier negative published reports on community care in the area.
5 Bearing in mind that it is difficult for street homeless people to get registered with a GP, this was remarkable (see Fisher & Collins, 1993).
6 This application form had a total of over 50 (substantive) pages which had to be completed by the officer in charge of the case. It was hardly surprising that, given the substantial case load of members of the HPU, it was rarely completed properly.

4 Children

In 1989, 304 children were taken into care because of 'family homelessness', 5460 because of 'unsatisfactory home conditions', 3134 because they had been 'deserted by parent'[1] (H.C. Debs, Vol. 190, col. 364 (WA)). In the mid-1980s, few SSDs paid any attention to their relationships with housing departments, or those departments' responsibilities, in order to pursue the 'ordinary housing solution' (Tunstill, 1985). It was well known that 'many of the problems faced by families in housing need and at risk of losing their children, [were] caused by the "intentional homelessness" clause of the 1977 [Housing (Homeless Persons) Act]' (BASW, 1986, p.15). This was the case even though, under the Child Care Act 1980, authorities were required to consider alternative mechanisms of preventing children being taken into care. On leaving care, a child of 16 could be left to fend for themselves in the property market with limited support from the state.

In addition to these structural issues, it was and remains common for media and certain politicians to identify children, renamed 'youths', as the scourge of society. For example, the initial impetus for the attack on single mothers in the housing context centred on the under-18s. Peter Lilley's speech to the Conservative Party Conference in 1992, which referred to single mothers jumping the waiting list ('I have a little list ...'), was an attack on 16- and 17-year-olds. The *Panorama* programme which hastened in the 'back to basics' campaign specifically used 16- and 17-year-old women as examples of those who 'got pregnant to get a council house'. In this context, references to the 'nanny state' have greater resonance. These views were the genesis of headlines such as the *Daily Telegraph*'s 'Tory advice for pregnant girls: have an abortion' (Copley, 1995).

Nevertheless, there was (and remains) considerable evidence to suggest that lone mothers are particularly marginalized within the labour market, occupy the poorest accommodation and are thus more likely to require rehousing, with particular emphasis on state housing (see, for example, Forrest & Murie, 1991, pp.72–3; Millar, 1992; Gilroy, 1994; Lewis, 1995). Furthermore, there was no evidence that young women 'got pregnant to get a council house' (IoH, 1994; Ermisch, 1996) although such views were inspired by the 'underclass' theorists (see, in particular, Murray, 1994). It is often forgotten that the general causes of homelessness amongst young people are exacerbated by, for example, consistent reductions in welfare (particularly housing) benefits, decreasing employment opportunities, arguments which hasten the child's departure from the home, inability to find accommodation in the private sector because of decreased resources and lack of capital to pay a deposit or bond (see, generally, Thornton, 1990).

The scheme of the Children Act 1989 built on the Child Care Act's emphasis on prevention (in s.1) by prescribing a partnership between parents and the state. No longer was there to be the notion of 'voluntary reception into care' (s.2). Rather, duties were placed on SSDs to provide accommodation, given that certain conditions were satisfied, in partnership with both parents and the child. Provision was also made for cooperation between housing departments, among others, and the SSD. The first section of this chapter considers the effects of this for SSDs as well as the problems encountered by them in implementing the 1989 Act.

The 1989 Act also required the SSD to work in partnership with the HPU. The second section considers whether the requisite structures to facilitate this partnership were put in place by the 1989 Act. The argument is similar to that of the previous chapter in that it is submitted that the structures, such as they were, were inadequate for the task. This argument provides the background to the third section which details the court manoeuvres which occurred during and just after our fieldwork took place.

These changes in emphasis in the 1989 Act would, we believed before our fieldwork started, cause considerable problems for HPUs in considering their responsibilities under the homelessness legislation (Cowan & Fionda, 1993). The fourth and fifth sections of this chapter outline the data from our fieldwork which at the least challenged that assumption and provided further evidence of the way in which the notion of the appropriate applicant was constructed. The analysis of these data is split between the HPUs in this study which fell within, on the one hand, non-unitary authorities and, on the other hand, unitary authorities. The reasons for doing so are the same as in the previous chapter on community care, where the corresponding split was made: the statutory provisions have different effects (in theory) between the different types of authority; and implementation might have been better in unitary authorities because they work within the same administrative structure.

Social Work, the Children Act 1989 and Access to Housing

General Trends in the 1989 Act

Throughout the 1980s the SSD came under attack from New Right and other groupings because of the dominance of the 'professional' ethic in the service. Professionalism was seen by the New Right as an attempt by the SSD to increase their power base, thus legitimizing their existence, whereas many services could be provided by untrained competent officials (Brewer & Lait, 1980). In 1991, John Patten MP continued this theme when asking whether it was 'really necessary for some of our big cities to have approaching 10,000 or so social workers and related staff on their payrolls?' (in Cochrane, 1993, p.74). Together with this overriding New Right ideological position, 'at any one time [during the 1980s] social workers always seemed to be waiting for another inquiry report to be published just as the previous one was being digested' (ibid., p.82). During that period there were 18 inquiry reports into child abuse, all of which received a high profile in the media. The consistently inconsistent conclusions of these reports were classic examples of 'damned if we do [intervene], damned if we don't' (Clarke, 1996, p.51).

Nevertheless, the 1989 Act did legitimate the role of the SSD in child-related matters, giving them wide duties, but with the prospect of increased juridification and guidance. However, the ethos of the new legislation was radically different from the old. In introducing the Children Bill, the Lord Chancellor said that local authority 'services to families in need of help should be arranged in voluntary partnership with the parents, and the children enabled to continue their relationship with their families where possible' (H.L. Debs, Vol. 502, col. 489). So, with no extra resources allocated, the challenge of the 1989 Act for the SSD involved a change in role, from policing family relationships to partnership with parents, children, and other statutory and voluntary agencies, as well as a fundamental repositioning of the notion of social work with children. The latter had been partly influenced by the 'mixed economy of care'. This meant that the SSD was required to adopt a managerial role in the assessment of children and the purchase of the necessary services which, under the managerial guidance of the SSD, were to be provided by themselves and other private sector agencies.

Accommodation Duties and Powers in the 1989 Act

Consonant with this new relationship of partnership with parents, the 1989 Act placed duties on, and gave powers to, local authorities to provide accommodation (s.20) instead of receiving children into care in broadly similar circumstances. The notion of 'reception into care', contained in the Child Care Act 1980, was discarded because it was connected with an 'unwarranted association with parental shortcoming' (H.L. Debs, Vol. 502, col. 491 (6 December 1988)). Partnership was to be enhanced by providing that the child's wishes should be ascertained and taken into consideration (ss.6); further, the authority were not to provide accommodation if objections were raised by the person(s) with parental responsibility (provided they are able and willing to provide, or arrange for, accommodation themselves). As the Lord Chancellor explained, 'provision of accommodation in these circumstances should be seen as *a service* to the family *without any stigma*' (ibid., col. 491; my emphasis).

The Act prescribed a myriad of powers and duties to provide accommodation[2] to children 'in need'. In addition, all authorities came under a duty to identify the extent to which there are children in need in their area (Sch. 2, para. 1(1)), 'safeguard and promote the welfare' of such children and 'promote the upbringing of such children by their families' (s.17(1)). A child[3] is in need (s.17(10)) if

- the child is unlikely to achieve or maintain, or to have the opportunity of achieving or maintaining, a reasonable standard of health or development without the provision for him of services by a local authority under this part;
- the child's 'physical or mental health' (s.17(11)) or 'physical, intellectual, emotional, social, or behavioural development' (s.17(11)) is likely to be significantly impaired, or further impaired, without the provision for him of such services; or
- he is disabled.

The most significant of the accommodation obligations owed to a child in need by an SSD was the duty to provide accommodation where there was no person who had parental responsibility if the child was lost or abandoned or where the person who has been caring for the child is being prevented (whether or not permanently, and for whatever reason) from providing suitable accommodation or care (s.20(1)). This duty recurred after the child had reached the age of 16 if the child's welfare was likely, in the opinion of the SSD, to be 'seriously prejudiced if they do not provide him with accommodation' (s.20(3)). Further accommodation duties and powers were to be owed to children, even where they were not in need (see ss.20(4) & 24(6), for example).

The Act contained explicit reference neither to the type of accommodation which the SSD was to provide nor to whom the accommodation was to be provided. Given the ethos of the act and the nature of the duties, we had argued that the duties and powers could, and perhaps should, extend to the provision of independent accommodation to families wherever possible (see, for example, Cowan & Fionda, 1993). This was particularly because the purpose of the Act was to keep families together independently of state assistance (unless the latter was necessary). The quality of accommodation available to many SSDs was unsuitable for them to provide independent accommodation. However, the 1989 Act made provision for the SSD to request the assistance of, amongst others, the local housing authority. The local housing authority must comply with the request but only if *'it is compatible with their own statutory or other duties and obligations and does not unduly prejudice the discharge of any of their functions'* (s.27(2); my emphasis). The role of the housing authority was, therefore, perceived to be of critical importance.

Guidance under the 1989 Act

The guidance issued under the 1989 Act referred to the need for 'close liaison' between the SSD and housing department. It went on to add, 'This may best be achieved through the establishment of formal arrangements, particularly as social services and housing may be provided by different tiers of government ... They should between them agree the arrangements for referring young people to the housing departments' (DoH, 1990c, para. 9.81). Although apparently innocuous as a statement of good practice, this was the seed of discontent. What the guidance did not point out was the effect of the 1989 Act on the delicate bargaining position of each agency. On the one hand, the housing department had the stock of accommodation but it also had duties to its own applicants and others on the waiting list. On the other hand, the SSD came under more numerous accommodation obligations without appropriate stock to perform those duties but having increased bargaining power through s.27 of the 1989 Act. Be that as it may, the guidance placed great expectations on the developing relationship between these organizations, suggesting for example that 'The local authority's housing department may provide sheltered or halfway accommodation for young people leaving care and it may also wish to consider reserving some of its stock of conventional accommodation to meet the needs of young people leaving care who are capable of living independently' (DoH, 1990c, para. 9.83). If any of the HPUs in our sample had sheltered or halfway accommodation, it was either only in the process of development or it had been 'silted up'.[4]

Problems of the 1989 Act

Two particular problems emerged from the 1989 Act which affected the role of the SSD. First, there was the role-based dilemma. As with community care, the movement to partnership stigmatized the SSD because, implicit in the change of language, it suggested that the SSD was not 'the sole possessor of necessary expertise in the area'. Consequently, it undermined professional power and involved a movement to managerialism, less explicit than in community care but nevertheless apparent (see, generally, Langan, 1993). Nevertheless, considerable distinctions in ethos emerged between the 1989 Act and community care (Hallet, 1991) which necessitated a move away from generic social work to more specialized, specific roles (Clarke, 1996, p.52). In the context of child protection services, partnership has also been linked with the move to the mixed economy of care so that 'partnership is a structural response to a social policy position. In reality it is the manifestation of an ideology of the role of the state in the provision of social services: who pays and who provides' (Solomon, 1995).

Second, the lack of resources and the singular failure of government to provide definitions of need meant that SSDs were forced to prioritize their services to children. Prioritization necessarily involved the rationing of services, which particularly affected those at the bottom end of the list of priorities. It was perhaps unsurprising, in the light of the media pressure[5] and inquiries, that all the available research suggested that heading the list of priorities was child abuse.

> The public mood of lack of sympathy for families in difficulty and the support for authoritarian corrective action 'for the sake of the children' pushes social services departments more and more into a policing role where the overriding priority is to cope with the bombardments of child protection referrals. (Social Services Inspectorate, 1994, p.8)

In a study of priorities in Welsh SSDs' children services, Colton *et al.* found that, of nine categories of service, sexual and other abuse or neglect was given a significantly higher priority than all the other categories. 'Unsatisfactory home conditions' – with all the implications that the phrase has for rehousing purposes – was regarded as the eighth priority, just above 'poverty'. Partnership was regarded as 'costly and time-consuming' (Colton *et al.*, 1995; reflecting the national position: Otway, 1996; Parton, 1996). Otway suggested:

> Too many people are experiencing the child protection system who could possibly be more effectively assisted under the family support provisions of the Act. It is not consistent with the Children Act philosophy for the gateway to family support services to be closed until the problem is presented in terms of child protection and clearly misrepresents the nature of need presented to Social Services Departments. (Otway, 1996, pp.169–70)

Research conducted by CHAR, a housing pressure group, in relation to the effects of the 1989 Act on young homeless people tended to reflect these problems (McCluskey, 1993, 1994; Kay, 1994; there were also reports of seminars held by CHAR in various different regions of England). This research provided a valuable concomitant to our own fieldwork. Broadly, their results were as follows: most SSDs (75 per cent) assessed whether a 16- or 17-year-old would be entitled to accommodation under the 1989 Act. Rooflessness (59 per cent) and drug or alcohol problems (53 per cent) were the usual circumstances where such a child would not be entitled to accommodation: the former because it was perceived as a 'housing department problem' and the person would therefore be referred to the HPU; the latter because social workers viewed these people 'in negative and judgmental ways' (McCluskey, 1994, p.21).

Only 7 per cent of SSDs had access to their own self-contained accommodation and so links with other housing providers were crucial. Over half of the SSDs had developed joint policies with housing departments, although this figure was greater in unitary authorities (69 per cent in unitary authorities and 36 per cent in non-unitary authorities). The report recognized that problems might have been under the surface even where joint arrangements existed:

> The housing departments that participated in the second stage of the research identified that social services departments were often reluctant to enter into joint working. In some areas social services departments have not approached the housing department or, after making arrangements for referral under section 27, they have never referred anyone (McClusky, 1994, p.39 – even though evidence suggested that the numbers of street homeless children were rising in the area)

Evidence from six follow-up study areas suggested differences between local authorities, four believing that the 1989 Act had minimal impact (because, for example, it simply reflected current practice) and in two other housing departments it was felt that the Act had spurred the SSD into making contact. There were, however, different views as to the effect of the SSDs' response to the Act.

The Children Act 1989 and the Homelessness Legislation: towards Appropriateness

In seeking to show the operationalization of the appropriate applicant, it was suggested in the previous chapter that the construction of the relationships between the HPU and the SSD was critically important. The particular reason for the problems encountered by our HPUs in responding to community care was that the legislation did not encourage collaboration or partnership, partly because the concepts used by the two were in conflict. Exactly the same argument, for many of the same reasons, can be pursued in relation to the overlap between the 1989 Act and the homelessness legislation.

The potential conflict was recognized during the parliamentary debates leading to the 1989 Act. For example, Baroness David laid an amendment requiring no homeless child to be taken into care and that all such people should be provided with accommodation by the local housing authority. The Lord Chancellor's response was simply that the homelessness legislation catered for this and that the homelessness Code of Guidance would be updated to take the 1989 Act's provisions into account (H.L. Debs, Vol. 502, cols 1330-33 (20 December 1988)). Lord Prys-Davies attempted to insert an amendment to the 1985 Act requiring authorities to provide accommodation to homeless children in priority need if they might be the subject of a care order, the SSD would have to provide accommodation under the 1989 Act, or the child would have to be cared for by persons other than its parents. Such an amendment would have neatly sidestepped the intentionality provision of the 1985 Act. However, the Lord Chancellor answered that such duties already rested on the housing authority. Referring to what became s.27, 1989 Act, the Lord Chancellor argued that 'This request will effectively activate the housing authority's duty and I do not believe that this amendment adds to those provisions' (H.L. Debs, Vol. 503, cols 1402-5 (6 February 1989)). Finally, to effectively kill off any further debate, the Lord Chancellor said that 'the Department of the Environment is currently reviewing the homelessness legislation and any amendments at this time would be premature' (H.L. Debs, Vol. 503, col. 1404 (6 February 1989)).

No doubt the Lord Chancellor reported the views of Baroness David and Lord Prys-Davies to the DoE, as he undertook to do. However, the 1989 review of the homelessness legislation made only brief reference to the 'proper public anxiety about the possible dangers for young people on their own' (DoE, 1989a, para. 17) without further commenting upon the potential problems in coordinating the agencies within the bounds of the 1989 Act. Such a lackadaisical response, surely at odds with what they had only recently legislated against, meant that, when it came to redrafting the Code of Guidance, little was made of the 1989 Act.

The only substantive point made in the third edition of the Code was a glib reference that there was 'no formal correlation' between the priority need test of a single person's vulnerability (s.59(1)(c)) and the 1989 Act's in need criteria, although 'the two might be expected to arise in similar circumstances' and HPUs would need to have regard to the SSD's accommodation obligations (DoE, 1991a, para. 6.15).

A number of difficult problems emerge from this supposed correlation that were specifically related to the notion of appropriateness. First, as has been argued in earlier chapters, the homelessness legislation was not about defining housing need. It provided tools for discerning who is morally blameworthy. The criterion of priority need was neither about need nor about prioritization. Thus, even if this correlation did exist in most cases, it did not necessarily presuppose that children in need would fall within the parameters of the homelessness legislation. Put another way, the problem was that the ethos of the 1989 Act was of individual empowerment within a family structure (presuming that exists in each individual case), enhanced by a relationship of partnership (and paternalism) with the SSD. The ethos of the homelessness legislation was entirely different. While this might have been considered technical, the wording of the legislation suggested that duties to provide accommodation to a child in need occurred when 'the person caring for [the child has been] prevented (whether or not permanently, and for whatever reason) from providing him with suitable accommodation or care' (s.20(1)(c)). Thus the moral blameworthiness of the carer was irrelevant under the 1989 Act although not under the homelessness legislation.

Second, there were problems caused by the dwindling supply of accommodation available to the HPUs. The HPUs' priorities lay clearly with those people who fell within the criteria of the homelessness legislation. In Chapter 2, it was shown how the HPUs in this study largely regarded themselves as 'gatekeepers' and this partially referred to a 'floodgates' type of argument. A particular problem was that potentially all persons under 18 who were homeless would be regarded as being in need. If that was the case, the HPU would not be able to cater for other client groups because the supply of available accommodation would be taken up catering for those covered by the 1989 Act. The Code provided no assistance on this point.

Third, the dilemma of the 1989 Act concerned the bargaining power of each agency. This problem underlay all other issues arising out of the act. Partnership was not only between the SSD and the family, but also between the SSD and the HPU. The 1989 Act provided a method of facilitating this partnership which appeared to create confusion as to which agency had the upper hand in the bargaining process which would almost inevitably arise out of the rationing situation. Section 27 enabled the SSD to request the assistance of the HPU, which would have to respond if the request was compatible with its statutory duties and obligations and did not unduly prejudice the exercise of its functions (s.27(2)). It was entirely unclear what the effect of s.27 might be (although lawyers were gearing up for challenges on the basis of it). Part of the problem was that the structure of the relationship as well as the way forward were extremely hazy. The redrafted Code did not help much:

The Secretaries of State are concerned to avoid any possibility that the implementation of the 1989 Act might result in children and young people being sent to and fro between departments or authorities. Each department and authority has a responsibility to those who approach it under its own relevant legislation. However, a corporate policy and clear departmental procedures in respect of collaboration between departments and authorities will help to ensure co-operation at all levels. (Ibid., para. 6.16)

The first two sentences defined the problem. The third sentence, with its emphasis on policies and procedures, as opposed to potential substantive issues, was hardly likely to assist.

At the time that our fieldwork commenced, judicial reviews were or had occurred. It might have been hoped that these would provide answers to these questions. However, as we see in the next section, such hopes were dashed.

Judicial (Re)stucturing of partnership

Section 27 before the Courts: General

Advisers seemed well aware of the wider implications and uses of the accommodation provisions of the 1989 Act. They also often seemed determined to use those provisions to their full effect. The issue was first given an oblique judicial airing in *R. v. Oldham M.B.C. ex parte Garlick; Bexley L.B.C. ex parte Bentum* (1993) 25 H.L.R. 319 in which Lord Griffiths, although rejecting an argument that two four-year-old children could make a homelessness application because they lacked the requisite cognitive ability, nevertheless referred to 'other provisions of our social welfare legislation that provide for the accommodation and care of children and the duty of cooperation between authorities in discharge of their duties' (at p.325; referring to ss.20(1) & 27, 1989 Act). As was observed at that point, three fundamental questions arose for discussion:

> First, are whole families capable of being housed together under the Children Act as they are under the Housing Act? Secondly, when are the duties of the housing department under both Acts compatible for the purposes of section 27(2)? Third, what is the effect of section 27 of the Children Act on local authority practice? (Cowan & Fionda, 1993, p.412, answering respectively 'yes',[6] unclear, unclear – see, further, below)

It was not long before the second issue arose fully. In January 1993, a local Shelter office offered advice to a family as well as to the Avon County Council SSD. The family had been found intentionally homeless by

Northavon District Council. Shelter's advice was that the SSD should provide a rent deposit as well as rent in advance so that the family could obtain private sector accommodation. The SSD refused to provide either but made a formal request under s.27 to the housing authority that the latter provide a private sector or, preferably, local authority tenancy. The housing authority refused, in a 'much criticised' letter 'no doubt drafted by a busy official at short notice' ((1994) 26 H.L.R. 659, 663). This letter argued that, as the Smith family had been found intentionally homeless, it would contradict their duties under the homelessness legislation if they provided long-term accommodation. It was this letter which formed the subject matter of the subsequent judicial hearings.

At first instance, Anthony Lester QC, sitting as a Deputy Judge, held that the housing authority had successfully argued that the request both would be incompatible with their own statutory or other duties and obligations and did unduly prejudice the discharge of any of their functions because of the size of Northavon's waiting list as well as the earlier finding of intentional homelessness (which was not challenged in these judicial proceedings) (unreported, 25 May 1993). However, on July 28 1993, the Court of Appeal allowed an appeal brought by Jimmy Smith (one of the family's children). Northavon's letter had shown that they had not actually considered responding to any of the requests made by the SSD:

> Avon's letter required Northavon to consider the Smiths' position afresh in the light of a new consideration, namely the judgement of the responsible authority that the children were in need and required to be housed. I think Northavon should have considered the matter afresh and not have regarded the finding of intentional homelessness as conclusive, as it seems to have done. I very much doubt if, on such consideration, Northavon could properly have considered it as other than compatible with its own duties and obligations to house the Smiths, but it might be (depending on the detailed facts, particularly the state of its own housing list) that to provide its own housing to the Smiths would have unduly prejudiced its general function of managing such housing in a fair and orderly way. ((1993) 25 H.L.R. 663, 672)

The interregnum between the Court of Appeal and House of Lords judgments (given on 14 July 1994) coincided with our visits in LA1-LA8. Consequently, it requires some consideration (see, further, Cowan & Fionda, 1994b). It seemed that, as the HPU is part of the housing authority, any request for housing would always be compatible with their duties and obligations. The only way to exclude the duty would be to argue that their waiting list was such that they would be unable to exercise their 'function of managing such housing in a fair and orderly way'. The HPU would be required to consider a whole different set of questions, on a wider scale than the enquiries required by the 1985 Act.

Not only this, but the subtle balance of power between the HPU and SSD had been shifted in favour of the latter. Before the judgment, it could be argued that the HPU had the upper hand, as it had access to the stock of accommodation as well as being able to ration that access through the homelessness legislation. The Child Care Act 1980 had not affected that, but the 1989 Act did question it, without providing any answer. If the SSD were to be entitled to call upon an allocation whenever they wished, and the HPU had to respond, questions would be raised about whether the 1985 Act enquiries would be relevant at all, unless the waiting list was blocked.

Subsequently, the House of Lords, on the other hand, pursued more of a policy-based approach. Lord Templeman gave vent to the common judicial concern about 'jumping the waiting list'. Indeed, the 1989 Act effectively gave some families an opportunistic second chance at the jump.[7] In the light of these motivations, the House of Lords decided that the letter did in fact 'clearly assert' that the HPU could not comply with the request because otherwise the exercise of their functions would be unduly prejudiced. If the matter had been left here, the only issue would be whether the waiting list was sufficiently large to justify the refusal of the request. No further enquiries would be necessary. However, Lord Templeman added:

> The social services authority are responsible for children and the housing authority are responsible for housing. The two authorities must co-operate. Judicial review is not the way to obtain co-operation. The court cannot decide what form co-operation should take. Both forms of authority have difficult tasks which are of great importance and for which they may feel their resources are not wholly adequate. The authorities must together do the best they can. ((1994) 26 H.L.R. 659, 666)

Lord Nolan hoped that,

> as a matter of normal practice a social services authority, faced with the problem of children who are threatened with homelessness, will explore the possibility of obtaining council accommodation informally and in a spirit of mutual co-operation rather than by an immediate formal request, unsupported by any offer of contribution, under the provisions of section 27. (Ibid., p.668)

These comments smacked of a lack of awareness of the relevant issues, abnegation of judicial responsibility, laissez-faire, and complete divorce from reality. HPUs and SSDs were effectively left to their own (de)vices to seek out local solutions to what were, apparently, local problems (for further comment, see Cowan & Fionda, 1995).

Issues in Unitary Authorities

Earlier than the *Smith* case, the Court of Appeal heard argument in a similar case concerning a unitary authority in which housing and the SSD fall within the same administrative structure. Such authorities were generally in London and the metropolitan boroughs at the time of our fieldwork, although they were subsequently extended to other areas by the Banham Commission and Parliament. This case, *R. v. Tower Hamlets L.B.C. ex parte Byas* (1993) 25 H.L.R. 105, was in fact an application for leave to move for judicial review – an initial hearing to decide if an application has any merit so that it can proceed to the main hearing. The particular problem faced by the applicant in this case was that, as the two departments were within the same administrative structure, 'it seems to me quite unarguable that the requesting authority can itself be the authority to which the request is addressed. You cannot ask yourself for help' ((1993) 25 H.L.R. 105, 107 *per* Hoffman LJ). This 'short point of construction' therefore was answered against the applicant.

Whether or not this decision was correct, it masked a more difficult and subtle question. The duties in the 1989 Act of assessment and provision are owed by the 'local authority'. The definition of local authority used by the act (s.105) includes metropolitan and London boroughs. On this basis, it could (and no doubt will) be argued that unitary authorities are required to make the relevant assessment and satisfy the relevant duties. As HPUs and their housing departments fall within the structure of the unitary authority, if the child approaches them first, this means that they will be required to consider the child and the family not only in the context of the 1985 Act *but also* in the context of the 1989 Act. This seems the logical interpretation of the 1989 Act and also, as it happens, neatly sidesteps the *Byas* argument.

The 1989 Act in LA1-LA10

Almost all the non-unitary HPUs in our study had, at an early stage, appreciated that the potential impact of the 1989 Act was that, if taken to its extreme, it could effectively undermine the duties potentially owed to a proportion of their case load as well as override their current decision making. For example, as one officer in LA6 expressed it, there would be no point in making the relevant exhaustive enquiries as to whether an applicant was intentionally homeless if the SSD simply referred the applicant back to the HPU to be housed. Indeed, most officers felt that the 1989 Act actually forced professional jealousies to the surface for this reason. No doubt because of this, a siege mentality was adopted in many of the HPUs and officers expressed themselves in typical war-based language when questioned about the effects of the 1989 Act.

Fear of the potential impact of the 1989 Act meant that, of LA1-LA10, only LA5 and LA7 had not at least entered into negotiations with the SSD as a precursor to some more formal agreement. Of those that had entered into negotiations on a formal agreement, sometimes referred to as a protocol, or actually had such an agreement in place, experience was mixed. This ranged from a litigious situation in LA1 through to a (surprising) nil effect in some other of our study authorities. Both experiences suggested that the legislation itself actually caused and enhanced these poor professional relationships and this, therefore, had an impact upon the assessment criteria. So, both experiences also show how the organizational interaction affected the type of person whom the HPU would regard as an appropriate applicant.

As in the previous chapter, HPUs in our study adopted administrative solutions to combat their perception that applicants who were believed to form part of the community care client load were being accommodated too early, without appropriate care packages in place. Precisely the same views were expressed in relation to 16-18-year-olds. Indeed, these views were given greater weight because, in the opinion of many of our interviewees, it was *unfair* that their first experience of independent accommodation should be tarnished for reasons beyond the applicant's control. The administrative solutions which were sought to combat this perceived problem were of a different variety from those adopted in relation to community care.

This section concentrates initially upon the way the authorities entered into their relationships with the SSD, how the agreements were drafted, and finally the effect of the agreement: 'entering the relationship'. Consideration is then given to the methods used by our HPUs to deal with referrals from the SSD: 'firefighting'. Finally, I look at whether the HPUs' interpretations of the key concepts in the 1985 Act were affected by the introduction of the 1989 Act and also the effect of any formal referrals under the 1989 Act from the SSD to the HPU: 'exiting from the relationship'. It will become apparent that, from an early stage, the HPUs in this study had mostly sought to avoid taking on obligations to under-18s because it was believed that they were inappropriate.

Entering the Relationship: the Effect of Altered Priorities

As a general rule, it was the HPUs in our study which began negotiations with the SSD, largely because of the perceived potential impact of the 1989 Act. HPUs believed that the 1989 Act had changed the balance of the relationship between SSDs and HPUs in favour of the former. Every HPU seemed familiar with the progress of the *Smith* case. Seeking a formal position meant that they would be able to outline and teach the SSD the obligations of the HPU towards homeless 16–18-year-olds, using their own existing practice as the starting-point. At no stage was there ever a suggestion that the HPU would manipulate its own criteria to take the 1989 Act into account. The only exception to this general rule was LA1, where the 'Policy Development Unit' of the county council had drafted a formal agreement which had been accepted by the Policy Section of LA1.

Furthermore, if the HPU position was made clear particularly as regards the supply and type of available accommodation, many felt that this would stem the possibility of referrals. Nevertheless, many of our interviewees reported to us that they had to explain not only their own obligations but also the relevant provisions of the 1989 Act. Some were concerned that these explanations would cause the SSD to give greater recognition to the role of the HPU, which would be met with a commensurate increase in applications referred directly from the SSD without any assessment having been made by the SSD.

Completed agreements The scope of the completed agreements reflected the success of the HPU in doing this, although agreements had only been completed in LA1, LA2 and LA8. LA2's experience had been significantly more positive than the others'. A positive relationship had been developed from initially poor communications between the organizations: they had 'battled it out' and generally improved their working arrangements. A flow chart of the relevant procedure had been produced which required most of the child applicants' cases to be passed to the authority's own community care development officer (who was not in post at the time of our visit).

LA8's overall experience, on the other hand, was negative. The formal agreement was described as being basic as it only covered referral mechanisms between HPU and SSD. Officers in LA8 were unsure whether the agreement had even come into effect and the required referral forms had not even been produced. In the discussions which led to the agreement being formed, the SSD's attitude had been that current (that is, pre-1989 Act) policy would not change. Apparently, the SSD's view was that the initial concerns would simply fizzle out. Thus the agreement had been shelved in practice.

The position in LA1 was entirely different. This was not altogether unexpected because the policy had derived from the policy section of the SSD. None of the HPU officers felt that this agreement reflected the reality of the 'on the ground' situation. Neither did they believe that it related to the SSD front-line officers' situation. Their principal concerns were twofold: they would have to house those that they had found intentionally homeless on the basis of referrals from the SSD;[8] and the referral agreement suggested that they were inadequately trained to assess 16–18-year-olds and that a better assessment would be done by the SSD. However, HPU officers believed that the SSD had little appreciation of the homelessness legislation and that the HPU would be expected to house people after inadequate enquiries had been made.

'In the process of' drafting agreements Five authorities were 'in the process of' drafting their referral agreements (LA3, LA4, LA6, LA9, LA10). LA9's concerns about the 1989 Act had led them to the door of the SSD but they subsequently found, over at least two years, that the effect of the Act on their practice was minimal or that they were able to put the SSD off referring applicants to them. This reflected the more general experience of officers in this category who believed that formalizing any agreement would be counter-productive.

LA4, on the other hand, already had mechanisms in place and was simply waiting for the formality of the agreement to be completed. Similarly, LA10 was in the pilot stage of its joint agreement. Their joint agreement was being drafted by the senior homelessness officer and two interviewing officers, together with all their counterparts in the SSD. They had produced a pilot referral and assessment form, which was currently in operation. Particular problems had been observed, in contradistinction to the other authorities, because the number of 16–18-year-old applicants had significantly increased.

LA3 resented the need for formal agreements and methods of referral, preferring informal mechanisms, such as the telephone. Its first contact with 1989 Act had been when the SSD had written a patronizing (in its view) letter to them explaining the effect of the 1989 Act and instructing them that the HPU were under a duty to house a particular applicant under the 1989 Act. The HPU's approach had been similarly to set out the statutory provisions of the 1989 Act, including s.27, followed by a refusal to house that applicant. On the other hand, informal approaches to the HPU by the SSD were usually met with a more understanding response. The result of any such application entirely depended upon the way in which the SSD presented it. The senior officer in the HPU explained that, just before our visit, there had been serious arguments about the way the relationship was developing.

No agreement Of the two other authorities which had no agreement and were not in the process of drafting one – LA5 and LA7 – the most success was being experienced by LA5. In previous chapters, it has been noted that the senior homelessness officer in LA5 had always had good relationships with the SSD because of his past, undisclosed experience, as well as his favourable interpretations of the homelessness legislation criteria. In similar vein to LA3, he wished to proceed informally but, in any event, he suggested that the Children Act had effectively legitimized his pre-existing practice of accepting all under-18s. He had taken steps to ensure that the SSD referred applicants in a structured way because, as he felt that he was overburdened to an unrealistic degree, he thought that he could use the 1989 Act to persuade the SSD to take over the assessment obligations. They would therefore have to conduct the relevant enquiries.

In LA7, the story was different. The officers in LA7 had a uniformly poor relationship with the SSD. The senior officer felt that the SSD was not as harsh in interpreting their legislation as the HPU and was not convinced that she could offer any assistance. This was partly because of her post-1989 Act experience of the SSD, which, it seemed to her, would rather a person was homeless than dealt with by the HPU. While there always had been a referral form, once this had been completed and sent to the SSD, the HPU often did not hear from the SSD again.

Section 27 Referrals: 'Firefighting'

All of the HPUs, whatever stage they had reached in their agreements, had experience of referrals from the SSD under section 27. Their responses seemed to be independent of any agreement or draft agreement, but were institutionally based: either they would refuse to accept the referral or, in three cases, HPUs suggested that they would 'play the game'. 'Playing the game' involved referring the applicant back to the SSD under section 72 of the 1985 Act. It was the preferred approach in three of the smaller HPUs in our study (although some of the larger HPUs had considered this, suggesting that this was common practice in authorities not part of this study). These authorities did not appreciate that this counteracted the original purpose of the homelessness legislation (see Chapter 2) or that this was almost certainly unlawful.[9] However, for them, it was a *legitimate* basis for challenging what they considered to be an illegitimate course of action.

Refusing to accept the referral was justified either on the basis that the applicant would have been intentionally homeless, that the housing department's waiting list was already full, or that the HPU owed no duty under the homelessness legislation to the applicant. Such arguments were almost certainly diametrically opposed to the effect of the Court of Appeal judgment in the *Smith* case, which was well known to the HPUs.

However, the arguments had their genesis in a number of reasons, which broadly approximate to the characteristics of appropriateness. First, it was felt that, if one applicant were allowed through the net, this would create a precedent for others to follow. Therefore the best approach would be to attempt to stem the tide, or close the floodgates, at the very beginning. Second, there was considerable disquiet expressed by our interviewees about applicants either having 'a second chance' through the 1989 Act if they would not have been entitled to housing under the homelessness legislation. There was a parallel with the government's own justification for repealing the homelessness legislation: the notion that homeless people jump the queue for housing (see Chapter 8). However, this was a concern rooted in the assumptions created by a supply deficit. Third, concern was expressed that most of the applicants who were referred would be unable to keep the obligations and responsibilities that are inherent in independent accommodation. HPUs generally felt that a 'revolving door' solution would reward nobody and therefore they strenuously objected to referrals.

LA1's position was different because of the method used to formulate the policy. In addition to all of the above, three further principles influenced LA1's firefighting approach. LA1's principal concern was the operationalization of the referral procedure. Having been told that they were incapable of assessing a child for accommodation, they considered the welfare assessment reports made by the SSD inadequate. Indeed, the common view was that those assessments carried no other information than applicants made available to the HPU. A further concern was that, if the applicant was previously unknown to the SSD, welfare assessments would include the line that the SSD would take no further interest in the case, other than on a 'duty basis'. Equally, referrals to LA1's HPU were generally not being made according to the procedure and did not have the formality which the joint agreement required. Finally, it became clear to the HPU that the SSD was being guided, not by its own criteria or by their joint policy, but by a local firm of solicitors, who were involved in practically all the referrals. Frequently, officers regarded the referrals as stage-managed by this firm.

LA1's response to this intrusion was atypical when compared to the other authorities in our study because the HPU involved the authority's legal department. The latter wrote a series of strong letters to the SSD suggesting that the SSD adopt the formal procedure, many of the SSD's assessments seemed *ultra vires* and many of the assessments made had given inaccurate or insufficient evidence. What followed, though, was a further referral from the SSD of a 17-year-old single mother who had rejected accommodation offered by the HPU under the homelessness legislation.[10] The HPU's annoyance over this case was caused because they believed that the accommodation originally offered had been acceptable; the referral had been made by a duty social worker who had not followed the correct procedure and provided inadequate information; and the referral had been initiated by the local firm of solicitors.

This was the final straw. LA1's solicitor immediately sought counsel's advice on the referral. When counsel suggested that the case might be distinguishable from *Smith* and that there was a 50 per cent chance of success, LA1 refused to accept the referral, knowing that this would be challenged by way of judicial review proceedings. This was the position at the time of our visit.[11]

Exiting from the Relationship: the Effect of the 1989 Act on Decision-making Practice

From general concern to nil effect For most of the HPUs in this study, after rejecting the first few referrals, their immediate concerns had proved ill-founded or, to put it another way, their firefighting had been successful. It became apparent to the HPUs that the SSDs were seeking alternative mechanisms for the provision of accommodation to this client group, which generally involved the provision of rent deposits and similar financial assistance. In LA8, where this had become the SSD's current practice, the senior homelessness officer believed that this was because such expedients involved a simpler, quicker, more effective solution, without the rigmarole of arguments or discussions with the HPU. The opinion in LA9 was that the SSD had been forced by the negative response to reprioritize and now perceived housing difficulties as a lesser priority. After some threats from the SSD of formal referrals – usually from 'new' social workers – LA6 had no experience of them (partly also because they had always threatened, by way of response, to use section 72). Thus the general result was a nil effect.

However, LA4 and LA10 were different from this norm. LA4, a small rural Conservative-controlled authority, was operating joint working processes with the SSD. These processes seemed to involve the HPU officer imposing his own value base on applicants within this client group. He had severe reservations, though, about the policy's resource implications. This officer regarded successful applicants, from the under-18 client group, to have attributes which closely aligned with his personal philosophy. They were required to want to progress, look for a job and have a solid basis for the future. This approach was also guided by the local expediency. It was explained that support strategies for individual applicants were simply unavailable in the area. Consequently, any person who would not help themselves, and might cause estate management problems, was a liability. The officer's reservations revolved around the significant increase in the number of applicants within this client group, which he attributed to successful applicants informing their friends. The simple administrative expediency he adopted to cope with this increase was to contact parents when approached by the applicant to find out if the applicant's reasons for leaving were genuine or not. Often the threat of this was enough to ensure that applicants returned home. The officer believed that this was because those applicants were not genuine (although such a conclusion was not merited – compare the approach adopted to violence to women).

LA10's pilot scheme had caused an increase in the number of applicants within this client group as well as an increase in referrals from the SSD. The senior officer's view was that this increase was a direct result of the resource constrictions of the SSD which led it to see the HPU as an organization onto which they could offload their clients. It had begun using section 72 to refer these applicants back to the SSD and, furthermore, was another authority which had noticed the SSD using rent deposits and funding assured shorthold tenancies. There was, therefore, some thought being put into redrafting the pilot scheme, as well as reconsideration of its aims.

Effect on decision-making Other than in LA1, LA4 and LA10, the effect of the 1989 Act was minimal. No authority admitted that the Act had changed their interpretation of the homelessness criteria. So, for example, while one might have believed that the notion of 'in need', so prominent in the 1989 Act, might have affected the HPU's interpretation of the 'vulnerability' criterion, this had not occurred. The process had remained stagnant. Indeed, many authorities adopted a further administrative step to their procedures when considering applications from this client group by always considering whether there could be a reconciliation between the applicant and their previous carer.[12] Two other motivations guided these principles. First, it was believed that often independent accommodation was not suitable for these applicants. However, secondly (and more effectively stressed by interviewees), it was believed that applicants themselves would be unsuitable for the type of accommodation on offer largely because there was insufficient after-care support for applicants once housed. When provided with independent accommodation, applicants were left to fend for themselves, or set up, in the opinion of our interviewees, to fail. Consequently, once again the different institutional objectives had combined to work against applicants.

Effects of the 1989 Act on inter-agency working Other than in LA4 and the pilot scheme in LA10, none of the non-unitary HPUs in our study were involved in joint planning. Indeed, when asked whether they were involved in facilitating the planning process required by the 1989 Act (Sch. 1, para. 1), this was greeted with a sense of bewilderment. Nevertheless, in contrast to the data collected on community care, it was said that much of the earlier confusion and annoyance caused when the 1989 Act was first implemented in their area had been watered down to respect for each other's resource limitations (except for LA1). While the 1989 Act had promised much in terms of providing access to accommodation, it was realized that this expectation was incapable of being met. Rather than continually battling it out, they simply ignored each other. The potential inherent in the *Smith* case for sides to be drawn was ignored because it required too much blood to be spilt. So, after some initial bloodshed, the sides withdrew to lick their wounds. The battle had ended in a draw.

'An Open Secret': the Children Act in LB1-LB5

While our study non-unitary authorities had been involved in a stand-off with the SSD on the implementation of the 1989 Act, our unitary authorities were involved in open warfare (referred to by one officer as an 'open secret'). The general feeling of LB1-LB5 towards the effect of the 1989 Act was entirely negative in terms of its practical effect, although most authorities referred to the ideology of the 1989 Act as sound. The fact that each department fell within the same administrative structure actually caused many of the arguments that had ensued and, further, many HPUs had sought to avoid the interference of the SSD in their practice by administrative expediency. Whereas many of the non-unitary authorities had heard little about the 1989 Act after its immediate impact, LB1-LB5 had generally sought to limit their involvement with the SSD by other means.

Entering into Relationships

Policy formulation All of our unitary authorities had entered into some form of relationship with the SSD as regards the implementation of the 1989 Act. In general terms, this was for similar reasons to those experienced in LA1-LA10. All HPUs had initially considered that the 1989 Act might have a dramatic effect on their pre-existing working practices. These relationships sometimes formed part of the bureaucracy of homelessness decision-making practice so that, on their being approached by a person under 18, that person would be referred directly to the SSD either for an assessment of their 'need' (LB1 and LB2) or so that the SSD might effect a reconciliation with the applicant's family (LB5). LB3 operated a panel of professionals to assess the applicant when considering an approach from a person under 18.

LB4, on the other hand, after setting up a joint working party with the SSD to discuss the relevant issues, had come to the conclusion that the 1989 Act was not as radical as had initially been perceived. This was assisted by the fact that the SSD's criteria in relation to their 1989 Act assessments were so severe that few applicants would be caught in their net. Consequently, there was no need for the HPU to alter their interpretations of the homelessness criteria. This was all in their policy manual (dated 27 November 1991), which also contained the following comment from a DoE official:

> No housing authority would be required to go beyond its existing statutory duties and, indeed, for many authorities with the number of households becoming homeless during the course of the year exceeding the number of lettings becoming available there is little prospect of offering assistance for this particular vulnerable group.

As LB4's housing situation was precisely that – they were the second hardest pressed of all our HPUs – the senior managers had decided that there was nothing to fear from the 1989 Act. This stance was approved by the Councillors.

The only authority with a formal written 'procedure note' (in this case) was LB1. This agreement promised much in the way of reciprocal assessments, formal reasoning as to whether the applicant was successfully found to be 'in need' or 'vulnerable', the institution of a formal panel and consideration of how aftercare might be provided. The procedure had been drafted by the authority's legal department in consultation with the director of housing, the director of the HPU and their 'opposite numbers' within the SSD. All our interviewees in LB1 agreed that the procedure was unworkable and had adopted alternative informal procedures, which also seemed to be failing.

The only success story was LB2 but only when dealing with applicants leaving the authority's care. In line with their policy of encouraging officers to take up specialisms, applications from children leaving care had all been assigned to one officer. The officer had redrafted the application form, developed the relevant and necessary relationships, and was succeeding in placing each such applicant in the authority's own accommodation. Both this officer and the senior officer (who had initially been responsible for this until a period of sick leave) took the view that the authority had institutionalized these children in the first place and that therefore they were under a countermanding responsibility to continue providing accommodation. Thus more favourable decision making was regarded as a necessity.

Initial problems and unreasonable demands The striking thing about the HPUs' experience of the 1989 Act was that all policies seemed to be failing for the same reasons, many of which overlapped with the causes of the failure of community care. Two potent reasons were, first, concerns that the

SSD was unclear as to its obligations and, second, that accommodation was not prioritized by the SSD unless there was a child abuse element. For example, all officers continually expressed the belief that the SSD had prioritized child abuse above everything else so that the SSD was unable to consider their accommodation duties. This was believed because either no assessments were being completed by the SSD or because any assessment that was made was woefully late or inadequate. Furthermore, when the HPU tried to involve the SSD in the assessment process by attempting to refer the applicant to the SSD, the SSD often refused to accept any responsibility. On the other hand, when dealing with a case which had a child abuse element, the SSD would continually be involved.

Many of our interviewees also expressed the same doubts as officers in non-unitary authorities as to whether the applicants were capable of taking on the obligations of independent accommodation. There was considerable anecdotal evidence that applicants were 'set up to fail' and also the belief that, for the SSD, this was desirable because at least the applicant had been given the opportunity. The HPU officers all reacted strongly against that sentiment. Finally, it was often said that HPU officers' main contact with the SSD occurred when the latter telephoned asking either for a house or for supported accommodation. As the HPUs had no access to the latter and the former were restricted (generally) to applicants to whom the HPUs owed a duty, these telephone conversations were viewed as a serious irritation. They only made clearer the HPUs' limitations.

There were other problems which were solely related to the implementation of the 1989 Act. For example, most HPUs appreciated that the SSD operated under severe resource limitations. However, it was believed that this led SSDs to attempt to avoid their obligations. In LB3, for example, the senior homelessness officer had reacted angrily when asked by the SSD to do the assessments of 'need' because she felt that this was a classic method used by the SSD to ignore their responsibilities.[13] LB1's policy had caused confusion from its inception. The SSD had apparently believed that it involved simply sending clients to the HPU without any social care assessments. Consequently, there was plenty of confusion as to the roles and responsibilities of officers, and the procedure was ignored. Additionally, their SSD child services department had decentralized, so that there were six area offices. HPU officers suggested that each area office argued about which was to take responsibility in each case.

Similar confusions as to roles and responsibilities were exhibited in LB2, although officers interviewed there felt that the SSD did very little with applicants because of their resource problems. LB3's panel had, in all but name, become a mental health panel because of the finite level of accommodation available. Consequently, only the most difficult cases were referred and these usually involved 'behavioural problems'. Other applicants were referred from one office to the other. This 'yoyo effect' was also the general practice of LB4, so that no department accepted responsibility for the client group.

LB5's policies had been in operation before the 1989 Act had come into force because of several well-publicized child abuse scandals. At the time of our visit, understandably perhaps, it was generally felt that the only time the SSD would become involved was when there was an abuse issue. The under-resourcing of the SSD was very much in evidence. All HPU officers had to conform to certain centrally imposed deadlines in relation to each case. However, it was often impossible to contact the relevant officer in the SSD in the relevant time and assessments took too long to produce. In response to these pressures and to avoid confrontations with SSD officers, the general practice was simply to process applications without any SSD input or involvement.

Firefighting

While the Code paid particular attention to the possibility of reconciliation between child and former carer, it seemed clear that, when a child approached the HPU to apply for housing, the child would have to be assessed according to the relevant criteria. LB4 and LB5 adopted a 'firefighting' approach by attempting a reconciliation *before* accepting a homelessness application. This was entirely a matter of administrative expediency or gatekeeping, not only for the reasons outlined above, such as the potential inability to cope with independent accommodation, but also because it was feared that too many acceptances from this client group would severely reduce their ability to cope with other client groups.

In LB5, all 16–18-year-olds who approached the HPU directly would be directed to an SSD-organized scheme (hereafter 'the scheme'). The primary purpose of the scheme was to seek a reconciliation between child and former carer wherever that was possible. If that was not possible, only then would the child be referred back to the HPU with an assessment of their 'need'. Originally, the HPU believed that the 1989 Act would mean that the child would be in priority need and automatically housed. This was their policy for a short period, but it was subsequently changed because the HPU believed that too many of their clients were using the system to gain access to the borough's accommodation. After that point, the usual approach was to place the child in bed and breakfast accommodation for a short period. The quality of this accommodation was such that few applicants came through this route. This was a method of testing the applicant's 'genuineness' (see, for similar practices, Chapter 6).

LB1, LB2 and LB4 had a rather different method of firefighting, reflecting a concern that they might be challenged. Rather than HPUs facing the possibility of having clients with children, whom the HPUs had found intentionally homeless, referred back to them under the 1989 Act, these clients were usually found accommodation in the private sector with assured shorthold tenancies. These policies only operated where there were children involved and were entirely generated by fears of the potency of the 1989 Act. This, in their view, neatly avoided the possibility of any form of challenge from the SSD under the 1989 Act. In LB1, this approach was doubly satisfying because the housing department was jointly funded with the SSD. The HPU was therefore able to dip into this joint fund and provide the rent deposit which came out of both departments' budgets. In each case, the SSD were not told where the clients were placed because the purpose of the policies was avoidance, not of their obligations, but of any contact with the SSD. This was their means of exiting from the relationship.

Exiting from the Relationship: Effect of the 1989 Act on Decision Making

Other than the above policies, only two authorities accepted that the 1989 Act had affected the way they viewed the homelessness criteria: LB2 and LB4. In LB4, only the senior homelessness officer admitted this, partly because of her view of the new role of the HPU and particularly in the light of the proposed changes to the HPU (the proposed merger with the SSD considered in Chapter 3). Nevertheless, this officer seemed entirely unaware of the accommodation provisions of the 1989 Act, interpreting our questions about them in a different way (even when these questions were specific).[14] It was, in any event, clear that the other members of the HPU were unaffected by the 1989 Act when considering a homelessness application. The senior officer in LB2 directly appreciated the relevance of the 1989 Act's accommodation provisions and suggested that his interpretation of the 1985 Act had been appreciably altered, particularly in relation to intentionality and priority need. However, he was adamant that his acceptance criteria should always reflect any potential estate management problems. Because of this, young people were often turned away from the HPU.

A specific research question was asked of each interviewee in our unitary authorities' HPUs. This related to the possibility that the Act required them to make the relevant 'in need' assessments when a person under 18 approached them. Unsurprisingly, each interviewee felt that they lacked the necessary experience, training and time to make these assessments. Many of the HPU officers in our study were acutely aware that, in contrast to the SSD's training, they were simply thrown into the job of assessing applicants for housing. Only the senior officer in LB2 appreciated that this might have been the intention of the 1989 Act, but his view was that such an obligation was impractical. Consequently, the 1989 Act had little effect on the assessments made by the HPUs.

Conclusion

This chapter has shown how the notion of appropriateness was manipulated by the homelessness decision makers when confronted by the apparently changed priorities created by the Children Act 1989. The approaches adopted mostly involved an attempt at initially stemming the flood of potential applicants referred by the SSD. It appeared that they had been remarkably successful at doing so. After initial concern about the effect of the 1989 Act had led HPUs to develop closer links with the SSDs, these links mostly slipped into obscurity and were replaced by a stand-off.

If one wished to seek the reason for this failure, it has been argued that one would not need to look further than the 1989 Act itself. As different interviewees continually stressed, the 1985 and 1989 Acts concerned the same issue but had different criteria. Whilst the Code tentatively suggested that 'in need' might in practice arise in similar circumstances to 'vulnerability', this did not answer the fundamental point. That was simple: the ethos of the Acts was entirely different and so it was not readily apparent how they might work together. This was particularly the case because both government and the courts failed to provide a structure within which cooperation could be facilitated. It was hardly surprising, then, that the HPUs could not, and would not, tailor their interpretations of the homelessness legislation because otherwise this would have entirely abrogated their responsibility to their other clients.

Notes

1. Both these could include circumstances which, in the context of the 1985 Act, would be regarded as homelessness.
2. It should be noted that the Act draws no distinction between the provision of short-term and long-term accommodation; see, further, DoH (1990b, para. 2.25).
3. A child is a person under 18 (s.105(1)).
4. 'Silting up' is a process whereby there is insufficient 'move-on' accommodation to cater for those living in temporary accommodation. Consequently, the temporary accommodation effectively becomes permanent.
5. Our own anecdotal evidence of this comes from within LA5, where we interviewed an SSD officer in the children team. This officer demanded to see our accreditation, insisted on telephoning our institutions and refused to allow us to tape record the interview. This was explained by the (understandable) fact that she was, at that point, being

harassed by local and national media as a result of a child abuse case with which she was dealing.
6   Cf. *R. v. Tower Hamlets L.B.C. ex parte Byas* (1993) 25 H.L.R. 105, 107, where this proposition was doubted. However, in the *Smith* case (see below), our position was assumed to be correct.
7   See, for example, Lord Templeman's comments that, if successful, the Smiths would destroy the fairness of the allocations process and cause bitter resentment ((1994) 26 H.L.R. 659, 662); the HPU could not provide accommodation to the Smiths 'without breaking the rules which applied to persons on the waiting list. There was no reason why the housing authority should pay for temporary accommodation when the social services authority declined to do so' (p.663).
8   This was a slightly disingenuous argument because LA1 housed most of their intentionally homeless client load as it was. Nevertheless, the problem arose here because the matter was taken out of their hands and placed in the hands of an agency who would have little regard for their own obligations and current practice.
9   This practice was no doubt unlawful because the effect of section 27 requires at the very least an exercise of a different discretion and the consideration of different questions; viz., is the request compatible with our own statutory or other duties and obligations? Does it unduly prejudice the discharge of any of the functions?
10 Once suitable accommodation had been offered, that discharged the HPU's duty under the homelessness legislation. This applicant was therefore using the Children Act to challenge the offer.
11 The following year, leave was granted for judicial review, but LA1 subsequently settled the case.
12 Three authorities ran the 'homeless at home scheme' under which the applicant remains at home until a property becomes available from the waiting list. In these cases, the primary issue was always whether a reconciliation could occur in order to put the applicant through the scheme. This would also avoid the necessity of placing the applicant in temporary accommodation, often because this was considered unsuitable for these applicants.
13 This may well have been an example of the SSD attempting to use the wider definition of 'local authority' in s.105 of the 1989 Act. The HPU officer's reaction may therefore have been defensive but reflected her belief that homelessness officers were not social workers and were not trained to do the assessment.
14 The officer believed that we were asking about the changes in the 1989 Act to the way in which parental responsibility for a child can be arranged without a court order. The officer's problems with this were that it made it much more difficult when considering whether a parent was in priority need as a result of the residence of a dependent child (s.59(1)(b)). Our questions became more and more specific until we directly asked about the accommodation provisions in the 1989 Act. Only at this point did this officer respond directly, but to little effect. It seemed relatively clear that the officer either did not know of the provisions or that she was attempting to mislead us. As this officer was completely honest and representative on all other issues, the former interpretation is to be preferred.

5 Racial harassment

The London Research Centre found that, in a survey of 1000 ethnic minority households across London, one in 14 black or Asian households had suffered harassment in or near their home (London Research Centre, 1993). A DoE questionnaire study of local authority housing departments found that racial harassment and violence was spreading, occurring in 67 per cent of local authorities which responded to the questionnaire. However, in the year 1989/90, the reporting of such incidents had decreased, although this was apparently due to a delay in collating the relevant statistics (DoE, 1994d, paras 40-45). All the available research and evidence suggested that there was and is a considerable under-reporting of incidents of racial harassment. In some of our study areas, we heard of significant numbers of racially motivated incidents of one sort or another, including arson attacks, violence, abuse, vandalism, graffiti and excrement put through letter boxes. Nevertheless, our HPUs uniformly reported extremely low numbers of applicants claiming that they were being subjected to racial harassment.

The response to the unquantified level of racial harassment was to encourage agencies to work together, combined with an exhortation on local government and other housing providers to develop and use legal remedies. Working together, so prominent in the community care legislation and Children Act, in this context did not appear in any legislation. Rather, it appeared in guidance and research reports. This approach was taken to encourage, as opposed to command, local authorities to adopt authority-wide policies, gather and make better use of statistics, and work effectively with other agencies such as the police and voluntary organizations (Home Office, 1989, 1991a; DoE, 1989b, 1994d). The aims were the prevention of racial harassment as well as unifying the institutional response to it. Thus the required response was, or should have been, institutional. In each document, local authorities were reminded of their obligations under s.71 of the Race Relations Act 1976, to discharge their functions with due regard to the need to eliminate unlawful racial discrimination, and to promote equality of opportunity and good race relations.

Underlying this programme was a belief in the legal process. In the housing context, it was continually suggested that the perpetrator of the racial harasssment should be evicted and the applicant should be entitled to protective remedies. A number of authorities therefore required their tenants to sign 'racial harassment' covenants, breach of which would enable the authority to bring an action for possession; ordinary implied covenants given by the local authority landlord and express covenants not to commit nuisance were probably sufficient, in any event.

However, it appeared that this faith in both the institutions and the legal process was misplaced. In one study, many authorities had a 'stated policy that legal action would be taken against perpetrators of racial harassment' but the authorities then 'largely fail[ed] to translate these into effective and sustained legal action against perpetrators' (Bridges & Forbes, 1990, p.8). An advice line was set up as part of the study, under the auspices of the Legal Action Group, but by 1990 only 30 local authorities had made use of the service. Further research showed that only 10 authorities were using the legal process and that these authorities were responsible for only 25 cases (Bridges & Forbes, 1990). The subsequent DoE questionnaire study showed that, out of 54 per cent of respondents willing to issue notices seeking possession against perpetrators of racial harassment, 48 per cent had not in fact issued any at all (DoE, 1994d, p.18).

Even when such notices were issued, courts apparently found great difficulties in the definition of racial harassment and the burden of proof. Applicants appeared to have little faith in the effect of injunctions or non-molestation orders. Many local authority legal advisors did not seem to want to have recourse to the legal process and, in any event, rarely collaborated with housing departments (Bridges & Forbes, 1990, pp.2-5). Often, also, it was suggested that those subjected to the harassment were unhappy to identify the perpetrator, or the latter was too young to be dealt with in terms of housing (cf. Cooper & Qureshi, 1994, p. 252).

There is also a history, documented within a series of Commission for Racial Equality investigations and academic texts, of housing departments operating forms of 'institutional racism'; that is, there is 'evidence of racial inequalities in housing linked to local institutional practices' (Ginsburg, 1992, p.109). This is suggested by allocation policies (CRE, 1986, 1989; Henderson & Karn, 1987; Sarre *et al.*, 1989; and, generally, Ginsburg, 1992), even in areas such as Hackney and Lambeth where allocation systems themselves had been devised to avoid such conclusions (Jeffers & Hoggett, 1995). Smith summarizes the extent of the housing inequality in the following terms:

> Barriers in access to mortgage finance and to the tax subsidies associated with ownership are paralleled in the public sector by disadvantage at the points of

entry to, allocation of and transfer within a diminishing stock of council housing. These processes all help to reproduce the racial inequalities that are expressed in, and moulded by, residential structure. (Smith, 1996, p.99)

Indeed, in one study of the London Borough of Newham's response to racial harassment, it was suggested that 'Initial anger [of those subjected to the racial harassment] towards the perpetrators was in many cases rapidly redirected towards the police or the council once a case had been reported. Our respondents spent significantly more interview time talking about this issue than about the incidents themselves' (Cooper & Qureshi, 1994, p.248). This was because of an initially over-ambitious view of what could be done by these agencies as well as a belief that too little was being done.

These institutional and legal problems form the backdrop to the discussions in this chapter, which considers why so few people who have been subjected to racial harassment used the homelessness legislation in our study authorities. In the first section, answers are sought, on the one hand, from within the homelessness legislation itself and, on the other hand, from central government policy, including the role seen for housing in the various Home Office and DoE documents, as well as the supposed lack of clarity within the concept of racial harassment. The second section details how certain of the HPUs in this study did, in fact, respond to racial harassment; the third section considers the implementation of the HPUs' policies and procedures (if any).

There are, however, two further introductory remarks which are required to distinguish this chapter within the structure of this book. First, the previous two chapters were concerned with the interaction between two pieces of legislation, both of which apparently seemed to guarantee at their heart some sort of access to housing. The appropriateness ideology of the HPUs operated differently, although for similar reasons. This chapter marks a structural divergence within this book because here, and in the next chapter where violence to women is considered, we are discussing allocation only within the context of the homelessness legislation itself. So the statutory relationships required in the community care legislation and the Children Act have less of an emphasis here. That is not to say that partnership or the 'multi-agency approach' was still not regarded as the essential response. However, in these instances it involved no explicit external threat to the criteria employed by homelessness officers.

Second, at the heart of this chapter lies a fundamental dichotomy for the HPU. In the previous two chapters, and indeed in Chapter 6, HPUs were seen to be engaged partly in reducing demand from within the client groups or else requiring other agencies to provide appropriate support. In this chapter, the dilemma was whether to respond to a problem which did not appear to exist statistically on the basis of their past experience and thereby potentially increase demand for the diminishing supply of accommodation. Furthermore, if the extent and nature of the problem was unknown, it would have been difficult to anticipate the effect of policies or how many resources would be required (see also H.C. Home Affairs Committee, 1994, paras 20-23). If they did so respond, in some areas this might be likely to run contrary to the gatekeeper ideology exposed in Chapter 2. This puts a slightly different 'spin' on the following comment:

> We want to emphasise that although the longer term aim of introducing a policy is to bring about a reduction in racial harassment, an initial *increase* in the number of reported incidents should generally be regarded as a positive achievement. The rise is likely to indicate that staff have become more skilled at recognising racial incidents and/or that victims are reporting a higher proportion of incidents because they have more confidence in the agency's willingness or ability to respond. (Home Office, 1989, para. 62)

Thus, the response was always likely to resolve to the appropriateness ideology.

Three Problems

Problem 1:What do We do with the Victim?

Although the government was attempting to stamp out the paternalistic state, they were in many ways *imposing* a solution on the housing problems of the 'victim'.[1] The starting-point was an apparent paradox. If the household suffering the harasssment was moved, this could be seen as a victory for the aggressor(s), which might have an impact upon the next household that moved into the vacant accommodation. Furthermore, if the household suffering the harassment was moved, this could lead to no-go areas and, indeed, ghettoization of estates, leaving subsequent housing applicants with a 'more restricted choice of housing and [they] will be more likely to receive poor accommodation' (Commission for Racial Equality, 1987, p.20; London Race and Housing Forum, 1981, pp.6-8). This issue was put as follows by the DoE:

> Giving a transfer to a victim may relieve the stress for that individual but may make things more difficult for other black people wishing to live on that estate in future. Moreover, it very publicly rewards the bad behaviour of the perpetrators by giving them exactly what they wanted. There is also a need to guard against the presumption that black tenants falsely claim racial harassment in order to obtain transfers. (DoE, 1989b, para. 62)

On the other hand, if nothing were done, this might only exaggerate the harassment.

Underlying the Home Office response to racial harassment, then, was the belief that the perpetrator should be *punished*. The housing department's role, within this construct, was partly to evict the perpetrator and subsequently, where necessary, to find that person and their household intentionally homeless (Home Office, 1989, paras 172-3). From the Home Office perspective, such a response was not seen as problematic. On the other hand, the person subjected to the harassment should make use of the civil remedies such as injunctions and non-molestation orders (cf. Barron, 1990). Local authorities should include anti-racial harassment clauses in agreements and give greater publicity to their policies. The assumption was that such persons would not wish to be rehoused, or that they should not be rehoused unless the circumstances of the harassment were severe (even though these assumptions tended to fit nicely with the solution to the paradox). As the DoE good practice guidance suggested:

> Much must depend on the report of the investigating officer. If investigation confirms that the harassment alleged is real and the victim is genuinely under stress as a result, then a transfer should be offered to the victim as of right. In other cases, the recommendation should be strongly influenced by the risk perception of the victim. (DoE, 1989b, para. 63)

So the rehousing options depend on the officer's perception of the 'victim's' perception of risk.

Problem 2: Defining Racial Harassment

It was always assumed that considerable problems existed in defining racial harassment. Although the Criminal Justice and Public Order Act 1994 created an offence out of harassment per se, the central problem concerned whether it would be possible to prove the racial element to any such offence. The Racial Harassment Bill 1985 was unsuccessful for this reason (although the Association of Metropolitan Authorities did adopt a similar definition to that which appeared in the Bill: AMA, 1987, pp.1-2). As has already been suggested, considerable problems emerged with the enforceability of racial harassment clauses in tenancy agreements. Most evictions due to racial harassment were in fact carried out on nuisance or rent arrears grounds (Fitzgerald, 1989, pp.100-101).

Most definitions therefore paid particular attention to the perceptions of the person who had been subjected to the harassment and might accurately be described as 'victim-centred'. So, for example, the CRE adopted the following:

> Racial harassment is violence which may be verbal or physical and which includes attacks on property as well as on the person, suffered by individuals or groups because of their colour, race, nationality or ethnic or national origins, *when the victim believes that the perpetrator was acting on racial grounds and/or there is evidence of racism.* (CRE, 1987, p.8; emphasis added)

The Association of Chief Police Officers in England and Wales provided an enormously influential definition which found favour in each of the government reports on racial harassment (Home Office, 1989, para. 14; DoE, 1994d, p.x): 'Any incident in which it appears to the reporting or investigating officer that the complaint involves an element of racial motivation, *or any incident which includes an allegation of racial motivation made by any person*' (emphasis added).

Within each definition, the 'victim's' subjective perceptions provided the crucial evidence. While this might provide a useful starting-point for the compilation of statistics, criminal lawyers would undoubtedly disapprove because insignificant attention is given to the intentions of the aggressor. Apparently, this was an important reason why racial harassment clauses in tenancy agreements were rarely used in civil proceedings as well (Fitzgerald, 1989, p.101). In other words, these definitions provided unhelpful criteria in terms of court proceedings because they took account of the complainant's perception as to the motivation of the aggressor.

Problem 3: Constructing the Appropriate Applicant and 'Victim-centring'

The second paradox suggested above has a particular resonance in the context of the homelessness legislation. For, even if the person believed that they had been subjected to harassment with racial overtones and perceived a sufficient threat to wish to be rehoused, it was unclear (at best) whether the homelessness legislation could itself accommodate such perceptions. This was partly because the HPU interpretation of the homelessness criteria paid little, if any, attention to the perceptions of those wishing to be rehoused. The 1985 Act itself required the HPU to consider the blameworthiness of the applicant in the light of the supply of available accommodation in the area. On that basis, the only relevant perception was that of the HPU officer responsible for the decision. If the belief that there was widespread abuse of the homelessness legislation were added to this equation, then even greater vigilance was required by HPU officers to ensure that the less deserving applicants slipped through the net. To put it another way, if the applicant thought that they were appropriate, this was irrelevant to the homelessness decision making practice.

Indeed, one could argue that the homelessness legislation itself discriminated against those subjected to racial harassment. Whereas violence or threats of violence occurring within the home were enough to ensure that a person was deemed homeless (s.58(3)(b)), violence or threats or other forms of harassment taking place outside the home were not. In the latter case, the applicant would have to show that it would not have been reasonable for them to continue to occupy their accommodation (s.58(2A)). While the Act did not sanction a referral to another authority in a case of 'domestic violence' (ss.67(2)(c) & 67(3)), applicants fearing non-domestic violence had no such presumption in their favour.

The Code of Guidance did make specific reference to racial harassment (although without any definition of it). However, most of these references were extremely bland. For example, 'Authorities should also consider applications from those at risk of harassment or violence on account of their gender, race, colour, ethnic or national origins' (DoE, 1991a, para. 6.17). The only provisions of the Code which directly addressed racial harassment in the context of appropriateness almost entirely negated the victim-centred approach. HPUs were exhorted to take into consideration six factors in considering whether it would have been reasonable for an applicant to continue to occupy their accommodation. In the section referring to 'violence or threats of violence from outside the home', it made the following point: *'The authority will need to consider* the seriousness of the violence, or threats of violence, the frequency of occurrence and the likelihood of reoccurrence. Violence or threats of violence could include racial harassment or attacks' (para. 5.8(c); emphasis added). As this only concerned violence or threats of violence, it would only refer to a minority of racial harassment complaints because many do not involve either of these. The most often reported incidents of racial harassment involve racial abuse, which was more than twice as likely to be reported than cases involving violence (DoE, 1994d, paras 50-1). Furthermore, the Code suggested that racial violence should be considered in the same way as all other aspects of violence without separate consideration being given to the racial element. Thus, the marginal importance of the homelessness legislation in cases of racial harassment was reinforced by this lack of consideration as well as the singular contrast with the 'victim-centred' approach.

Responding to Racial Harassment

Statistics and Expectations

Table 5.1 shows the ethnic composition of each of the areas in this study, the proportion of each ethnic group occupying local authority accommodation and the ethnic composition of the local authority's accommodation. These percentages can be judged against those for England as a whole (where *n* equals England). As a general rule, the proportion of white people occupying local authority accommodation is significantly less than live in the area. This is skewed in the opposite direction for Afro-Caribbeans and Asians. It is therefore clear that, if the effect of the right to buy has been that generally the better properties have been sold off, leaving an unappealing rump, this disproportionately affects Afro-Caribbeans and Asians. These statistics also suggest that, as has been well documented, ethnic minorities have consistently been allocated the worst quality housing, which have tended to be flats in high-rise buildings, because only the best has been bought (Forrest & Murie, 1991, pp.65-85).

It is little surprise that LB4 and LB5, our inner London study areas, show significantly larger proportions of Afro-Caribbean and Asian people occupying local authority accommodation than the national average, both as a proportion of the ethnic group and in the authority's stock itself. The paradoxical effect of the dispersal policies of the 1970s, which aimed to move black households to better homes and neighbourhoods, was 'a *greater* borough specific concentration of black households than in previous years' (Smith, 1996, pp.99-101). It also appeared that Caribbean households had been moved from one tenure to another in the same area, and allocated public housing at a time when standards were falling (see, generally, Peach & Byron, 1994, a study of the effect of the right to buy on Caribbean tenants). Equally, it is little surprise that, of our non-London authorities, the Midlands urban authorities showed a substantially greater proportion of ethnic minorities. Early settlements concentrated in these areas as well because of the higher labour requirements and these have remained constant (Peach, 1986).

It might therefore be expected that applications to the HPU due to racial harassment would be most prominent in LA1 and LA2, of our non-London authorities, and all our London authorities, with the possible exception of LB3. In respect of the authority's own property, ethnic composition suggested that applications to the HPU due to racial harassment would be higher in LB4 and LB5, because a significantly larger number of ethnic minority households were accommodated in this stock. On the other hand, larger communities of ethnic minorities might ensure less harassment (for example) because of greater syncretization or, alternatively, fear of larger-scale reprisals.

Statistics of Racial Harassment in Study Areas

Only LA1 was able to provide complete statistics of the percentage of

Racial harassment 105

Table 5.1 Ethnic composition of study areas

	Ethnic composition of area, and proportion of each in local authority accommodation (%)						Ethnic composition of local authority accommodation (%)		
	White	Prop. in l.a. accomm.	Black African/ Black Carib.	Prop. in l.a. accomm.	Indian cont.	Prop. in l.a. accomm.	White	Black African/ Black Carib.	Indian cont.
n	95.5	19.5	1.5	37	3	12.5	95	3	2
LA1	92	33	4	41.5	3.5	12	93	5.5	1.5
LA2	80.5	30.5	2.5	34	17	9.5	91	3	6
LA3	99.5	30							
LA4	99.5	14.5							
LA5	99.5	6.4			0.5		99.5		0.5
LA6	99	22.5							
LA7	99.5	11							
LA8	98.5	16	0.5	13.5	1	0.5	99	0.5	0.5
LA9	95	22.5	1.5	19	3	11.5	97	1.5	1.5
LA10	98	27.5	0.5	29	1.5	0.5	98.5	0.5	0.5
LB1	88.7	15.5	5.5	19	5.5	11.5	89	7	4
LB2	85.5	11	4	13	11	5	90	5	5
LB3	95	97	1.5	19	3	5.5	97	1.5	1.5
LB4	75.5	22.5	15.5	39	8.5	19.5	68.5	24.5	7
LB5	75	32	19	56	5.5	35	66	29	5.5

Note: n = proportions for whole of England; incomplete rows involve negligible (i.e. less than 0.5 per cent) proportions; all percentages rounded to the nearest 0.5 per cent.

Source: OPCS (1993).

applicants accepted as homeless by the HPU owing to racial harassment (3 per cent). None of the other authorities compiled these statistics, mainly because they were not required by the DoE on quarterly return forms. LA1 were able to provide them because they were required by the local councillors and their policy to do so. The remainder of the evidence is, therefore, anecdotal.

Six authorities were able to say that no applicant had alleged that they were being racially harassed in the area. This was the case in LA3-LA8. The range in other non-London HPUs was from 'hardly any' in LA9, to 'a few' in LA10 and 'about one a month' in LA2 (where the statistics suggest that there was a significant Asian population). In our London HPUs, 15-30 per annum were the usual figures suggested by LB1-LB3, but only slightly larger numbers were suggested in LB4 and LB5. These totals represented a tiny proportion of the officers' case load.

It was often suggested to us that most cases where racial harassment was involved in the authority's own accommodation were dealt with by the estate management office and, where necessary, affected households would be rehoused through management transfer systems. Thus applicants who approached the HPU would be diverted to estate management offices covering the relevant area. These policies were particularly apparent in LA2, LB4 and LB5, which would suggest a reason for the insignificant number of applicants. Estate management offices would have a wider variety of possible responses because, for example, most tenants had anti-racial harassment clauses in their tenancy agreements (or the authority was in the process of drafting them) and some had authority-wide policies on racial harassment, supposedly operating the 'victim-centred approach'.

Applicants recorded as having approached the HPU alleging racial harassment would therefore mostly come from the private sector (although a proportion of these would also be referred to the estate management offices in LB4). None of our interviewees in areas where there was a significant ethnic minority population suggested that racial harassment did not occur in the private sector. Rather, they claimed that racial harassment was either rare in the private sector or that it was rare for a person to leave their private sector accommodation because of racial harassment. This was possible, although the statistics given in the introduction to this chapter suggest that such a solution was probably too easy. An equally plausible suggestion was, as is expressed in the next section as well as in Chapter 6, that it was more likely that HPU officers would expect applicants from the private sector to take greater advantage of civil law remedies, particularly where the violence or harassment occurred outside the home, before a homelessness application would be considered. The data which this study draws on provide insufficient evidence to justify any other inference.

While the other chapters in this book detail HPU policies which attempted to *reduce* the number of applicants from within the client groups and there was a general HPU withdrawal because of limited supply, some HPUs were beginning to adopt policies and take part in other processes which could only increase their case load from applicants alleging racial harassment. On the other hand, some of the more typical gatekeeper beliefs were exposed. One officer in LA9 also suggested that, were a more openly positive approach to be adopted, it might lead to applicants alleging racial harassment when it had not occurred (compare the views expressed in Chapter 6).

The HPU as 'Proactive'

LA1's approach had for some time been proactive. Certain officers ('race workers') were employed partly to publicize the HPU's policy on racial harassment within their own community. One race worker was currently employed to deal with the black community and one post (dealing with the Asian community) was yet to be filled. The other members of the HPU (including interviewers and senior officers) were predominantly white. The race worker felt that the community were largely cynical about the role of the HPU. Whenever she had attempted to explain the homelessness legislation to the community, there had been an extremely negative reaction. It had apparently been felt that the legislation itself was discriminatory. Furthermore, this officer felt that the current rate of 3 per cent of applicants found to be homeless as a result of racial harassment did not reflect the numbers of people in the community who left their accommodation for this reason. This officer suggested that members of her community did not come to the HPU, partly because they did not think that they would be believed, partly because the officers in the HPU were predominantly white and partly because other members of the community had been offered poor-quality accommodation in the past. A further important point (also suggested by many of our interviewees in London HPUs) was that applicants often experienced greater racial harassment when the HPU had housed them in temporary accommodation.

In two other smaller authorities in this study, LA3 and LA8, the HPUs' approach might also merit the 'proactive' label. These authorities had a proportionately smaller ethnic minority population than most other areas and had experienced no applications due to racial harassment. At the time of our visits, senior officers were drafting standard racial harassment clauses for local authority tenancy agreements. Other than those isolated examples, HPUs regarded themselves as reactive bodies with little role to play. Prevention was considered to be the responsibility of other agencies.

The HPU and the 'Multi-agency Approach'

The government's response to racial harassment required all agencies to work together and cooperate with each other. A number of benefits were seen to flow from this approach:

> Increased awareness of the problem and its extent; increased understanding and contact between agencies; useful opportunity for constructive debate; enables individual agencies to make their own response more effective, by encouraging co-ordination and helping to avoid overlapping and conflicting activities; improved information flow between agencies; allows ideas and experiences to be shared; enhanced commitment to a rigorous response. (Home Office, 1991a, p.29)

LA1's councillors had imposed such a multi-agency approach within the authority. This had been achieved, not only by requiring each agency to adopt a proactive role, but also through the publication of a leaflet on racial harassment and the imposition of certain other procedures on each individual agency. These are considered in the next section.

More generally, it seemed that considerable problems lay in the way of full HPU involvement in the process. On the one hand, it seemed that HPUs had a vital role to play in any such multi-agency approach, as a rehousing agency. Indeed, if all other agencies within the authority and the area were working together, it would surely have been anomalous if the HPU were not part of it. On the other hand, it was difficult to see what role HPUs could or should have played. Within their local authority, our study HPUs had little, if any, estate management role (although the effect on the estates was a consideration that HPUs might take into consideration on some applications: see, for example, Chapters 3 and 4) but regarded themselves as an agency which provided access to housing. Indeed, there was a belief, noted above, that there was not a significant problem of racial harassment in their private sector or, at least, they did not hear of any significant problem. Furthermore, the Home Office's multi-agency approach had not even ascribed a role to the HPU, treating the whole issue as one of estate management (Home Office, 1989, paras 166-72). As not even the homelessness Code of Guidance provided a reference to the multi-agency approach advocated by the Home Office, the HPU was seemingly left without a role.

The limitations of HPUs in this context had been plain in those areas where there had been successful applications from those alleging racial harassments. Certain areas in those authorities were very clearly no-go areas (particularly in LA1, LA2, LB4 and LB5) and often applicants would refuse any accommodation offered by the HPU at all. There was also the experience of racial harassment in some temporary accommodation provided by the

HPU. These HPUs had therefore been forced to become aware of the ghettoization of some of the estates in the area. If the ethnic minority population of an area was low, then accepting a rehousing duty might only transfer the problem to other estates. If racial harassment was a common complaint within the authority's own housing stock, then it would be relatively difficult to find any accommodation within that stock to meet the applicants' needs. Thus the role of the HPU was similar to a type of estate management (see also Sarre *et al.*, 1989). HPUs in this study believed that there was little that they could do to avoid enhancing this effect because of their role as a rehousing authority, which was required to respect the wishes of successful applicants in their choice of future residential area.

Nevertheless, some HPU officers did in fact participate in multi-agency panels, which would provide a coordinated response to individual cases of racial harassment. This was centralized amongst three of our London authorities (LB1, LB3 and LB5) and only in respect of the authority's own tenants. Membership of the panel in all cases included police officers, the borough solicitor, the estates management and other senior housing officers. Additionally, in LB3, social services had a representative on the panel. The procedure adopted was different in each authority. So, for example, in LB1, the applicant was not present; their case would be presented by the estate officer after that person had conducted their own investigation; the panel would then decide the best course of action. On the other hand, in LB3 and LB5, the applicants themselves would present their case (through an interpreter if necessary) to the panel. The panel then decided how to resolve the situation, taking the victim's perceptions into account.

From this brief summary, it is clear that these procedures masked quite different approaches. LB1's panel represented a bureaucratic, paternalistic solution largely outwith the confines of a victim-centred approach. On the other hand, LB3 and LB5's panel adopted a broader victim-centred approach although, particularly in LB3, the HPU representative believed that very often the situation was 'six of one and half a dozen of the other'. All the officers sitting on the panels felt that the police were doing as good a job as possible and did respond (for example, by increasing their presence in an area) after the panel hearings. Nevertheless, it was also believed that there was significant mistrust within the local communities of the police.

The possible solutions that the panels offered were both reactive and proactive, helping to prevent further cases of harassment in the area. For example, letters would be sent out to each tenant on the estate warning them of the consequences of committing racial harassment. This was believed to be particularly efficacious where the applicant victim did not know the identity of the perpetrator. On the other hand, it was significant that no perpetrator had been evicted after the panel hearing, whereas it was possible for the applicant to be moved immediately. This was the case even though it was the avowed intention of all panels to deal with the perpetrator. Indeed, one anomaly of LB3's panel (which seemed to go unnoticed by our interviewee) was that, where a panel recommended a transfer, this could be done as soon as a suitable property became available. On the other hand, if the applicant's fear was such that temporary accommodation needed to be provided immediately, that household would then be placed in the waiting list system and the applicant would wait alongside everybody else.

Panels were not the only way of dealing with racial harassment. Neither, for many reasons it seemed to us, were they the best method. First, they only considered harassment on their own estates and not in the private sector and so they seemed to be a simple extension of the management role. Second, while in general they could be convened relatively quickly (usually within two days), sometimes it was impossible for the senior officers to be present and, therefore, junior officers would be deputed to sit on the panel. This might have suggested to the applicant that racial harassment was not taken seriously enough. A further result was that only the most qualitatively serious cases were referred to the panels, which might not have reflected the applicant's perception. Third, although there were undoubted benefits in centralizing racial harassment cases, these panels only operated when a specific complaint was made. Our observation, and some interviewees as well, suggested that officers might not have been able to identify some disputes as racial harassment cases as opposed to (say) a simple neighbourhood dispute. Fourth, in our view, the existence of a panel did not negate the obligation on each individual agency to have its own policies and procedures so that potential applicants did not slip through the bureaucratic net. Finally, the success of the applicant depended on how well they were able to express themselves as well as, in LB1, the officer presenting the applicant's case.

Policies, Procedures and Appropriateness

Policy Manuals

While many HPUs apparently adopted the victim-centred approach, there were internal contradictions in their approaches, mainly because the nature of racial harassment meant that it usually occurred outside the home. As has already been observed, the homelessness legislation draws a distinction between violence or threats of violence inside and outside the home. The homelessness legislation was, therefore, in many ways an inappropriate vehicle itself for responding to racial harassment.

These internal contradictions found their most evocative form in LB4's redrafted policy manual. The first sentence of the section on 'homelessness through violence or harassment' suggested that LB4's policy was to operate a victim-centred approach. However, a page later, the manual referred to the question of whether it was reasonable for the applicant to continue to occupy their home (s.58(2A)). After a sentence which repeated the Code of Guidance relating to the nature and frequency of attacks (see above), heavy reliance was placed by the manual on whether they could have been averted by police or legal intervention, thus supposedly enabling the applicant to remain in that accommodation. Furthermore, the manual suggested that applicants should be told that they would be 'better off pursuing legal remedies rather than waiting a number of years in temporary accommodation for rehousing, with all the upheaval entailed in moving from one temporary accommodation address to another'. Such a comment might appear reasonable, but there is plenty of evidence (considered in the next chapter) that this puts potential applicants off (see, for example, Hague and Malos, 1993).

A similar 'prevention' stance was taken by LB2 in their policy manual. Applicants would only be accepted as homeless if there was a 'serious risk of violence' or a 'clear risk'. As regards priority need, readers of the manual were informed that the form and degree of the harassment was critical as well as appropriate evidence.

The constraining factor in each case was (unsurprisingly) considered to be the legislation itself, which placed a significant barrier against fully incorporating the victim-centred approach. Although the clear aim of both policy statements was the prevention of homelessness, both placed obstacles in the way of such applicants. For example, while many of our HPUs accepted that legal remedies were largely irrelevant in cases of non-racially motivated violence to women because of their limited efficacy, heavy reliance was placed upon them by the same HPUs in this context. Indeed, often their effect might lead to an exacerbation of the conflict. A cynical interpretation of these manuals, therefore, might suggest that they were attempts at gatekeeping potential applicants from this client group. 'Appropriate' applicants would use the remedies but then they would not need to make a homelessness application or would not be accepted as homeless (further problems with these remedies are considered in greater depth in the next chapter). This was a particular form of 'no criming' - taking no action and not recording - potential applicants (see also Chapter 6).

Other HPUs which had policies on racial harassment, such as LA2 and LA9 outside London and LB1 and LB5 inside London, did not place such an emphasis on legal remedies. However, their approach was similar. The first consideration was whether there was evidence of harassment from various sources, such as the police or social workers, which substantiated the legislative requirement that the former accommodation be 'unreasonable to continue to occupy'.

These types of responses were the norm, but an exception occurred in LA1, where the authority had adopted a unified approach to racial harassment within which the HPU were to play an important role. Any applicant claiming racial harassment would automatically be interviewed by a senior homelessness officer together with (if requested) the race worker. The applicant's case would also be communicated to a specific, dedicated section of the authority which would carry out its own enquiries in conjunction with the HPU. These enquiries would centre on the perpetrator. The victim-centred approach meant that the applicant should automatically have been placed in temporary accommodation, if this was requested. Rehousing would follow but it was accepted that these cases might take longer than other applications because of the necessity to provide a safe area.

Generating the Policies

HPUs often gave as a reason for not developing any specific policies to racial harassment that there were insufficient numbers of applicants claiming racial harassment to merit a separate policy. LA1's policy was generated centrally as a result of councillors' pressure to respond to the issue. The government literature approved of this 'filtering down' of policy making. The direct contrast was with LB2. The senior homelessness officer responsible for drafting the policy manual suggested that, until just before our visit, it had been 'professional suicide' to be seen to respond to racial harassment. This was apparently because councillors' perception had been that racial harassment was a problem in other areas and not in LB2. The senior homelessness officer felt that this was a wafer-thin excuse, particularly because other boroughs on LB2's boundaries had serious problems and London boundaries were largely illusory. As it happened, the different derivation of these policies was probably a significant factor in determining whether their implementation was successful.

From Policy to Practice

Other than in LA1, applicants alleging racial harassment who were the authority's own tenants were, seemingly without fail, told to report the allegations to the estate management office (and thus 'no-crimed'). From there, the HPU would have no contact with the case unless requested by the estate management office. Indeed, in such cases, the only responsibility on the HPU was to provide temporary accommodation. Such applicants would therefore not be recorded on the homelessness statistics.

It has already been suggested that the main body of applicants came from the private sector. These applicants would in all cases be required to show that they had responded to the racial harassment in some way. For example, this could be proved by having reported the matter to the police or other branches of the authority. HPU officers would then check these sources. The main division between HPU approaches, as well as between officers with each HPU, was caused largely by the different rationales for requiring proof. Some HPUs required proof of the harassment to ensure that the applicant was not abusing the system. This was particularly true in LB1 and LB5. Others, for example LA10 and LB3, required proof so that it might be used against the perpetrator. Others regarded proof as unnecessary in many cases and only required it when they did not believe the applicant.

Most officers interviewed by us suggested that they usually had a 'gut feeling' when an applicant was lying or only recounting half the story (see Chapter 6). However, many of these officers also believed that, in racial harassment cases, applicants had usually tried every other avenue and regarded the HPU as the last resort. Consequently, there was sometimes plenty of proof available, even if not required. Depending on the gravity of the allegations, the applicant would be offered temporary accommodation to avoid the necessity of going back to their accommodation.

However, many applicants had not contacted the statutory agencies, perhaps because of the correct or incorrect belief that nothing would be done by them, as well as the belief that such agencies were racist (see Cooper & Qureshi, 1994). So, for example, even though LA7 had no experience of applicants alleging racial harassment, the homelessness officer had entered into discussions with the police because the police had apparently treated all such cases as 'civil issues' and would not therefore involve themselves. Many of our interviewees in areas where there had been allegations by applicants of racial harassment believed that the police had not responded appropriately. Sometimes this perception had been mitigated by the police representative on the authority's panel, but even then it was accepted by interviewees that the community placed little faith in the police. These perceptions about the police suggested a further operational contradiction because the evidence most often sought by HPUs was from the police. In Cooper and Qureshi's study, it was suggested that the main body of reporting had been to local non-statutory organizations such as pressure groups. It was a striking fact that few HPUs in our study seemed to seek out this evidence.

Not only was proof an issue concerning whether the applicant was homeless, it was also of considerable importance in ascertaining whether a single applicant fleeing racial harassment was in priority need. Single applicants usually have to show that they are in priority need because they are vulnerable 'due to ... some other special reason' (s.59(1)(c), 1985 Act).

Although the Code suggested that applicants fleeing racial harassment should be found temporary accommodation, it did not provide that all such applicants should have an automatic priority need. So, for example, LB4's requirement that applicants used the legal process as a tool to prevent homelessness was mitigated by the suggestion that, if such attempts proved useless or illusory, the applicant would have an automatic priority need. If there was sufficient proof, the applicant would be deemed to have a priority need. On the other hand, no such presumption was made elsewhere in our study. This is in strong contrast with the case identified in the next chapter, where HPUs often believed that it was 'the law' that single women fleeing violence were vulnerable.

Intentional homelessness was a key issue which was reflected partly in policy manuals and partly in our interviews. For example, in LB2 and LB4, if applicants alleging racial harassment were to give up their accommodation without having first sought legal redress, it was likely that the consequence of that action would be a finding of intentional homelessness. In other circumstances, where there was no proof of racial harassment, a similar result was likely. The reason for these responses was that the harassment or violence would have to be sufficiently serious - within the interviewing officers' perception - to justify the applicant leaving their accommodation when the supply of accommodation was drying up.

The appropriate applicant thus had a different identity when applications were considered where racial harassment was alleged. The victim-centred approach was largely ignored in practice, HPU officers preferring other approaches. These other approaches appeared to be fairly crude attempts at restricting the numbers and types of person to whom duties might be accepted. The abandonment of the victim-centred approach, which (it has been argued) was a natural consequence of the approach adopted in the homelessness legislation, led to applicants who claimed that they had left accommodation because of racial harassment being regarded as inappropriate.

Abandoning Prescribed Policy

It was noted above that LA1, in marked contrast to our other HPUs, operated a particularly proactive policy imposed on the authority generally as a result of councillors' influence. In essence, part of the policy involved 'fast-tracking' the applicant through the homelessness procedure under the guidance of a senior homelessness officer, a race worker attached to the HPU, the authority's own Race and Housing Unit and the estates management section. At the time of our visit, this institutional benevolence was in the process of becoming almost entirely dismantled within the HPU.

The policy would only be activated if the applicant mentioned the magic words 'racial harassment'. Apparently, if the applicant alleged that they were being harassed, little attempt would be made to draw out of the applicant the additional racial element required to set the policy in motion. Consequently, the matter would be dealt with as a neighbourhood problem or 'nuisance'. This practice concealed a significant degree of hostility by HPU officers to the imposed policy.

Officers had been provided with no specific training when the policy was introduced and so had little appreciation of its significance within the authority. Consequently, while the written policy was truly victim-centred, officers would still consider whether they believed that the violence was serious enough to warrant accepting an application. So, in these circumstances, there was little difference between LA1 and the other authorities in this study, although it was clear that a finding of intentionality would never be made in these circumstances (were an application to be accepted) because some of these decisions could only be made by the councillors themselves.

In any event, the race worker was extremely sceptical about the policy. She believed that it was not rigorously enforced and its practical application depended entirely upon which officer conducted the interview. So, for example, one senior officer said that he would rely on the qualitative assessment of the race worker although, as far as he was concerned, the harassment would have to be serious enough to warrant accepting such a case. The race worker's function when the client was being interviewed had developed into an advocacy role, partly as a result of her feelings about the HPU and the authority. So, while normally the minimum proof required would be a police statement, in these cases generally the applicant's story would be accepted at face value.

However, this worker was often only asked to sit in on an interview where the applicant had specifically used the 'magic words'. She believed that many applicants did not use them because they might have felt humiliated or because they were not encouraged to use them by the (white) interviewing officers. Furthermore, they probably also would not have appreciated the significance of the words for the HPU's practice. Consequently, on many occasions, the race worker was effectively locked out. Once she was in the interview room, the only other obstacle was that the harassment or violence would have to be serious enough to the interviewing officer to warrant an application.

Other officers felt that policies imposed upon them by Councillors did not take account of the reality of the situation. Therefore their effect would be avoided wherever possible. This should be contrasted with the HPU's different approach to (non-racial) violence to women considered in the next chapter, which was generated by a groundswell within the HPU itself. That policy's effect was likely to be carried through.

Conclusion

As with the previous chapters, the government-inspired approach to issues – partnership between agencies – was unsuccessful in our study authorities. Whereas in Chapters 3 and 4 we saw that HPUs took action of differing types which marked out which applicants would be appropriate, it seemed that few applicants claiming racial harassment would in fact be deemed appropriate. Government and locally inspired policies which placed the 'victim' at their heart were routinely ignored because the homelessness legislation's notion of the appropriate applicant could not abide such a contradictory philosophy.

There were three particular reasons for ignoring these policies. First, so few applicants actually claimed that they were being racially harassed and thus there was no particular need for HPUs to respond. The next chapter suggests that, when a significant number of applicants allege the same problem, HPUs will often respond by imposing negative policies. Second, the HPU was a rehousing agency which, if it did rehouse every person who claimed racial harassment, would end up effectively ghettoizing certain areas and thus paradoxically also creating an undesirable result. Third, a direct result of the limits of the HPU was that other agencies were better equipped to deal with any problems and thus potential applicants would be diverted to them. In this way, HPUs effectively diverted any potential demand.

The final point which requires further thought (outside the scope of this book) is that it seemed to be assumed by government that racial harassment only operates in the public sector. Thus the relevant DoE reports only discussed the role of local authorities. Furthermore, the specific remedies introduced in the Housing Act 1996 (Part V), partly to deal with the growing nuisance problem, only affect the public sector. Such an assumption emphasised the Conservatives negative perception of this tenure.

Note

1 The word 'victim' is often used in official reports to describe a person to whom another causes violence or who is harassed or threatened by another person. Underlying this terminology, then, is that the person is a 'victim' because their skin colour is different or because a person is female. Thus, for example, she is a victim who is beaten because she is female or she is a victim who is beaten because she is black. The word 'victim' is therefore entirely unnecessary and also has a debilitating accent. Wherever the context permits, I therefore avoid using this word.

6 Violence to women[1]

The original intention of Stephen Ross MP, who initiated the homelessness legislation, was that there should be no doubt that battered women *should* be regarded as homeless under the 1985 Act (see H.C. Debs, Vol. 926, col. 902 (18 February 1977)). Nevertheless, the history of HPUs' abuse of the homelessness legislation in cases of violence by men against women is nothing short of shameful.[2] A study of local authority practice in 1981 suggested that, of 207 applications under the Act, 32 per cent of women applying from a refuge were found not to be homeless, 24 per cent were regarded as the responsibility of another authority (from which the women had escaped), 9 per cent were defined as not in priority need,[3] and 8 per cent were found intentionally homeless (Binney *et al.,* 1981, pp.78-85).

If one believed that this practice had been rooted out as the legislation as well as the crime has become better known, one would be mistaken, for later studies have drawn similar conclusions, albeit that local authority reasoning might have become more 'sophisticated'. For example, Thornton's study of local authority policy found that many local authorities required applicants to make use of domestic violence legislation as proof of the violence and also as a long-term solution to their housing problems (Thornton, 1988, pp.71-3). It also became apparent that there were wide variations between HPUs' practice (Niner, 1989, p.28) and within HPUs (Loveland, 1995, pp.180-90). Malos and Hague's in-depth study of the local authority response in three HPUs suggested that HPUs were using techniques, of some of which they were unaware,[4] to avoid responsibility to applicants in these circumstances (Hague & Malos, 1993). The House of Commons Home Affairs Committee also found that the intentional homelessness provision had been used to avoid long-term responsibility to women leaving a violent partner. They regarded this practice as 'nonsense' and recommended that it should end (House of Commons Home Affairs Committee, 1992, para. 131).[5]

The concomitant of all this research has been that which found that women are over-represented in the public, local authority, housing sector. This is unsurprising, given two related aspects of the research which has been conducted. First, public housing provision has been both residualized, by the various methods of acquiring public housing, and marginalized because the majority of this accommodation is occupied by those being supported by the state (Forrest & Murie, 1991, pp.65–85). Second, it is by now a commonplace observation that women have the weakest economic power and consequently rely on local authority housing (see, generally, Woods, 1996; McRae, 1995). The average income of women is two-thirds the average of men, there is evidence to suggest that women are discriminated against by building societies (Watson, 1988) and on relationship breakdown it is more likely for women to move into local authority tenure (Bull, 1994).

Further research suggests that women and men have different conceptions of 'house' and 'home', which can be related to the causes of violence to women. Most research suggests that one particular cause of violence lies in the patriarchical attitudes of males (see Dobash & Dobash, 1980, 1992; Hague & Malos, 1993). Further, the belief that an English*man*'s home is his castle does not equate to the views of women. In her anecdotal study, Darke suggests that women's feelings about the home 'are a mixture of affection, reciprocated towards the home as a nurturing environment, and resentment at the demands of the home' (Darke, 1994, p.11); or, as Woods suggests, 'the safe haven versus the site of exploitation' (Woods, 1996, p.65). Watson suggests that the division of labour within the home provides a further argument that 'once the relativity of the concept of homelessness is recognised, and the structural position of household members in relation to the home is taken into account, one individual in a household may be potentially homeless, according to a broad definition of the term, while another is not' (Watson, 1985). Indeed, it has been suggested that the cycle of abuse occurring in the home means that homelessness can be perceived as a *solution* (Tomas & Dittmar, 1995). On these arguments, there is a vast untapped demand for rehousing.

Some HPUs have made strides towards meeting these needs and repairing the previously negative perceptions. Maguire argued that:

> The coercive and controlling nature of these judgments [made by HPUs in relation to women leaving violent relationships] are exposed by the reality that they are not inevitable. While authorities with the political will *can* (and sometimes do) respond adequately to women at risk of violence it is possible for all to do so. I argue that this is because local authorities share an ideology of women's subordination with other state agencies that they find it impossible to treat women at risk with respect and dignity. (Maguire, 1988, p.42)

This identified and emphasized the institutional ideology as the dominant decision-making tool. For Maguire, therefore, the requirement was for an attitudinal shift from a male-dominated perspective.

On the other hand, while an attitudinal shift might have been crucial and resulted in more informed, positive policies, the principal problem was that the homelessness criteria actually encouraged local authorities to adopt these attitudes. The requirement to consider why the applicant left their previous accommodation combined with the resource issues propagated, justified and enhanced unfortunately negative interpretations. This was particularly the case when a significant proportion of an interviewing homelessness officer's case load was made up of cases where there was at the least a suggestion of violence, or threats of violence, against women. In our study, officers suggested that between 15 and 30 per cent of their case loads involved these circumstances. Thus, in many ways, this chapter represents the apotheosis of the idea of appropriateness.

The government's approach has been, in essence, to sidestep neatly both issues by using the 'inter-agency cooperation' terminology and practice, thus suggesting its alchemical significance. In contrast to other areas covered in this book, this inter-agency cooperation was to grow organically locally without any significant central control. The suggestion was that government would simply sit back and adopt a coordinating role without providing any finance (or that finance would be diverted to other purposes). This has led to some scepticism about their commitment to the process (see Hague *et al.*, 1995, p.3; 1996, p.79).

After setting out the relevant pieces of the legislation and Code of Guidance, these inter-agency initiatives are the starting-point for the analysis in this chapter. At the time of our fieldwork, nationally these initiatives were in their infancy and this was reflected in the responses of our HPUs. Nevertheless, some general points can be made about their effects on HPU policy. Attention is then drawn to the ways in which our HPUs used their equivalent of 'no-criming' cases of violence to women (that is, avoiding obligations by not recording applications), thus providing an institutionalized 'solution'. Finally, consideration is given to the study HPUs' interpretation of the criteria in the homelessness legislation. Our fieldwork data suggest that there have been no significant advances from the earlier studies. Indeed, it might be suggested that, as practices had evolved, so they had regressed. However, in the context of dwindling resources and gatekeeping required by HPUs, this should not be surprising.

The 1985 Act and Code

The 1985 Act

In two particular instances, the Act made express provision for those who had or were suffering from violence. A person was deemed to be homeless if 'it is probable that occupation of [the accommodation] will lead to violence from some other person residing in it or to threats of violence from some other person residing in [the accommodation] and likely to carry out the threats' (s.58(3)(b)). A number of important points can be drawn from this. First, the subsection covered not only violence but also threats of violence which were likely to be carried out. Second, the violence or threats did not need to have been carried out at the time any application was made under the Act. Third, this only applied to violence or threats of violence which occurred *within* the home. Thus the distinction between violence within and outside the home had a well established import within the jurisprudence of the homelessness legislation. Why this occurred remains a difficult proposition to answer. The particular concern of Stephen Ross MP, who brought forward the original bill, was with 'battered women'. Nevertheless, there appears to be little if any qualitative distinction between the effect of violence in different areas. In many ways, it reflects the well-rehearsed maxim that an English*man*'s home is *his* castle and therefore reflects the masculine view of violence.

An imporant by-product of the *Puhlhofer* amendments in 1986 was that local authorities came under a duty to consider violence which took place outside the home because that might make it 'unreasonable to continue to occupy the accommodation', so making the applicant homeless (*Hammell* v. *Kensington and Chelsea RBC* (1988) 20 H.L.R. 666; *R.* v. *Broxbourne B.C. ex parte Willmoth* (1989) 22 H.L.R. 118). However, this represented a far more stringent test, providing difficult lines of enquiry. So, in other words, if there had been or was likely to be violence or threats of violence within the home, the applicant was deemed homeless. If there had been violence or threats of violence outside the home, the applicant's homelessness status depended upon the HPU's interpretation of the reasonableness criterion. The fallacy of this distinction could easily be exposed: if a cohabitant committed an act of violence on another cohabitant, the latter would be homeless. However, if this act of violence was committed by the same person outside the property after being ejected from it, the more difficult barrier of reasonableness fell to be decided.

The second area where there was explicit provision for cases of violence was in relation to the local connection provision. While the Act provided a general discretion to refer applicants to alternative authorities if the applicant had no local connection with the authority to which an application was made, this discretion was over-ridden if the applicant or 'any other person who might reasonably be expected to reside with him will run the risk of domestic violence in that other district' (s.67(2)(c)). The definition of 'running the risk of domestic violence' was related to the person with whom the applicant might have been expected to reside but for the violence or threats of violence (s.67(3)).

There was no other specific provision covering cases of violence to women in the Act itself. This perhaps reflected the view of Stephen Ross who believed that the 'housing needs [in such cases] may not necessarily require the allocation of a permanent tenancy of some kind' (H.C. Debs, Vol. 926, col. 902 (18 February 1977)).

The Code of Guidance

The following are the particular points which the Code brought to the attention of HPUs:

(a) Wherever possible, officers of the same sex, preferably trained to deal with these specific cases, should conduct the interview. Proof should not be sought from the alleged perpetrator (para. 4.6).
(b) As regards violence from outside the home, the authority was required to consider the seriousness of the violence or threats of violence, frequency of occurrence and likelihood of recurrence (para. 5.8(d)).
(c) Authorities should respond sympathetically to applicants claiming violence from within the home. They should inform applicants of the available civil remedies but not require them (para 5.9(c)).
(d) While there was nothing explicitly suggesting that applicants who have been subjected to violence or threats should be regarded as in priority need, the Code went almost this far by suggesting that, 'wherever possible', accommodation should be available for those who have suffered violence at home or were at risk of violence if they returned home (para. 6.17).
(e) The Code accepted that, in relation to intentional homelessness, it would not normally be reasonable to continue to occupy accommodation where there had been violence or threats from within *as well as outside* the home. In parenthesis, the Code advised that applicants should not be regarded as intentionally homeless if they had not used the civil court system (para. 7.10(b)).

Inter-agency Cooperation and the Development of Policy

The History of Inter-agency Working[6]

Whereas, in relation to racial harassment, inter-agency cooperation had been stimulated by a series of Home Office research reports and the role of other organizations, such as the Runnymede Trust, the process had a different genesis and mode of operation in relation to violence to women. Initially, inter-agency cooperation on violence to women stemmed from the development of the refuge movement in 1972 (see, generally, Dobash & Dobash, 1992, ch. 3; Hague & Malos, 1993, ch. 2) and the subsequent formation of the Women's Aid Federations. The Home Affairs Committee noted, from evidence provided from practically all coordinating agencies, that less than one-third of the refuge places recommended in 1975 had been secured by 1992 (para. 129).[7] So the need to work with other housing providers has been caused by the general 'silting up' of places in refuges, which were initially only meant to provide a short-term breathing space, and the need for sufficient, decent quality, 'move-on' accommodation. There is also considerable evidence that the availability of accommodation is a crucial determinant in whether or not a woman leaves a violent situation (Dobash & Dobash, 1992, p.62). Hague and Malos suggest: 'To get clean away from a violent relationship ... means first and foremost having somewhere safe and permanent to escape to. Temporary accommodation in refuges becomes merely a dead end, the hope it offers a charade, if there is no permanent accommodation available afterwards' (Hague & Malos, 1993, p.109).

Combined with the structural and economic inequalities, the importance of local authority accommodation becomes a vital link. Thus, local refuges needed to work with the local authority and vice versa. This informal networking of organizations occasionally developed into a number of fora, operated differently throughout the country, with different lead organizations as well as principles (see, generally, Hague *et al.*, 1995, 1996).

While inter-agency cooperation has been working informally, there has been a parallel movement by government to involve itself (albeit somewhat belatedly) in coordinating this work. This began in 1986 with a Home Office circular but was reinforced with a further Home Office circular in 1990 (Home Office, 1990). This called for the police to take a more active role in securing immediate protection for women (para. 8); urged chief officers to consider setting up domestic violence units (para. 10); and provided advice on appropriate action to be taken (paras 11-29) including the recommendation that all police forces should issue policy statements (para. 11); finally, chief officers were 'invited' to liaise with other agencies, amongst other invitations (para. 30). The Home Affairs Committee subsequently recommended that an intergovernmental working group be formed to consider joint responses and ensure that appropriate priority be given to coordinating the response of various agencies to violence to women (para. 132). At the same time, an influential report was published by Victim Support on inter-agency working (National Inter-Agency Working Party Report, 1992).

As part of the government's strategy, the Home Office was made the lead agency. In 1995, a further circular was produced (Home Office, 1995) which provided working definitions of 'domestic violence', evidence of its extent, the government's approach and details of good practice in inter-agency fora. It provided a summary of the role of various agencies in 'domestic violence'. This circular was published after our fieldwork was conducted. The DoE's statement of its role is characteristically obscure but it seemed to create excessive expectations of the role of the homelessness legislation. Their statement suggested that 'Women with children, or women *who are vulnerable as a result of domestic violence are in "priority need", and they should be considered unintentionally homeless if they are fleeing from violence or the threat of violence*' (para. 7.71; emphasis added). The Act made no such promises and, while the Code went this far, this statement overstated the role which could be played by the homelessness legislation.

The Relationship between Fora and Policy Development

The impression that has been given so far in this chapter is of an organic development, swelling up and involving all agencies. However, in Lyon's study of the beginnings of a forum in Liverpool, the housing section had two meetings with only two people present (Lyon, 1995, p.204). Kewley's study suggested that there were structural and institutional problems in the housing participation in a forum in Hull, including the limited accommodation available to the local authority as well as the government's general policy of privatization (Kewley, 1994, ch. 2). A more general study, developed by Hague *et al.*, found that local authority housing and social services departments were usually involved in fora but that 'Housing departments [were] also absent in some areas despite their responsibilities in regard to homelessness and domestic violence' (Hague *et al.*, 1996, para. 4.5). The depth of a local authority's involvement in this work appeared to depend upon the genesis of the forum. Sometimes, for example, the forum developed from the local authority which would therefore give sufficient priority to it (see the example of Bristol in Hague *et al.*, 1996). One of the important findings of that research was that, beyond networking between organizations, inter-agency fora could speed and assist in the development of policy and practice.

Within our study areas, only two HPUs might have been said to have been involved in these fora, although for very different reasons. LA1 had been involved in empirical research, conducted the year before our visit, on the HPU's policy and practice in relation to violence to women. While being ambivalent about their policies, the report had heavily criticized the officers' interviewing techniques. This report had inspired the authority generally to reconsider and revise its practices on violence to women. The HPU, as part of this overall campaign, had become involved in rewriting its policy on domestic violence.

However, there were other reasons for doing this. The only other written policy they had was on racial harassment (which was generally not being put into practice: see Chapter 5) which had been developed by the authority, as opposed to being an HPU initiative. The drafting of the violence to women policy came about, more pertinently from their own perspective, because the women's groups in the area, including Women's Aid refuge, constantly challenged the HPU's approach to violence to women. It was hoped that drafting a new policy, which would eventually be circulated to all agencies including the women's groups, would avoid these challenges because the policies would be better known and appreciated. This generally justified having a written policy on violence to women but not on other areas (except for racial harassment). A further pertinent reason for drafting the policy was the perception, which was confirmed by conversations between officers, that different interviewing officers would approach their cases differently. Therefore the need for consistency became apparent.

The policy was, at the time of our visit, at second draft stage. A senior officer had taken responsibility for drafting it but each draft would be circulated to all HPU officers for comment. The first draft had been heavily amended as a result of this process. It was also clear to us from our interviews and observations that all HPU officers felt strongly about this issue and wished to develop a fairly generous policy. This general 'pulling together' as well as the observations of the interviewing officers meant that it was likely that the policy would be liberally interpreted by them. By no means, however, could the policy have been described as 'generous'.

Although there was no forum in LB2 yet in operation, it was possible that one might develop from the specialisms being created within the HPU. The senior officer, sounding a note of caution, suggested that Councillors had little time for the issue. However, the officer responsible for this specialism had already made contact with various organizations, such as the women's refuge and the local domestic violence unit (hereafter 'DVU'). She was developing a training package in concert with the refuge as a first step.

Other than these two possible examples, none of our other HPUs was involved in formal fora. One might speculate that the reasons for the limited involvement by HPUs in our study as well as in other studies related to HPUs' belief that their involvement could only be on their terms and only through their legislation. Policies might be developed but the gatekeeping role, and particularly the need not to open the floodgates, provided the critical limitation.

Informal Networking and Policy Development

It became clear throughout our study areas that there was a considerable degree of informal networking, which had a commensurate effect on policy development. As Hague *et al.* suggested in their mapping study, 'In many areas surveyed, excellent inter-agency relations existed, often due to the efforts of Women's Aid and of other agencies over many years. ... In such cases, there may well be no need for more formal inter-agency work' (Hague *et al.*, 1995, p.15). Whether or not the second assertion can be sustained, our HPUs all reported excellent working relationships with local refuges. Many also had attended training courses arranged by, or on behalf of, Women's Aid. This became apparent, for example, from our HPUs' general belief that civil remedies were 'not the worth the paper' they were written on (the title of Barron's work (1990)).

So HPUs would generally accept all applicants who came from refuges and they used the refuges themselves as a discharge of their duties to provide accommodation pending their enquiries (for similar data in a different context, see Pahl, 1985, p.89). All the HPUs in this study, with the exception of LA4, had one or more refuges in their area. In LA4, refuges from nearby areas were quite happy to receive women from LA4, either driving to the HPU to pick them up or arranging with the authority for a taxi. Occasionally, women referred from refuges would be interviewed by the senior officer in the HPU (although this would not apply to applicants who approached the HPU directly). In LA9, where this practice occurred and the senior officer was male, the interviewee would be accompanied in the interview by a worker from the refuge. Consequently, significantly better treatment would be apparent in these cases. In LB3, a person who had been involved in setting up the refuge 18 years before was now working part-time in the HPU itself, suggesting that there was a symbiotic element to the relationship as well as with the HPU's policy.

Whether these relationships had caused the HPU to reassess its policy and practice, like LA1, was more uncertain because, combined with these perceived excellent relationships, there was a belief amongst many officers that certain applicants saw a claim of violence as the easiest way of gaining access to local authority housing. Further, many officers could cite examples of cases where the battered female returned to the violent partner, or took the partner back and subsequently returned to the HPU. The succeeding sections of this chapter cast some doubt upon the assertion that these relationships were always excellent, as well as on their more general effect on policy development.

Whilst relationships with the local refuges were described positively, relationships with the police (all our HPUs referred to DVUs in their areas) were described negatively by all areas. Two examples from the litany of complaints should suffice in this context. In LA7, the senior homelessness officer reported to us that particular problems still occurred with the police 'no-criming' violence to women and treating situations 'as a domestic'. In LB2, the officer who adopted responsibility in cases of violence to women reported that, when she met the officers in the DVU, they were full of the 'old' attitudes. Police officers would be required to do a stint in the DVU, as opposed to wishing to be stationed there. As the policy in LB2 was to refer applicants to the DVU for advice, this caused particular concern to this officer who, in fact, rarely referred her clients to it during this period.

Threshold Tests: Avoidance and Evasion

In the introduction to this chapter it was noted that violence to women made up 15-30 per cent of our interviewees' case load. Whereas in LA1 and LA2, the statistics produced by the HPU attested to the fact that this category represented the second largest proportion of their acceptances (27 per cent and 20 per cent, respectively), other HPUs' acceptance rates were generally lower. For example, LB3's HPU report to councillors on homelessness acceptances contained no statistics of acceptances in cases of violence. Given the general unreliability of statistics, not much weight should be given to any of these statistics. Here, for example, possible reasons for the distinctions might be any of the following: violence to women was rare in some authorities (which could not have been a possibility, even though LA1 and LA2 are urban authorities); that LA1 and LA2's policies were more generous than other areas; that different methods of compiling the statistics were used between and in each authority;[8] or that other authorities may have adopted a 'no-criming' approach.

It was a commonplace observation by interviewees that a suggestion of violence by applicants was regarded as the 'easiest' way of gaining access to accommodation under the homelessness legislation. The proportion of female applicants claiming violence, the perception that such claims were sometimes not genuine and the system was therefore being abused, (in some cases) the belief that successful applicants sometimes return to their violent partners, all militated in favour of placing further obstacles (or gatekeeping techniques), in the way of applicants. This was not always the case, but even in authorities with relatively 'generous' policies, where it was believed that an applicant was abusing the system these obstacles would arise in an ad hoc way. In other words, appropriateness was related to whether the interviewing officer believed that the applicant's story was genuine, and not the legislative concepts themselves. In determining whether the applicant was in the 'most deserving' category, it was necessary to work out whether the applicant's story was *genuine*. This process was often referred to as the 'gut feeling'.

Many officers claimed that, with sufficient experience, it was possible to root out those applicants who were attempting to abuse the Act by lying about violence. The reference to a 'gut feeling' implied that there was no evidence for drawing such a conclusion other than the applicant's demeanour and explanation. Nevertheless, the way a person presented themselves depended on their ability to articulate their fear as well as being able to explain their situation. Those running away from violent situations are not always in the best position to do so. On the other hand, many of our interviewees stressed that they would be unhappy about returning an applicant to a violent situation. Where this 'gut feeling' was evident, it appeared from our interviews that greater evidence would be required in the initial interview. There were also suggestions that in some cases officers would adopt a more adversarial interview technique. The interview would often then be followed up by more rigorous enquiries. The greatest difficulties were experienced with those applicants who presented themselves to the HPU without any evidence at all, whether in the form of documentary proof or through contact with other agencies. Many HPU officers said that they were wary in these situations and would adopt alternative strategies, such as those outlined below.

Injunctions, Non-molestation Orders and Excluding or Ousting the Violent Partner

There was well-documented evidence that female applicants fleeing violence were faced with considerable problems throughout the process of seeking legal representation, applying for injunctions and other protective remedies, and in having a power of arrest attached to any order made (Barron, 1990; Barron & Harwin, 1992). This research also suggested that, without a power of arrest, many police officers would not become involved. Also the effect of these civil remedies was open to doubt in many cases, with many violent partners seeking out the complainant and committing further acts of violence to her even when any of these civil remedies were in operation. Nevertheless, there had always been evidence to suggest that some HPUs, usually within London, require applicants to seek these remedies. This was the case even though the Code of Guidance noted that they 'will not necessarily deter people' (para. 5.9(b)).

Violence within the home All HPUs in our study offered advice, usually at the initial interview, about the civil remedies that could be obtained in relation to violence which occurred both inside and outside the home. About half of our HPUs also handed out lists of solicitors who would provide, in the view of the senior officer, good quality legal advice. The Code suggested that HPUs may take this step 'but should make clear that there is no obligation to do so if s/he feels it would be ineffective' (para. 5.9(b)). This proviso was mostly adhered to by authorities and appeared in all policy manuals. However, as Malos and Hague have suggested, the way in which this advice was received was entirely dependent upon the way in which it was delivered. So it may well be that some applicants believed that the interviewer was suggesting that this was a requirement of the HPU. While our interviews with HPU officers did not bring this to the fore in cases of violence within the home, it may well have been that, when faced with an applicant whom they did not believe was genuine, this sequence occurred.

LB1, however, had adopted a slightly different, more transparent, technique. About 18 months before our visit, there had been a sudden rush of cases in which applicants had alleged violence within the home. At that time, all such applicants were accepted for accommodation under the Act, having been given advice to see a solicitor. Few applicants apparently took that advice. Councillors (at that time, Conservative) had decided that this policy could not continue and approved a different, more negative policy. Applicants approaching the HPU claiming violence within their home were placed in temporary accommodation (if there was no other safe accommodation available) on the proviso that they saw a solicitor within a certain period, usually about a week. This was a test of the person's genuineness. Applicants were also strongly advised to obtain an injunction against their violent partner, as there had been many occasions when the violent partner had tracked the applicant down and committed acts of violence at the temporary accommodation (which was often shared). In any event, the applicant would be told to contact the HPU as soon as they had sought the legal advice. If this had not been done within the appropriate time frame, the temporary accommodation provided by the authority would be cancelled. If the applicant had sought legal advice, the HPU would contact the solicitor to see what action was being taken. If no civil action was being taken, the reasons for this would be required. If these were satisfactory – for example, the applicant was too frightened – at that point, an application would be taken from the person.

Although many policies in HPUs were applied in piecemeal fashion, if at all when the officers had no say in their formulation, LB1's officers applied this procedure rigorously. Indeed, two officers interviewed suggested that they would give the applicant a 'standard lecture'. This lecture also suggested that they *required* injunctions, as opposed to merely visiting a solicitor. Needless to say, the result of this policy was that the number of applications from this client group had sharply fallen. One of the joint senior officers attributed this to the fact that the general economic malaise had lessened, and not to the effects of the introduction of this policy. However, it became clear that this policy was widely known in other areas (having been mentioned by two of our other London boroughs in interviews) and so presumably also well known within the local community, including the refuges in the area, who might therefore steer their potential applicants to other authorities which operated more generous policies or with whom they had a better relationship.

If LB1's position might have been thought anomalous within our study, there was evidence of other authorities requiring civil remedies to be used, although this was in piecemeal fashion and often where the applicant had no proof and/or there had been fewer violent attempts and/or there was a question in the interviewing officer's mind as to the good faith of the applicant. Often this would also be contrary to express policy statements. For example, in LB4, the policy manual had adopted a 'victim-centred approach' to cases of violence, including racial harassment, under which the 'victim's' word was to be accepted (see Chapter 5). One senior officer in this authority said that, where there was no apparent evidence of violence, the applicant would always be asked why they had not applied for an injunction (even though this officer was aware that injunctions were often worthless).

In LB2, the policy manual which was in the process of being completed explicitly said that injunctions and other civil remedies were not required. All interviewing officers accepted this except one who believed that an ouster or exclusion order was required when applicants were living with husbands (as opposed to cohabitees) or were in the process of divorce proceedings. In LA6, where there was no policy manual, injunctions were sometimes required where the interviewing officer was concerned about the applicant's truthfulness because otherwise it was suggested that it would be unfair to those on the waiting list.

In LA7, where there was no policy manual, the senior officer suggested that all interviewing officers dealt differently with cases where violence was alleged. This officer believed that she would be more wary if the applicant was not going to see a solicitor because, in her view, if the applicant was applying for housing, the applicant should also be willing to take other measures. In LA9, the policy manual did not contain much relevant information outside the Act or the Code on violence. One officer suggested that, where a property had been left, she expected applicants to 'secure' the property by taking all legal steps possible.

Violence outside the home Without exception, all HPUs regarded violence outside the home as an entirely different matter in practice, requiring either greater evidence or use of civil remedies. Indeed, whilst many HPUs, when discussing violence from within the home, regarded injunctions and the like as often useless, these civil remedies somehow gained greater efficacy simply because the violent acts took place outside the home. Such views were no doubt supported by the difference in emphasis in the legislation between violence within and outside the home. This was the position in most HPUs. So, while LB4's statement drew no significant distinction between violence within and outside the home, it appeared from our interviews that most officers believed that there was little they could do in cases of violence outside the home and adopted a 'no-criming' approach. This was the most extreme example of the distinction in operation, although the results in other authorities would be similar. For example, LA6's HPU suggested that no automatic temporary rehousing would occur but that they would 'monitor' the situation. How this would be done was unclear, although the interviewee inferred that monitoring would occur when the person reapplied.

In other areas, people claiming violence from outside their home might be dealt with by the local authority's area offices and not by the HPU (even if they were from the private sector). This was the case in LA10, even though the senior officer admitted that the distinction between inside and outside the home was extremely difficult to make in practice. This practice achieved a shift in responsibility from HPU to the area office which would find itself making the usual homelessness enquiries. In LB3, the HPU believed that their resources were so constrained that there was little they could offer and so, rather than employ themselves in these cases, the authority's tenants would be put through their management transfer scheme. Others were seemingly ignored. LB3's HPU would not automatically accept an application in these circumstances unless the risk to the tenant was serious and legal remedies had been pursued.

These and other examples mask an important qualitative distinction that was required by the legislation and accepted by most HPUs. Violence occurring within the home would, it was believed, be more deeply felt by individuals than outside the home. Equally, and a view with which perhaps more sympathy might be felt, there was occasionally a view expressed that removing the 'victim' would simply reward the perpetrator (cf. Chapter 5). Even so, there seemed little if any justification for ignoring the wishes of the occupant who had made the difficult decision to leave their home and apply as homeless.

Joint Tenancies

It is now regarded as clear law that any one joint tenant can surrender a tenancy *(Greenwich L.B.C.* v. *McGrady* (1982) 81 L.G.R. 288;

Hammersmith and Fulham L.B.C. v. *Monk* [1992] 1 A.C. 478). This provided a major boost in combating violent situations and appeared in many HPUs' policy statements on violence. Equally, it provided a simple way for HPUs effectively to categorize cases of violence as 'no-crime'. Advice in these cases, particularly where the accommodation was local authority-owned, would be to surrender the tenancy and possibly also seek civil remedies. No further action would be taken with private sector tenants, although, with their own tenants, the estate management or area office would be asked to take a major role in implementing this.

Owner Occupation

Many policy statements drew attention to the situation where an owner occupier claimed violence as the reason for making an application under the Act. In these cases, those policy statements also referred to the question whether the applicant would be better advised to seek protection through civil remedies. Often HPU officers would be required to work out the equity due to the applicant (no mean feat bearing in mind the difficulties faced by the judiciary and academics in this area). Where there was a substantial equity, HPUs would sometimes only offer temporary accommodation until the property could be sold. There were also suggestions in two HPUs that applicants in these situations would be told that accommodation provided by the authority would not match the standard that they had previously enjoyed. This might have had a similar effect to applicants being told that they could wait for a long time before being rehoused: that is, returning to a violent partner (see Binney *et al.*, 1981). Similar results might be extrapolated from LB4's new draft policy statement which contained the following: 'The applicant should be told they may be better off pursuing legal remedies rather than waiting a number of years in temporary accommodation for rehousing, with all the upheaval entailed in moving from one temporary accommodation address to another.'

'See if They'll Go to the Refuge'

One other way of weeding out those about whom there was a gut feeling or instinct that the person might be abusing the system was for the HPU to offer the applicant a place in the local women's aid refuge. This technique was used in LA8 and LB4 to test the genuineness of the applicant. In LA8, this was a particularly useful test – the senior officer expressed his 'cynicism' about cases of alleged violence in our interview – partly because the local refuge was known to be overcrowded and, in his view, a generally unpleasant place. In LB4, if the person did not accept a refuge, an added degree of scepticism would attach to the person's story and alternative options, such as civil remedies, would be discussed with the applicant.

'See if They Go Back'

Those whom the HPU did not believe, or had given rise to a degree of scepticism about their allegations, would be offered temporary accommodation. This would be for a slightly longer period than usual and would be set to test whether the applicant returned to their violent partner. However, two HPUs used this period more positively. In LA2, this period was specifically designed to give the applicant some breathing space and to decide what to do. LB3 was a further example. If the interviewing officer did not believe the applicant's story, the person would be placed in temporary accommodation, which was of a reasonable standard, without taking an application but nevertheless attempting to ensure the person's protection. However, research has always suggested that the quality of accommodation offered initially, as well as the possibility of 'move-on' accommodation, is one determining factor as to whether a person returns to a violent relationship or situation. If bed and breakfast was offered, as some HPUs did in some cases, this might well hasten a return to violence (see, generally, Dobash & Dobash, 1992, ch. 3).

General Perspectives

Throughout the preceding discussion, attention has been drawn to specific policies and procedures, some used only on occasion. These have all been methods used by HPUs to negate or bypass any potential application, and have served their attempts to weed out non-genuine applicants. The objection to these policies and procedures must be the initial assumption that a proportion of applicants were abusing the Act. A number of our interviewees, in describing the characteristics of the type of person believed to be lying, could equally have been describing an entirely genuine person who felt uncomfortable describing and discussing their situation. It was believed that mendacious applicants could be rooted out by one means or another, although in the process it seemed clear that many genuine applicants would be caught in the same net.

An Englishman's Home is His Castle

It has already been noted that, where a person has been subjected to violence, or threats of violence, within the home, that person should be deemed homeless (s.58(3)(b)). The legislation referred neither to the qualitative effect of that violence or threat nor to the quantity of violence required. Indeed, the only requirement was a belief that the violence *would* happen or that the threats were likely to be carried out. The principal problem for the HPUs in this study was whether or not there was evidence of the violence or threat. In a number of cases, as might be expected, there would be little or no proof short of physical imprints where, for example, the woman had simply run away from the accommodation without taking any of her belongings with her. Furthermore, women might not report what had happened to them to any agency which the HPU could contact. The second problem for HPUs was setting the level of violence or threats which would enable the applicant to fall within the deemed homelessness category.

Policy Statements

We have already seen how, if there was little proof and/or the HPU officer did not believe the person, the officer would attempt to avoid the responsibility. Equally, where there had been referrals to the HPU from Women's Aid or other refuges, the person was more likely to be believed. The natural consequence of an HPU officer's belief that an applicant's story was not genuine was that more in-depth enquiries would be made, as well as more searching questions being asked in interviews. This was the case even in HPUs which offered a 'victim-centred' approach to issues of violence. Broadly, four authorities might be said to fall into this category: LA1, LA2, LB4 and LB5. No doubt a truly 'victim-centred' approach required the applicant to be believed, accepting that there will be little if any evidence of the violence or threats (see Chapter 5 for further consideration). Nevertheless, there were clearly limits to this approach which were exhibited in policy statements and actual practice in these authorities, depending on the way in which the applicant presented their story as well as on the officer conducting the interview.

Indeed, on this point, many policy statements actually contradicted themselves. The most openly victim-centred was LB4's policy. At one point this suggested that there should be little questioning of the applicant's story. Corroboration of the applicant's statement should not be required and, if there was no corroboration, this should not have affected the credibility of the applicant's story. The policy statement went on, however, to suggest that the applicant's *reasons* for not providing corroboration should be ascertained and noted on the file, and that the application might therefore be rejected on this basis.

LA1's draft policy statement was similarly contradictory – indeed, it was riddled with contradictions both of law and of practice. For example, it was noted that, *where there was no evidence*, the woman's story should be believed *unless there was evidence to the contrary*. How there might be evidence to the contrary if there was no evidence provided by the applicant was mystifying. This policy statement also attempted to define the types of violence or threat which would allow the applicant to fall within the deemed homelessness category. Where the violence was 'not serious enough' or was 'not likely to reoccur' so that 'it was reasonable to continue to occupy' the property (*sic*), the applicant would not be assisted although she would be told that she could reapply at some other time. This was entirely contrary to the statutory category of deemed homelessness (s.58(3)(b)).

All other policy statements simply recited the Code of Guidance, without much more advice being given to interviewing officers.

Practice

Practice differed not only between the HPUs but also within the HPUs, as well as depending upon how the applicant presented their version of events and the process through which the applicant arrived at the HPU. Implicit within these different permutations was the observation that the way in which the interviewer approached the applicant's version of events would depend on all of these factors. For example, as we have seen, applicants approaching the HPU from the refuge would almost certainly be treated more sympathetically and also would be given added credibility. However, the general theme that emerged from our interviews was that, if there was any doubt as to the applicant's credibility, further and more in-depth enquiries would be made. This attitude starkly raised the two issues adverted to earlier: proof and quantity of violence.

There was a general belief that there was a certain threshold of actual violence beyond which an applicant would or should be accepted. If the violence had not reached this threshold, then the HPUs might consider that there was little that would or should be done other than offering the applicant some form of temporary accommodation in order to reconsider their position. This type of ad hoc practice was usually informed by the belief that 'a little violence' was not something which should require the person to leave their home, although some HPUs were more inclined to listen to what the applicant wanted than others. The senior officer in LA3, who espoused this position, went on to voice his concern that the way applicants were treated depended to such a large extent on the applicant's ability to articulate their version of events. The same position was adopted in practice with some applicants who were being threatened. The general rationale for this, which seemed to be considered by our interviewees, returned to whether it would be reasonable for the applicant to continue to occupy the accommodation. So this tended to merge with the notion of deemed homelessness.

The second issue – proof – caused the most difficulties. While our interviewees generally believed that it was possible to substantiate violence or threats through contacting the statutory agencies such as the police, domestic violence unit or social services, or by contacting the applicant's doctor, there were other cases where there would be no such evidence. The latter caused the most difficulty and involved the HPU officer(s) in the most heart searching. At root, the issue became whether the applicant's version could be believed. All HPUs accepted that some applicants would not have reported or discussed their situation with others, but suggested that this caused most of their problems. This was the reason why most HPUs used avoidance or evasion techniques. None of the HPUs required bodily marks to be shown to the officers, although some women were only too happy to show these, apparently because, in the officers' view, they had already been degraded to such an extent that nothing would bother them.

Again, the depth of the enquiries as well as the way in which the interview was conducted would depend on whether the applicant was believed. Where there were children involved, some officers would contact their schools, who apparently often provided helpful answers. Some would consider the applicant's housing history, which would occasionally yield some clues. The London HPUs in our study were more likely to be concerned by the lack of proof. For example, LB1's policy had been specifically designed to create the necessary proof. LB2 commonly referred such applicants to the police domestic violence unit for advice and assistance for similar reasons. When discussing the issue of proof, most of the officers in this study would finally suggest that they would have to accept the applicant's story and use the familiar homily that it was better to allow one person to abuse the system than to penalize the genuine (although their avoidance/evasion techniques were there to root out the non-genuine cases).

Outside the Castle Gates

All our HPUs were entirely aware of the legislative distinction between what takes place inside the home and outside the home. Indeed, most were also aware of the *Broxbourne* judgment, which required HPUs to consider whether violence or threats of it made the applicant homeless because it would not be reasonable 'to continue to occupy' the accommodation. However, the assistance offered in these cases depended upon the amount of proof involved and, indeed, to a much greater extent on the availability of civil remedies. There was a significant difference between the policies adopted in these cases and those adopted in cases of racial harassment (where there was such a policy). Officers would be much more limited in what they would offer and apply far more stringent tests before they would accept a person as homeless. There was a significant distinction in approach between our non-London HPUs and our London ones. The former would generally make the enquiries which the Code suggested (where these cases came to them, as opposed to being diverted to the area offices), although they would generally offer little unless there was significant evidence of a life-threatening situation. Our London HPUs would generally categorize these types of cases as 'no-crime'. For example, LB3 would put these applicants through their management transfer panel.

LB5 was, once again, slightly different. While all applicants suggesting violence within the home were channelled through to their 'family team' of officers (even if they were single), all those cases where there was an issue of violence outside the home were channelled to their 'special needs team'. This distinction was not always rigorously followed. The senior officer in the special needs team candidly admitted that she was losing the 'feel' of cases of violence outside the home. There was a large box in the corner of her office marked 'Broxbourne' which contained all the relevant application forms. Her position was that, unless there was significant proof of a serious threat or violence that had already occurred, it would be reasonable to return to the accommodation. However, she was extremely unhappy about this decision. The policy manual required not only what the Code suggested but also cogent proof as well as 'evidence of an "at risk" situation', although the definition of 'at risk' was left to the reader's imagination.

The situation in our non-London HPUs was more diverse. Some treated applicants in these circumstances similarly to those where there had been violence within the home. For example, officers in LA2 and LA5 suggested that, if a woman took the step of leaving her accommodation, taking only her children with her (if there were any), this would be sufficient evidence. However, others generally required greater proof, senior officers often referring to the Code's requirements.

Throughout our HPUs, the officers we interviewed had considerable difficulty drawing the distinction between inside and outside the home. This was particularly true where cases involving the latter were farmed out to area or estate offices. Even so, they all attempted to draw this distinction; but this suggested to us that the distinction was as artificial in practice as it appeared in the legislation.

Need and Priority

There was a sharp distinction exhibited between our London and non-

London HPUs on the issue of whether a single person fleeing violence, whether from within or outside the home, automatically fell within the priority need categories. It was an interesting finding from our non-London HPUs that, even though the within-outside dichotomy would be rigorously enforced when considering the applicant's homelessness, this would not be considered relevant when looking at whether the applicant had a priority need.

Often, we were told that it was 'the law' that a priority occurred in all these cases; some more legally sophisticated officers suggested that the Code required this. However, neither the Act nor the Code does so. In seeking an answer to this apparent inconsistency, it is possible that a finger could be pointed at the way the DoE collected its statistics. The forms required authorities to say how many people had been accepted as vulnerable owing to, amongst other things, 'domestic violence'. The implicit suggestion within this was that all those fleeing domestic violence should be regarded as vulnerable. Whether or not this was correct, there were certainly some fairly liberal interpretations of the priority need categories being adopted by these HPUs. In part also this was because most of the non-genuine cases (in the view of the HPU officers) would have been weeded out by this stage and so they would be prepared to stretch the legislation. For example, three HPUs accepted these classes of applicants as in priority need owing to an 'emergency' (s.59(1)(d)).[9]

Within our London HPUs, the story was radically different. Only in LB4's policy manual was priority need automatically ascribed to those applicants without children fleeing violence, and this was ignored in practice. The result was that, unless there were other reasons why a person might be regarded as 'vulnerable', no priority need would result. LB2's senior homelessness officer did suggest that they would require less evidence of vulnerability in these cases, but this was the exception to the rule. The result of this was that most single applicants fleeing violence would be given a period of temporary accommodation only.

Intentionality

Few of our interviewees openly admitted that they would consider finding a woman fleeing violence or threats within the home as being intentionally homeless. Indeed, many interviewees suggested either that a hint of violence would override such a consideration or that 'the law' did not allow it. The explanation for the latter proposition was the Code, which was not so definite: 'It would not normally be reasonable for someone to continue to occupy accommodation if s/he ... (c) was a victim of domestic violence, or threats of violence from inside or outside the home' (para. 7.11). Nevertheless, our experience suggested that this sentence had an influence on policy which went beyond its apparent effect.

There may well have been a number of other explanations for this type of policy and practice. For example, by the time interviewing officers came to consider intentional homelessness, most of the non-genuine applicants, in their view, would have been weeded out by the diversionary techniques noted above. Officers in LB3 argued that an intentionality finding would never 'stand up in court' if challenged. Further, the time taken, and enquiries required, to make an intentionality decision generally militated against this necessity. This would be the case particularly where there was no direct evidence that the violence had occurred and equally no direct evidence that it had *not* occurred. Finally, there was the 'human' perspective. Officers consistently wished to portray themselves as human and believed that a finding of intentional homelessness would be inhuman in these cases.

There were, however, two exceptions. LA1's draft policy said that it would not normally be appropriate to find a woman in these circumstances intentionally homeless *unless the interviewing officer had reason to believe that the woman was lying about the violence*. This was yet another way of weeding out those whom the HPU believed to be non-genuine. Whether such a finding would ever be made seemed unlikely from our interviews with the officers. More generally, where an interviewing officer advised the woman to seek alternative remedies and the woman did not, a finding of intentional homelessness might result, depending upon the circumstances. Once again, then, the actual result of any application would be determined by the way in which the applicant explained their version of events.

Conclusion

This chapter has provided a further overlay on the notion of appropriateness. The significant numbers of applicants within this client group immediately differentiated the situation from that identified in Chapter 5 and provided a commensurate risk to the HPU's available resources. Thus the supply element of appropriateness was affected. However, this was linked to the belief that not all the applicants were genuine (or, perhaps, that there could not possibly be so much domestic violence in the area) and some should be weeded out. So, here, the most deserving applicants were those whose stories were believed by the interviewing officer or who passed the initial 'tests' of genuineness. The chapter contains explicit references to HPUs 'no-criming' certain potential applicants. Use of this terminology was inspired by techniques adopted by the police and criminal prosecutors. As Sanders has suggested, 'If a victim is perceived by the investigating officer to be undeserving, then his perception will structure the case to make it unprosecutable' (Sanders, 1988, p.366).

The central reason for this was the proportion of applicants who claim violence and the commensurate risk to the HPUs' resources. It appeared, though, that the HPUs in our study were more concerned that the available housing was allocated properly only to the *genuine* applicants. Once through that initial gate, there are, however, additional obstacles that must be overcome and it was apparent that, while some HPUs and our interviewees were more liberal than others within and outside the HPU, these obstacles can be – and often are – used negatively. Given the importance of adequate housing to women in this situation, which was as a general rule known to our HPUs, these practices were little short of disastrous.

Notes

1 It is far more usual that violence is committed by men against women than vice versa. Furthermore, restricting the terminology to 'domestic' violence is regarded in the literature as problematic; as the legislation draws a distinction between violence inside and outside the home, this is a further reason for this title.
2 It should not be forgotten that this mirrors the response of many other agencies to violence against women. For the police response, see Morley & Mullender (1994) and Grace (1995). During the 1980s, the police were 'no-criming' – that is, taking no action and not recording - violence to women within the home (Home Office, 1990, para. 13).
3 This was found even though the Code of Guidance then in effect recommended that single women fleeing domestic violence should be regarded as 'vulnerable'.
4 This included, for example, aggressive, adversarial interviewing techniques.
5 This was in direct opposition to the evidence of the Minister, Sir George Young, who had argued in evidence that 'It is for the local authority to treat each case on its merits, but in general the Code [of Guidance] assumes that victims of domestic violence should be treated as unintentionally homeless' (House of Commons Home Affairs Committee, 1992, Vol. II, p.257).
6 See Hague *et al.* (1996, chs. 1–2).
7 The Home Affairs Committee's report noted that refuges are funded from a variety of different sources. The Housing Corporation and Housing for Wales have funded refuges and 'move-on' accommodation through the housing association movement: see Charles (1994).
8 For example, if applicants had applied as homeless after staying with friends or relatives – usually the first port of call after leaving a violent situation – they might be recorded as such instead of as an application due to violence.
9 Section 59(1)(d). This reads as follows: '(d) a person who is homeless or threatened with homelessness as a result of an emergency such as flood, fire or other disaster.'

7 Towards *in*appropriateness

The appropriate applicant has so far been defined as the person who was *not morally blameworthy*. This idea of moral blameworthiness was related in the structure of the homelessness legislation to the *supply* of accommodation in the area. Earlier chapters have suggested alternative constructions which partly linked appropriateness to the structure of the relationships within the organizations involved in implementation of homelessness policy. Here the element of supply had been critical because the explicit issue considered by the HPUs in our study was how best to ration a restricted resource. For Loveland, this was precisely what the Conservative government had intended:

> In increasing demand for ... accommodation [under the homelessness legislation] by pursuing monetarist macro-economic and social security policies, while simultaneously curtailing its supply by eroding pluralism in central–local government relations, the Thatcher governments 'deliberately' ... fashioned a socio-economic context in which the objectives of the 1977 Parliament could not be realised. As such the [homelessness legislation's] retention *could plausibly be portrayed as an exercise in legislative deceit*. (Loveland, 1995, p.331; my emphasis)

This chapter marks a sharp divergence from the earlier discussion, which was to a large extent involved in searching out which applicants were considered appropriate by the HPUs in this study. From this point, our concern lies with the 'inappropriate'; that is, *constructing the types of person which society believes are so morally blameworthy that the issue of supply becomes irrelevant*. As Garland notes, the new criminology of 'responsibilization' (which I have linked with the earlier chapters in this book) has been linked with an entirely contradictory criminology 'which trades in images, archetypes and anxieties, rather than in careful analyses and research findings' (Garland, 1996). The following substantive chapters of this book suggest that the Conservatives manipulated newspaper discussions of housing in this way so that the critical issue of the lack of supply of low-cost accommodation could quite simply be avoided or obfuscated. The assumption which was adopted was that, if one were to provide low-cost housing, the *wrong* or inappropriate people, often characterized as feckless types, would abuse the system to gain access to it.

The most sensational and notorious use of this construct or language was the creation, fostering and explosion of the belief that single mothers became pregnant in order to prioritize themselves for housing through the homelessness legislation. In this way, single mothers were constructed as 'inappropriate'. That media construct is considered in the next chapter. This chapter provides scene-setting material. The linking of the single mother 'phenomenon' with housing, as a product of those people's fecklessness and willingness to abuse the system, was part of a wider campaign to hive off as many groups of apparently inappropriate people as possible. The next part of the strategy – the reduction of obligations to the homeless – was thus made more palatable to the adequately housed section of society. As the government suggested in its 1994 homelessness review, the reduction of obligations to asylum seekers in 1993 had been 'in many ways a precursor to the proposals set out in this paper' (DoE, 1994a, para. 14.4). Thus one needs to cast one's net wider than the single mother 'phenomenon' and seek out further types of inappropriate person.

In 1988, it was noted that Conservative Central Office had given its MPs a 'Homelessness Briefing Pack' which explained that

> the government's approach is designed to divide homelessness into a number of discrete issues, with a reasonable tale to tell on each, and to avoid treating it in general terms as a large amorphous issue which could only be approached by the injection of unrealistically large amounts of public money. (Travis, 11 November 1988, cited in Ginsburg & Watson, 1992, p.154)

The 'reasonable tale to tell' was linked with a process of criminalization or near-criminalization that, in turn, built and depended upon the 'scrounger-phobia' epidemics of the 1970s (see Golding & Middleton, 1982; Clarke, 1993). Those 1970s epidemics had enabled the Thatcher government to sweep into power in 1979 on a promise to 'act more vigorously against fraud and abuse' in a more cost-conscious environment, although one which had a differential effect between tax and supplementary benefit fraud (Cook, 1989). By the end of Thatcher's second term, it became apparent that, while welfare spending had remained relatively constant, expenditure on housing had halved as a result of the systematic destruction of public sector housing through, for example, the right to buy (Hills, 1991).

The general drift of Thatcher's housing policy was that as many households as possible should be accommodated in the private sector. This was first achieved through the right to buy and, when sales began to falter, by increasing discounts to those exercising this right. Measures were taken to increase the declining private rental sector through market principles and obliging local authority tenants to consider their options by forcing local authorities to increase the rent due. Other measures were taken to make it desirable for local authorities to divest themselves of all their property (see Mullins et al., 1993) or enable private sector and central government takeover of the 'worst estates', through the Housing Action Trust (Karn, 1992). Concentration on the private sector and the retreat from state provision were signalled by a changed discourse about the role of the state, symbolized by 'the emergence of "dependency" as an accepted assumption of the effect of state intervention' (Jacobs & Manzi, 1996). The provision of public housing therefore became a safety net for those who could not afford private sector housing or were incapable, through no fault of their own, of being housed in the private sector.

Just as 'scroungerphobia' was most evident in the media at a time of economic crisis (Golding & Middleton, 1982, pp.231-6), so housing 'scroungerphobia' has been most evident during a time of housing crisis. Housing scroungers did not exercise the Thatcherite duologue of self-reliance and personal responsibility. Instead, they invaded other people's private property (squatters and travellers), forced other people to hand over money (aggressive beggars) or came to this country in order to gain access to the generous welfare benefit system (asylum seekers and immigrants). Historically, there may be a link between each of these groups, for as Goodrich suggests:

> The legal image of the foreigner is already quite precise: she was alien, other, outlandish, extraneous and suspect. ... The associations of the stranger are insidious in the extreme and the definitions of foreignness and its consequences are multiple. Thus Aegyptians are defined as 'divers and outlandish people .. using no craft nor seal of merchandise ... [and who] use great subtlety and crafty means to deceive people of their money'. (Goodrich, 1994, pp.128-9)

In this chapter, my concerns in relation to each of these supposed groups are to outline three particular themes, albeit briefly. First, that these supposed groups were easy targets because they had always been subjected to persecution of one sort or another. Second, the characterization as *groups* made it possible for the government and the media to ensure that the group, as a whole, became associated with the identity of more traditional deviants. Classically, this would involve an identification with predominant notions of deviant youth, often described through the 'new age' culture, although this was not always the case. So the concern here is with the way in which the media labelled these groups as outsiders against whom society demanded and needed protection (see Becker, 1963; Golding & Middleton, 1982). Third, this characterization provoked a legislative or near-legislative response or, as Golding and Middleton suggest, 'the legislative, administrative and possible judicial responses to this cultural thrust reinforce its potency and provide a real shift in the structure of state responses to the definitions provided by the moral panic' (p.60; drawing on Cohen's classic text of 1972). The legislative responses have based themselves upon the (largely inaccurate) representations contained in the second theme. What has apparently been noticeably absent from this response has been judicial support for these responses, which, it has been suggested, has signalled the rise of the 'radical' judiciary. As part of the consideration in this chapter, I will be arguing that this supposed radicalism is a mere fiction. However, it has enabled the media to label the judiciary as 'liberals' and marginalize their sentiments as the views of the unelected.

There is a significant degree of interaction between the second and the third of the themes taken in each section of this chapter. The relationship between media and the process of government and law is, at least, complex. Hall *et al.* describe a process of news selection and reproduction of the *primary definers*, who are regarded as people in powerful positions who provide the *primary interpretations* which 'set the limit for all subsequent discussion by framing what the problem is' (Hall *et al.*, 1978, pp.57-60). If the primary definers are also the people who will be expected to provide a reaction to the news stories, then one might expect there to be a high degree of manipulation.

Nevertheless, the newspaper will also provide its 'own version of the language of the public to whom it is principally addressed' (*ibid.*, p.61); at the same time, the media also attempt to speak for the(ir) public, through presenting their dominant ideologies as consensus. The opposite is also true: certain news is deselected 'where it is dangerous to the *status quo* and when there is a high ownership of the media by precisely such interests' (Cohen & Young, 1973, p.20). Fowler puts it this way:

> In so far as the Press ... interests coincide with those of government, it has political motives for conveying approval of a stable, familiar ideology. Articulating the ideology of consensus is a crucial practice in the Press's management of its relations with government and capital, on the one hand, and with individual readers, on the other. And this is a *linguistic* practice ... Consensus assumes that, for a given grouping of people, it is a matter of fact that the interests of the population are undivided, held in common; and that the whole population acknowledges this 'fact' by subscribing to a certain set of beliefs. (Fowler, 1991, p.49; original emphasis)

One journalist interviewee suggested, more simply, that 'Readers like to see their prejudices confirmed' (Golding & Middleton, 1982, p.131).

Particular attention is paid to one particular newspaper in the following chapters: the *Daily Mail*. Sales of this newspaper in January 1997 were reported to have reached two million copies. It is a no-compromise newspaper that gives prominence to right-wing concerns (such as fear of the European Union, belief in institutions such as marriage and royalty, and, equally prominently, anti-scroungers). As an article in *The Guardian* suggested:

> And when the Daily Mail campaigns, a weak government falters, fudges and becomes far less keen on no-fault divorce and foreigners. Trace the latest Major lurch to the right and you will trace the push and shove of the Daily Mail ... that famous and growing constituency, Middle England, from the Essex provisionals to the Wilts officials, casts around for that confirmation and reinforcement of dearly held prejudices necessary for the peace of mind which produces a good stripe on the lawn and the bracing spasm of fury which gets it to the train on time in the morning. Increasingly, they pick up the Daily Mail. (Nevin, 12 February 1997)

A further aspects of presentation of the news by the media lies in the complexity of the material to be presented. This is particularly true of housing. For example, the concepts used in the homelessness legislation can hardly be described as simple. It is easier to say, as fact, that a pregnant teenager will be entitled to jump the housing queue than to provide a more complex analysis which will suggest the opposite. Thus stories become personalized and demystified, as with the *Panorama* television programme which took a group of teenage women who 'admitted' that they became pregnant to jump the housing queue (see, for analogies, Golding & Middleton, 1982, ch. 3; Cook, 1989, pp.15-19).

Squatters and Travellers

The conjunction of squatters and travellers here is for one reason of convenience and three other organizational reasons. The reason of convenience is that, within the structure of this book, they are marginal and therefore require to be dealt with on a marginal basis in the text. However, the success of the Majorite legislative policy of criminalization of these groups in the Criminal Justice and Public Order Act 1994 (hereafter 'CJPO') suggests that this was the thin edge of the wedge. The three other organizational reasons are, first, that the attack on squatters and travellers was partly an attack on youth (cf. Cohen, 1972), dressed up by using the 'new age' terminology: thus the Home Office Consultation document on squatting indicated that 52 per cent of squatters were under 25, 40 per cent between 26 and 40, and *only* 8 per cent over 40 (Home Office, 1991b, para. 9); second, both groups, in one form or another, formed part of the 'legitimate' homelessness population: travellers were *deemed* to be homeless in certain circumstances (s.58(3)(c)); squatters were also *deemed* to be homeless because they had no lawful right to occupy any property (s.58(2)(b)): thus criminalization could only lead to a reduction in the numbers of people who either labelled themselves or were labelled as squatters; third, the excessive criminalization in the CJPO led to immediate police concerns as to the desirability of the provisions' enforcement (Penal Affairs Consortium, 1994, pp.3-4). However, the distinction between squatters and travellers has been marked by the judicial response to the new legislation.

Squatting

English property law protects possession (Pollock & Wright, 1888). Landowners' actions to evict squatters are not based upon a superior paper title but upon an earlier right to possession. Squatters, in fact, take *legal* possession when they take physical control of premises with an intention to exclude all others. For property lawyers, therefore, squatting, or adverse possession (that is, adverse to the true owner's title), is an entirely natural process. Nevertheless, from an early time, 'squatting acquired fully its modern pejorative meaning of unjustified interference with others' exclusive rights' (Vincent-Jones, 1995, p.224).

At different times this century which have been punctuated by housing crisis, such as after the two world wars and in the early 1970s, a squatting movement has formed. At these times, media representation of the squatter has occasionally been positive. As Prichard suggests, squatters 'could be regarded as one product of a prevalent social unease particularised over the co-existence of much homelessness and numerous empty premises capable of habitation' (Prichard, 1981, p.1). Thus the squatting movement of the early 1970s was characterized by 'ordinary' families who had been rejected by the state (see, for example, Denning's references to the families in *Southwark L.B.C.* v. *Williams* [1971] Ch. 731) but who engaged in direct action as a result (Bailey, 1973). 'On the other hand, no holds were barred in condemnation of the "undeserving", such as the later single squatters, and the hippies who occupied the infamous 144 Piccadilly in 1969' (Vincent-Jones, 1995, p.228). Nevertheless, the squatting 'movement' had no uniformity or rationale and became 'limited, localised, occasional and defensive', as with tenant protests and, I would argue, for the same reasons (Cole & Furbey, 1994, pp.152-75). This made negative portrayals of squatting simpler.

Towards in*appropriateness* 147

These portrayals soon changed from the bland 'deserving/undeserving' into more general representations, which Vincent-Jones (1995) characterizes in five different ways:

– Squatters were an immediate threat to those ordinary homeowners who returned from holiday or doing the shopping to find their properties squatted. Such perceptions 'played a prominent role in the Government's case for further criminalization since 1991'.
– Squatters were jumping local authority housing queues.
– 'Squatters were freeloaders and scroungers, flouting society's work ethic and getting something for nothing in return.'
– Squatters often also wrecked homes.
– 'Squatters were a threat to dominant social values, undermining respect for property, public order, hard work and just reward.'

The only argument with any validity, to Vincent-Jones, was that squatters jumped housing queues, although even this must be regarded with some scepticism because many of these properties were regarded as 'short life' housing only (that is, they were to be demolished by the local authority when sufficient funds became available). Indeed, some of the major housing associations in England have developed out of parts of the squatter movement (see Millett J's summary of the formation of Shortlife Community Housing: *Camden L.B.C.* v. *Shortlife Community Housing* (1993) 25 H.L.R. 330, 334-5). So even this claim must be treated with a certain amount of circumspection.

It was with some surprise, then, that a reader of the Home Office Consultation Paper on squatting was confronted by the following:

There are no valid arguments in defence of squatting ... No matter how compelling the squatters' own circumstances are claimed to be by their apologists, it is wrong that legitimate occupants should be deprived of their property (para. 5) ... The Government does not accept the claim that is sometimes made that squatting is a reasonable recourse of the homeless resulting from social deprivation. Squatters are generally there by their own choice, moved by no more than self-gratification or an unreadiness to respect other people's rights. (para. 62)

The principles espoused by this paper as well as its claims remained unsubstantiated, suggesting that reliance had been placed on media representations as opposed to hard data. Indeed, the suggestion that has already been made above is that the numbers of properties squatted is directly related to the lack of available accommodation. Nevertheless, the results of the consultation paper were, first, easier and quicker methods of bringing actions to remove squatters; and second, the creation of a criminal offence out of a failure to leave premises within 24 hours of being served with a *civil, interim possession order.*

Travellers

The definition of the word 'gypsy' has always been suffused with a significant ambivalence, which also reflects societal ambivalence towards travellers themselves. By way of contrast to the law on squatting, the 1960s gave rise to a more enlightened approach to the 'true gypsy' than had previously been apparent. This enlightenment was represented by the Caravan Sites and Development Act 1960 and the Caravan Sites Act 1968. The latter, a private member's bill which had all-party support, placed a duty on non-county councils to provide sites for 'gypsies' to put their mobile homes. Even though there were some financial rewards for complying with this duty as well as the ability of the secretary of state to issue directions enforcing the duty, it appears that the duties were rarely successfully enforced (Beale & Geary, 1994b; Hawes, 1991). In part this was a result of problems in defining the word 'gypsy' in law (see Beale & Geary, 1994a; Barnett, 1995; Sandland, 1996).

One of the central reasons for introducing the Housing (Homeless Persons) Act 1977 was that the National Assistance Act 1948, s.21(1)(b), and the DoE circular, LAC 18/74, had proved unenforceable in practice. The definitions of the 1948 Act had proved too imprecise. Furthermore, local authorities routinely avoided their obligations. All of these reasons were evident in relation to the Caravan Sites legislation and, consequently, one might have believed that the obligations might have been strengthened. The CJPO actually repealed the 1968 Act without creating any further duties and indeed created certain further criminal offences (see the Public Order Act 1986, s.39, and Vincent-Jones, 1986, for the creation of earlier offences to combat this menace).

The apparent reason for this fall from favour has been the rise of a group known as 'New Age Travellers'. They were seen as a highly undesirable group of hippies who had dropped out of society and who therefore presented a threat to society's norms. The representation of this group within the media appears to have had a resonance within gypsy communities:

> One thing the government should understand is that New Age Travellers are not Gypsies. They should be called hippies, not travellers. Have you ever seen us smoking drugs, having acid house parties? You don't see Gypsies doing this. We're getting blamed for the hippies. They are educated people from posh houses. Many of them are on drugs. (Thomas & Campbell, 1992, p.4)

Local authorities themselves do not appear to have been so convinced that the distinctions were recognizable within the legal framework. In one study, 37 authorities suggested that New Age Travellers were not within it, whereas 19 suggested they were (Geary & O'Shea, 1995, pp.175-7). For Sandland, the real reason why the New Age Traveller terminology infiltrated that of 'gypsy' lay in the fact that the latter was incapable of any form of definition in the first place (Sandland, 1996; compare the views of gypsies themselves as presented by Thomas & Campbell, 1992, also on p.i-xiv). Whatever the reason, it was apparent that the creation of this ill-defined group enabled the media to relabel the group as something else, far less savoury to its readership.

The first sign of a 'radical departure' (Hawes & Perez, 1995, p.117) was a press release from the Conservative Central Office during the 1992 election campaign which suggested that 'there were between 2,000 and 5,000 New Age Travellers camping illegally in England and Wales, in addition to the 4,000 Gypsies not yet provided with official stopping places' (ibid.). On re-election, the government issued a consultation document (through the DoE) which contained, according to one commentator, the following 'familiar tones':

> the question of numbers (increasing at an unacceptable pace); the refusal to acknowledge differences in culture; the presence of a few who spoil it for the rest (and for whom the rest must pay); the denial of needs which do not conform to established norms; the cost of special provision to the exchequer and the tax-paying public; and the privileges afforded to a group which the majority of the population are denied. (Lloyd, 1993)

The consultation paper made the suggestion that gypsies should be syncretized within the private sector housing movement through greater ability to gain planning permission, for example (thus removing their deviancy): DoE (1992, para. 23). If this was not possible, access to public sector housing could be gained through the homelessness legislation (para. 26). Furthermore, 'a limited form of assistance' would be provided to enable gypsies to buy property (para. 28), thus fulfilling the Thatcherite dream and being the ultimate removal of housing deviancy. The cost of not fulfilling that progression was criminal deviancy under the CJPO, which gave increased powers to the police to direct travellers off property, seize travellers' vehicles and, as remarked above, removal of the local authority duties to provide caravan sites.

Judicial Reaction to CJPO: Travellers

In *R.* v. *Lincolnshire C.C. ex parte Atkinson* (unreported, 31 August 1995),

Sedley J held that local authorities would need to consider the provisions of the Children Act 1989 before they evicted travellers under the new powers in the CJPO. This was hardly a radical decision, bearing in mind that the DoE circular, LAC 18/94, 'Gypsy sites policy and unauthorised camping', said: 'The Secretaries of State expect authorities to take careful account of [the Children Act 1989 and the homelessness legislation] when taking decisions about the future maintenance of authorised gypsy caravan sites and the eviction of persons from unauthorised sites' (para. 10).[1] It was also conceded by counsel for all parties that this represented the law on the subject. Furthermore, all this decision required was for the council to reconsider its decision in the light of that Act.

Nevertheless, this decision was framed in strong language. Sedley J described the CJPO provisions as they applied to travellers as 'draconic'. He added that the welfare considerations inherent in the 1989 Act and the homelessness legislation were 'considerations of common humanity, none of which can be ignored when dealing with one of the most fundamental human needs, the need for shelter with at least a modicum of security'.

The modesty of the decision was not reflected in the following day's newspaper reports. These preferred to focus upon some scaremongering evidence provided by the local authority (the primary definer). *The Guardian* reported that one council affected by the ruling 'branded the new legislation "totally unworkable"' (Weale, 1 September 1995). *The Independent* quoted a representative of the Association of District Councils as suggesting that local authorities take eviction proceedings partly because they 'come under strong pressure from local communities to effect the [travellers'] removal as quickly as possible' (Jury, 2 September 1995). When (quite naturally under the doctrine of precedent) a second case was decided on the same principles as *Atkinson - R. v. Kerrier D.C. ex parte Uzell* (1995) 71 P & CR 566 - the *Daily Mail* entered the fray, arguing that the judiciary had organized a 'travellers' charter' and 'judges make it even harder to kick out New Agers' (Doughty, 7 November 1995).[2] The article proceeded by commenting that the decision 'will add to growing fears that liberal judges and European court decisions[3] are rapidly making it possible for travellers to park their caravans almost anywhere - with few legal remedies available either to councils or outraged residents'.

'Aggressive' Begging

Creating the 'Problem'

Vagrancy, of which begging forms part, has been a criminal offence since at least Tudor times, the current legislation dating from 1824 being explicitly designed to deal with problems caused by those returning from the Napoleonic wars (see Cranston, 1985, pp.66-9). Begging has thus nearly always been regarded as a deviant act. There are currently over 2000 prosecutions a year under this legislation. On 28 May 1994, at the crucial time between publication of the consultation paper on the homelessness legislation and the decision to go ahead with it, John Major drew attention to the problem of 'aggressive begging'. The supposition was that there was an increasing problem of begging with menaces. The Thatcher/Major notion of housing deviancy was particularly apparent with beggars. Begging, or street homelessness, is perhaps the most strident tale of the current housing crisis and one which often generates considerable concern. However, Thatcher's slant was rather different:

> Crowds of drunken, dirty, often abusive and sometimes violent men must not be allowed to turn central areas of the capital into no-go zones for ordinary citizens. The police must disperse them and prevent them coming back once it was clear that accommodation was available. *Unfortunately, there was a persistent tendency in polite circles to consider all the 'roofless' as victims of middle-class society, rather than middle-class society as victim of the 'roofless'.* (Thatcher, 1993, pp.603-4

Once again, rather than offering new solutions to that crisis, the government, this time joined and stimulated by the Opposition's linguistics, sought to provide further evidence of this group's deviance. This was through the epithet 'aggressive', implying that there was a dichotomy between the acceptable and unacceptable beggar.

The subsequent campaign, to which the then Shadow Home Secretary, Jack Straw, gave vent, was equally explicitly located in notions of criminality. He was manipulating a well-rehearsed theme. Straw's strategy, which formed part of the incipient bidding in the law and order auction from 1995 to the current time, was to 'reclaim the streets for the law-abiding'. This law and order auction has sometimes had Straw and sometimes Howard, the then home secretary, occupy the role as a primary definer. A little later, Tony Blair, leader of the Labour Party, declared that Labour was the party of home ownership, thus distancing himself from the begging debate at that time, as well as reorienting the party with more Thatcherite perspectives (see Meikle, 6 March 1996; Sherman, ibid.; cf. Littlejohn, 7 March 1996).

Straw castigated those who cause graffiti, 'squeegee merchants, winos and addicts' in the following terms:

> Graffiti is often *violent and uncontrolled* in its visual image and correctly gives

the impression of a *lack of order* on the street.

... the squeegee merchants who wait at large road junctions to *force on reticent motorists* their windscreen cleaning service.

The winos and addicts whose *aggressive begging affronts and sometimes threatens decent compassionate citizens*. (as reported by Travis, 5 September 1995; emphasis added)

In staking out this territory, Straw was apparently drawing upon comments made by the mayor and police commissioner of New York (Travis, 5 September 1995; Ford, 6 September 1995). An editorial in *The Guardian* regarded this as Labour 'giving up on the welfare state' (6 September 1995). The following day *The Guardian* gave prominence to a story about the 'forgotten homeless "victimised" by everyone' (Chaudhary & Bowcott, 7 September 1995). By the time Straw had defended his comments by reference to the failures of government policy, the damage had been done (Straw, 1995a, 1995b, 1995c, 1995d). A subsequent poll commissioned by *The Guardian*, conducted by ICM, suggested that 65 per cent of those asked would favour increased police powers, although only when more hostels were provided (Linton & Meikle, 11 October 1995).

Responding to the Problem

All of this provided an excellent impetus for five government departments to reconsider the vagrancy laws, a review strategy announced on 2 October 1995 (although the actual document was never published). The government's approach was to 'set targets for voluntary, state-funded agencies' which would 'cover the numbers of people they remove to hostel accommodation' (Meikle, 3 October 1995). The police would have been required to take 'a more pro-active role' (David Curry, the housing minister, reported by Meikle, ibid.) under what became known in Whitehall as 'sluice 'em down' policies (Travis & Meikle, 8 January 1997). The review was apparently punctuated with comments such as 'Begging is distressing for members of the public and visitors to the capital alike'. It might have added that begging is distressing for those that have to beg, but the government's view was summed up by Michael Howard, the home secretary, when he argued that 'There is no justification for anybody begging in this country when we have a welfare state'. He also suggested that Metropolitan Police figures show that 40 per cent of those prosecuted under the Vagrancy Act actually had accommodation, without specifying the type, quality and so on of their accommodation (Meikle & Travis, 4 October 1995). However, he was also drawing upon a well-worn theme that many beggars are wealthy enough not to beg (see, for example, Conan Doyle's Sherlock Holmes story with a similar image: 1994, p.147; Pyatt, 28 October 1996, cf. Johnston,

3 November 1996). Furthermore, he was avoiding the critical question: the lack of supply of affordable housing.

Apparently, the police 'blocked' the proposals, *The Guardian* reporting the decision thus:

> A Home Office (sic) review of the vagrancy law prompted fierce opposition from police organisations against involvement in a 'lock them up and hose them down' solution to a social problem.
> The decision was taken before the Princess of Wales's attack on society's attitude towards young homeless people last week. It reflects sensitivity at how the issue of homelessness is once more on the agenda despite John Major's assertion of a 'remarkable reduction' in the number sleeping rough. (Meikle, 11 December 1995)

While the matter was temporarily off central government's agenda, local solutions to the problems were being sought and given publicity. In May 1996, a police sergeant in Brighton 'discovered' a local bye-law from 1882, which might enable prosecutions of those described by *The Times* as 'squeegee *boys*' (Frost, 23 May 1996; emphasis added to suggest this was an attack on youth). This discovery was also reported with a certain amount of glee by the *Daily Mail*, which suggested that female passengers had abandoned their cars 'in fear at one junction where many of the screen-washers gather' (*Daily Mail* reporter, 23 May 1996). Slightly later, *The Mail on Sunday* reported that Winchester had 'fought back' against 'aggressive drunks and street alcoholics' by refusing to serve alcohol over 6 per cent by volume and through a scheme which encouraged people to put money into collection boxes rather than giving to individuals. The exaggerated success of the scheme was explicitly linked to the 'broken windows' ideology: 'The results were startling. Overnight the beggars and drunks disappeared from the cathedral grounds, and incidents of petty crime, drunkenness and urinating in the street fell away' (Henderson, 1 December 1996).

A Postscript

The 'aggressive' begging debate has not yet been consigned to the historical dustbin where it belongs. On the day that this section was being tidied up, Tony Blair's interview with the *Big Issue* was widely reported by the mass media. He said:

> Obviously some people will interpret this in a way which is harsh and unpleasant but I think the principle is: 'Yes, it is right to be intolerant of people homeless' ... I do buy the Big Issue occasionally *but I don't put that in the same category [as other begging]*. (Rogers, 5 January 1997; my emphasis)

Major accused Blair of 'breathtaking hypocrisy' (Deans, 8 January 1997), while the *Daily Mail* carried an item suggesting the return of the workhouse and Poor Laws for 'the homeless, vagrants and beggars' (Heffer, 8 January 1997). The by-lines of this article were 'humane' and 'prison'.

Britain Should be a Haven, not a Honeypot' (Howard, 12 December 1995)

Creating the Response

It is sometimes suggested that Britain's asylum and immigration laws have been (too) generous and that there has therefore been a need to define more carefully and restrictively who should be entitled to take advantage of these laws. In doing this, such people are radically rewriting history (see Goodrich, 1994; Dummett & Nicol, 1990). The post-war period has been a prolific time for xenophobia. However, the 1990s have witnessed probably the most significant legislative attacks on asylum seekers and immigrants. In access to public sector housing, legislation has introduced a crude method of reducing demand because, it was argued, such people came to Britain for its benefits, including public sector housing, and thus *abused* the system by taking that housing away from British nationals. Once again, then, a group of people were being accused to avoid the necessity to accept that there is a housing crisis.

The Asylum and Immigration Appeals Act 1993 began this legislative progression by imposing a duty on local authorities *not* to house those asylum seekers who had temporary accommodation, provided it was reasonable for them to continue to occupy their temporary accommodation.[4] Just three years later, the Asylum and Immigration Act 1996 took this matter further by disallowing local authorities from granting a tenancy or a licence to a person 'subject to immigration control' and further disallowed such a person from taking accommodation or assistance under the homelessness legislation. Earlier in 1996, regulations had also disentitled asylum seekers from receiving any form of benefit.

On the day that the 1996 Act was presented to parliament, Home Secretary Howard wrote in the *Daily Mail* that 'Britain has a proud tradition of providing refuge for those fleeing persecution' but 'only four out of every 100 people claiming asylum in Britain are deemed to be genuine refugees by the Home Office.' Furthermore, 'Peter Lilley has announced his intention to curb the availability of benefits to asylum seekers. This will not only reduce the burden on the taxpayer, *but will also deter would-be bogus asylum seekers from applying here*. Britain should be a haven, not a honeypot'

(Howard, 12 December 1995; my emphasis; see similarly, *Daily Mail*, 12 December 1995). Peter Lilley had estimated that £200 million would be saved by these benefit changes (although this was a tiny proportion of the welfare budget of £80 billion spent by the DSS). In any event, there were disagreements as to the actual figures involved (Ford & Sherman, 1996).

The main argument therefore appeared to be that the reforms would deter bogus asylum seekers and negate the perception that Britain had become a 'soft touch' (as the *Daily Mail* announced on its front page: Henderson & Gallagher, 1995). As the *Daily Mail* pointed out on 17 January 1996, 'record numbers are claiming political asylum in Britain'; 43 000 people took refuge in Britain in 1995 (Williams, 1996). This was echoed by a more reactionary opinion in *The Times*, which argued that 'No one has a right to asylum' (Anderson, 8 December 1995). That politicians and the *Daily Mail* regarded the link between bogus asylum seekers and welfare benefits as critical became more apparent when the government succeeded in overturning a House of Lords amendment to the bill, which would have allowed asylum seekers to claim benefits if they claimed asylum within three days of arriving in Britain. The *Daily Mail* commented that 'Ministers won a crucial victory last night in their battle to curb the flood of bogus refugees into Britain.'

The campaign by this newspaper, on the right wing of the Conservative Party, was heightened by its attack on one particular asylum seeker, Dr Mohammed al-Masari, whom it regarded essentially as undesirable and therefore not genuine. There were headlines such as 'Why do we give this bigot houseroom?' (Torode, 19 April 1996); 'The madness of letting this racist remain in Britain' (Torode, 18 June 1996); 'The bombers' friend' (Eastham, 28 June 1996); and in the *Sunday Times* a similar campaign was headed 'Saudi exile wants Rushdie whipped' (Malone, 21 April 1996). From the housing perspective, the *Daily Mail* continued the campaign with an attack on an illegal immigrant who succeeded in a claim for damages against Hackney L.B.C. for illegal eviction (Doran, 24 April 1996). A subsequent report in this newspaper selectively quoted from a Joseph Rowntree-funded research project to suggest that 'Immigrants "threaten housing crisis"'. The first paragraph of the report suggested that 'An influx of immigrants could contribute to a major housing crisis over the next two decades, a report warns today.' The campaign to have Dr al-Masari 'evicted' from Britain was unsuccessful, but for the *Daily Mail* 'the crackdown' on benefits produced immediate results: 'Asylum flood halved' (Doran, 3 July 1996).

The evidence suggests that Britain's 'proud tradition' in immigration policy has not entirely been a positive one. Equally, it was hardly surprising that people did not seek asylum in Britain when (a) the system of selection became harsher, (b) they became the objects of media hatred, and (c) all persons subject to immigration control were disentitled from gaining access to public sector housing.

Judicial Reaction

Asylum seekers Three cases stemmed from quasi-legislation (a statutory instrument) which passed through parliament: Social Security (Persons from Abroad) Regulations 1996, SI 1996/30. In essence, these regulations denied benefits to all asylum seekers who did not seek asylum at their port of entry to Britain. The first case involved a direct challenge to these regulations. Initially, the action was brought by a number of London boroughs against the Secretary of State for Social Security, but the action was taken over by the Joint Council for the Welfare of Immigrants.[5] When Brooke J held that the regulations could be challenged in judicial proceedings as *ultra vires*, the primary legislation (without any doubt correctly), the *Daily Mail* placed this in the context of its more general attack on the judiciary, giving column inches to the right-wing Conservative, Michael Fabricant, who attacked the role of the judiciary.[6] The article then (spuriously) suggested that Brooke J, a former chairman of the Law Commission, had stepped down from his role in the Law Commission 'after claims that the disastrous Family Homes and Domestic Violence Bill, which it inspired, would undermine marriage'.

The Court of Appeal decided by a majority that the regulations were indeed *ultra vires*. Simon Brown LJ, giving the principal judgment for the majority, argued that the benefit changes were inconsistent with the rights given to asylum seekers by the Asylum and Immigration Appeals Act 1993, because they would effectively stop asylum seekers gaining access to those rights (such as the right to appeal against decisions or having their cases heard by the Home Office IND).[7] He went on to add:

> Either that, or the 1996 regulations necessarily contemplate for some a life so destitute that, to my mind, no civilised nation can tolerate it. So basic are the human rights here at issue, that it cannot be necessary to resort to the Convention for the Protection of Human Rights and Fundamental Freedoms ... to take note of their violation.[8]

Nevertheless, he was also careful to suggest that 'Parliamentary sovereignty is not here in question' (ibid., p.401) and that 'No one could dispute the desirability of these aims' (that is, the aim of discouraging economic migrants from making and pursuing asylum claims so as to speed up the system to the advantage of applicants as well as the taxpayer) (pp.392-3). Waite LJ was more strident:

> The stark question that has ... to be answered is whether regulations which

deprive a very large number of asylum seekers of the basic means of sustaining life itself have the effect of rendering their ostensibly statutory right to a proper consideration of their claims in this country valueless in practice by making it not merely difficult, but totally impossible for them to remain here to pursue those claims. (Ibid., p.402)

There could only be one answer to this question. Both judges were concerned that, while spurious and unfounded claimants should be stopped, the regulations, by operating a type of scatter-gun approach, also affected genuine claimants. In this sense, the judgments could hardly be described as 'radical'. Indeed, Neill LJ, in the minority, was more persuaded by the 'powerful' facts that most unfounded claims would occur after the applicants had entered the country: 'it is equally clear that the legislation is not aimed at the *genuine* asylum seeker' (ibid., p.391; my emphasis).

The following day, the *Daily Mail* continued its attacks. An editorial argued that 'here was no measured assessment of a fine point of law. Instead, the judges seem to have indulged in spluttering, partisan propaganda of the kind one might expect in a party political broadcast' (*Daily Mail*, 22 June 1996). The main article was entitled 'Carry on claiming', taking advantage of the reworking of the (characteristically) British film parodies (Deans, 22 June 1996). The article granted three lines to Claude Moraes, the director of the Joint Council, and the rest to Peter Lilley's denunciation, as primary definer, of the ruling. Copious references were made to 'welfare tourists', but highlighted was Peter Lilley's assertion: '*I fear that if the law is left as it stands today we'll see a fresh flood of bogus claimants*' (emphasis added). The article concluded with a statement (under the banner 'Law and disorder') that the judiciary claims that it is interpreting the law, whereas 'Ministers and MPs fear there is an increasing tendency among judges to impose their own social and political prejudices on Government policy' (Deans, 22 June 1996). *The Times* by-line to its report of the judgment brought this out as well, setting the judges against Peter Lilley: 'Judges condemn Lilley for asylum benefit cuts' (Ford, 22 June 1996). Two months later, the judgment of the Court of Appeal was blamed by the *Daily Mail* for opening the floodgates to asylum seekers (government statistics published the day before 'proved' that there had been 780 more claims for asylum seekers in the month after the judgment than in the month before that), although there might have been other reasons for this increase. This gave the paper a further opportunity to cite Major's rebuttal of a Church of England attack, which had been put in terms of consensus: '"*The vast majority of people should agree* that these groups should not receive benefits at the expense of the British taxpayer"' (Doughty, 16 August 1996; emphasis added).

The second case, three days later, involving the same Court of Appeal judges, received less publicity, partly no doubt because it involved a point of statutory interpretation. The issue in *R. v. Kensington and Chelsea R.B.C. ex parte Kihara* (unreported, 25 June 1996) was 'whether the utter poverty and resourcelessness afflicting certain asylum seekers ..., now deprived of all benefits by operation [of the above regulations], is in law capable of constituting them "vulnerable as a result of ... other special reason" within the meaning of s.59(1)(c) of the Housing Act 1985' (*per* Simon Brown LJ).

This time the court was unanimous that the answer was 'yes'.[9] Once again, this was hardly a radical decision. On its facts, such a person must be vulnerable because they are 'less able to fend for themselves in finding and keeping accommodation' (the *Bowers* formulation); and there can be little doubt that the circumstances suggested an 'other special reason' (although Popplewell J, at first instance, had shrunk from such a conclusion).

In the third case, *R. v. Hammersmith & Fulham L.B.C. ex parte M* (*The Times* 10 October 1996), the issue was whether accommodation could be provided under s.21(1)(a), National Assistance Act 1948, to applicants who were 'destitute and faced the dilemma that [they] must either starve without a roof over [their] heads or return to the country from which [they] had fled'. Collins J, at first instance, argued that he

> found it impossible to believe that Parliament intended that an unlawful asylum seeker, who was lawfully here and who could not lawfully be removed from the country, should be left destitute, starving and at risk of grave illness and even death because he could find no one to provide him with the bare necessities of life.
> If Parliament really did intend that in no circumstances should any assistance, other than hospital care, be available to those asylum seekers, it had to say so in terms.

It appears from the report that the only novel part of this decision was that s.21(1)(a) includes a duty to be provided with *ordinary* as opposed to residential accommodation (although the distinction does not appear to have been argued before the judge). Otherwise, the judgment is entirely in the usual mould of considering the legislative intent of the 1948 Act ('to ensure that no one would be left destitute because of an inability to fend for himself') and interpreting the subsection in the light of this as well as the amendments to it.

The Times suggested that the result of the case was that 'High Court rules that asylum seekers may claim benefit', but this was clearly inaccurate (Gibb, 9 October 1996). The issue was housing and basic subsistence. The

Daily Mail regarded the judgment as 'a rebuke to Michael Howard' (Doran, 9 October 1996), also inaccurately. An appeal against the decision was 'under way ... triggered by an angry Government response'. The article also canvassed the views of the Immigration Service Union, which usually adopts a stringent approach to asylum seekers (see Dummett & Nicol, 1990, p.235). Unions are usually perceived as anti-government and therefore, if they were to agree with the newspaper's stance, would add legitimacy to its primary views. Here the union suggested, in bewildering fashion, that 'Many [asylum seekers] hide in the backs of lorries or deceive immigration staff, so I'm not sure that the judge's logic is correct.'

The 'HIV foreigners' In *R.* v. *Westminster C.C. ex parte Castelli & Tristan-Garcia* (1996) 28 H.L.R. 616, the Court of Appeal decided that applicants from the EU, who had overstayed in Britain after being given limited leave to remain and not having been told that they would be removed, were entitled to housing under the 1985 Act. For the newspapers, this drew together two negative themes. First, the applicants were regarded as 'benefit tourists' even though both had attempted to work but had been unable to find employment. Second, they were both HIV-positive. Neither theme played any part in the decision, which considered their immigration status in the light of European legislation. The homelessness legislation was yet to include the notorious 'habitual residence' test, which operates in the field of social security, as a precondition. In other words, there was nothing particularly radical about this decision. The basic issue was whether the earlier Court of Appeal judgment in *R.* v. *Secretary of State for the Environment ex parte Tower Hamlets L.B.C.* (1993) 25 H.L.R. 524 applied to the applicants' case. As that case involved those unlawfully in Britain and the applicants in this case were lawfully here, the two cases were readily distinguishable.

However, *The Times* covered the case on its front page under the banner, 'HIV foreigners win housing battle' (Murray, 22 February 1996). The article quoted Julian Brazier, a right-wing anti-Europe MP, as saying, 'This is one more example of Euro-legislation and Euro-practices creeping into British courts'. The *Daily Mail*'s banner did not mention the applicants' HIV status, but placed the decision within the 'battle' between ministers and the judiciary: 'Judges' blow to war on benefit tourists' (Hadfield, 22 February 1996). However, it went on to say that 'both *HIV victims* [were] funded by legal aid' (emphasis added) and further that the decision had 'exposed a massive loophole in the Government's crackdown on "benefit tourists" who sponge off the state.' This was also the focus of *The Guardian*'s report (Travis, 22 February 1996). None of these reports referred to the fact that the 'habitual residence' test, which was at the forefront of the government's response to 'benefit tourism', caught out 25 757 benefit claimants in 1995, of whom 5431 were British nationals (Brindle, 14 February 1996; NACAB, 1996).

Conclusion

The media have played a significant role in the creation of negative perceptions of supposed groups as feckless, non-genuine abusers of the state. In doing so, they furthered subsequent punitive government action, most notably in relation to squatters and travellers. A similar position was almost reached in respect of begging. The punitive reaction was reached in relation to asylum seekers and immigrants by the cutting off of their livelihood. However, I have also sought to argue that a by-product of this has been a *legitimation* of the housing shortage or crisis (whichever term is most applicable). For, by castigating certain sections and portraying them as the most undeserving, one is also arguing that they are not deserving of accommodation; so the issue of its supply was routinely avoided in the debates. It seemed that the implicit belief was that there would be enough accommodation to meet the needs of other, more worthy, groups.

Adverse judicial decisions were portrayed as radical but, it has been argued, that portrayal was unconvincing. However, it is is clear in retrospect that these decisions have only served to marginalize the judiciary, given further ammunition to the media, which have used them to provide a further boost to government policies. In considering this reaction, particular attention has been paid to the *Daily Mail* because it has been in the forefront of these portrayals. This newspaper has been closely linked with a defining role in the propagation and legitimation of government policies (even though often it is too reactionary for the government's taste).

Notes

1 Having argued in Chapter 4 that the practical effect of the Children Act on our study authorities was virtually nil, its greater and perhaps initially unintended effect here is ironic.
2 Note in this title the disassociation of the term 'New Agers' from 'Travellers'.
3 The *Daily Mail* is notoriously anti-European and therefore its readership would identify this as another example of European excess. At that time, *Buckley* v. *UK* had been referred to the European Court of Human Rights by the European Commission. *Buckley* became an example of that rare case, a success by the UK government in the ECHR.
4 The homelessness Code of Guidance was amended to take both of these considerations into account.
5 *R.* v. *Secretary for Social Security ex parte Joint Council for the Welfare of Immigrants*

[1996] 4 All E.R. 385. As Simon Brown LJ explained in parentheses: 'The Secretary of State has now reached agreement with local authorities to pay them a substantial part of the costs involved and thereby bought off judicial review challenges to the 1996 regulations, which the authorities themselves had instituted' ([1996] 4 All E.R. 385, 395).
6 The decision 'brought calls from some Tory MPs for an investigation of the powers and role of the judiciary' (Eastham, 6 February 1996).
7 He appears to have been influenced in his approach by evidence given to the Social Security Advisory Committee: [1996] 4 All E.R. 385, 398.
8 His Lordship also referred to *R. v. Eastbourne (Inhabitants)* (1803) 4 East 103, decided 'nearly 200 years ago', in which Lord Ellenborough CJ had argued: 'As to there being no obligation for maintaining poor foreigners before the statutes ascertaining the different methods for acquiring settlements, the law of humanity, which is anterior to all positive laws, obliges us to afford them relief, to save them from starving' (at p.107).
9 Several important comments were made as to the meaning of s.59(1)(c), which go beyond the scope of this book.

8 Reforming the homelessness legislation: uses of *in*appropriateness

The enduring success of Majorism was that, in pursuing Thatcherite housing policies, the Conservative Party was able to reform housing law beyond what Thatcher could even have attempted. Three separate Conservative governments have reviewed the homelessness legislation. The first review was never published (although a summary can be found at H.C. Debs, Vol. 23, col. 317w (13 May 1982) *per* Michael Heseltine). The second review, published by the DoE in 1989, provided the following reasoning:

> *the majority of households who get help through the 'homelessness' route are people with a genuine urgent requirement for housing, who would expect to receive a high priority in any needs-based system of housing allocation. ...* In theory, a case can be argued for repealing the special 'homelessness' legislation, since this can lead to a misleading impression that homelessness is a distinct housing phenomenon, separate from the generality of housing problems. ... the government recognise that there remains a need for the 'long stop' mechanism of the homelessness legislation to help people who are in urgent need, and cannot resolve their housing problems for themselves. *They believe that the legislation has done the job that Parliament intended of it, and therefore they do not propose changes to the statutory framework.* (DoE, 1989a, paras 45(b), 46, 47; emphasis added)

These comments were hardly a ringing endorsement, but they seemed to reflect an unhappy adoption of the belief that the homelessness legislation catered for those who most needed housing (cf. Chapter 2). Less than five years later, though, a subsequent Conservative government, with John Major at its helm, performed a *volte-face* and provided a devastating critique of the legislation. Such a radical change might be explained by the widespread belief that the 1989 review planned to include amendments which subsequently appeared in the 1994 review (see Hoath, 1990a, 1990b; Dwelly, 1990). In other words, the 1994 review was taken 'off the shelf' and 'dusted down'. It might also be explained by the fact that two key sets of protagonists of the 1994 review were Conservative councillors in the London boroughs of Wandsworth and Westminster, often regarded as the 'flagships' of the Conservative administration (see H.C. Debs, Vol. 236, col. 310 (26 January 1994) *per* John Battle; see also Cowan & Fionda, 1994a, p.612).

There were two further critical backdrop elements to this. First, there was the success of the government policies resulting from the vilification of the supposed groups considered in the previous chapter. This created and fostered the relevant atmosphere. Second, the impact of the 'New Right' underclass theorists, especially Charles Murray, added to this atmosphere. In 1989, the *Sunday Times* invited the 'distinguished' American sociologist, Charles Murray, to Britain to consider whether the American phenomenon of the 'underclass' was being replicated. In 1993, Murray returned, once again at the behest of the *Sunday Times*. Murray considered three aspects of British life to suggest that the underclass was developing in 1989 and had bloomed by 1993: crime, illegitimacy and economic inactivity among working *men* (see Murray, 1994, p.2). By 1993, all had increased on the statistics from 1987. The married, affluent, well-educated part of society, which he described as 'the new Victorians', 'will edge back towards traditional reality' (ibid., p.15), whilst the rise in illegitimacy – amongst a group of people which he described as 'the new rabble' – would lead to 'more crime, more widespread drug and alcohol addiction, fewer marriages, more dropout from work, more homelessness, more child neglect, fewer young people pulling themselves out of the slums, more young people tumbling in' (ibid., p.18).

This chapter provides an alternative slant on the process of reviewing the homelessness legislation, which builds on the previous chapter's analysis. That chapter argued in part that the suggestion that some people were so *inappropriate* enabled the government to avoid discussing the supply-side deficit in the housing equation. Precisely the same argument is used here, although directly in the context of the homelessness legislation. Here I will be arguing that the government drew upon two established myths about the homelessness legislation in order to suggest (they never publicly argued this) that their proposed reforms would have a narrower effect than they, in fact, would have done. That is, the media were used to make the suggestion that the government's proposals would penalize specific supposed groups of people. These supposed groups of people were, and remain, commonly associated with notions of fecklessness and non-genuine abusers of welfare legislation. Both have been part of the folklore of the homelessness legislation for some time. However, the beliefs that 'single mothers got pregnant to get a council house' and that 'homeless people are queue jumpers' rose in a crescendo during 1993-6. Often these two factually incorrect statements were conjoined so that the portrayal was of teenage 'girls' becoming pregnant so that they could jump the queue for housing.

The government's ability (as primary definers) to foster these sentiments enabled them to avoid discussion of the thrust of their proposals, and of the critical question of the deficit in supply of low-cost accommodation. There was an important link between these two propositions, for the thrust of the proposals was essentially to reduce demand for the very accommodation which was in short supply. The specific proposals themselves had little to do with single mothers or stopping the majority of homeless people from jumping the queue. This is the theme of the first section of this chapter where the government's general rationale for the abolition of the homelessness legislation is considered, together with the specific proposals contained in the consultation paper.

This provides the context for the discussion in the second section, which considers the significance of the single mother and queue jumper. It will be argued that both notions, as well as the idea that single mothers became pregnant to get a council house, were inaccurate. The third section argues that, nevertheless, both notions played a key part in the reporting of the government's proposals, which were often portrayed, by broadsheet and tabloid newspaper alike, as stemming the tide of single motherhood. The point which I wish to stress here is that this was not the government responding to media pressure through legislation (as with, for example, the 'dangerous dogs' debacle or the knives/guns debate) but the media reporting government plans inaccurately. The central reason for this (mis-)reporting was the political climate at that time, which had been coloured by the apparent failure of the 'back to basics' campaign and questions about John Major's leadership (he having described some members of the government as 'bastards').

The government itself actually focused more clearly on the belief that successful homeless applicants themselves were *abusers* because they were able to jump the housing queue. In other words, the 'system [had been] designed to be exploited' (Murray, 1994, p.22). In the fourth section, I will be arguing that this was also the position that the judiciary had adopted so that, rather than base their decisions on the legislative policy of the homelessness legislation, their interpretations finally resembled more closely the government's 1994 Consultation Paper. In other words, it will be argued that the judiciary, far from being 'radical' or left-wing liberals, were in fact propounding government policy before its introduction in the Housing Bill. The judiciary were therefore a willing tool of the reactionary right, and vice versa.

Reforming the Homelessness Legislation

The Rationales

The DoE's Consultation Paper, issued on 21 January 1994, provided the rationales for the government's proposals. They presented a total contrast to the bland assertions in the 1989 review which had influenced the government's belief that 'the legislation has done the job that Parliament intended of it' (DoE, 1989a, para. 47). The 1994 Consultation Paper made proposals for reform to

> ensure fairer access to all parts of the rented housing sector. These include measures to prevent homelessness, *to remove the distorting effect that the present provisions have on the allocation of housing, and to ensure that subsidised housing is equally available to all who genuinely need it, particularly couples seeking to establish a good home in which to start and raise a family.* (DoE, 1994a, para. 3.1; emphasis added)

At the 1993 Conservative Party conference, Sir George Young, then the housing minister, put the same issue as a rather starker choice. He argued that the homelessness legislation did not

> sit comfortably with the values we share; with the self-reliant society we want to promote; and whether it represents the fairest way of allocating housing; ... *How do we explain to the young couple ... who want to wait for a home before they start a family ... that they cannot be rehoused ahead of the unmarried teenager expecting her first, probably unplanned child?* (Young, 1993; emphasis added)

It followed that the rationale for reforming the homelessness legislation appeared to involve three separate strands. First, the homelessness legislation had a distorting effect on housing allocation. This was substantiated by arguing that the number of homelessness applications had increased to the extent that 'in some areas - particularly in parts of London - it is almost impossible for any applicant ever to be re-housed from the waiting list' (DoE, 1994a, para. 2.6). Statutory homeless people were entitled to a 'reasonable preference' on the housing waiting list: s.22, Housing Act 1985. Furthermore, homelessness applicants were housed on average six months more quickly than applicants who waited on that list (ibid.). DoE research had proved this (although see below). Thus the government argued that there was a 'perverse incentive' for people to have themselves declared homeless (para. 2.8) because that legislation was a '"fast track" into social housing' (para. 2.9) and not a 'safety net', which was what the government believed it should be (para. 1.1). It was therefore 'unfair' (para. 1.1). The queue jumping argument was defined in terms of cause (the homelessness legislation is a 'fast track') and effect (more people wanted to be found homeless).

The second strand was that accommodation was not being allocated according to 'genuine need' or 'real housing needs' (para. 2.4). A marker was put down in the opening paragraphs of the consultation paper, with the suggestion that 'establishing a home – particularly as a place to raise a family – is a matter for which *married couples want to feel personally responsible*' (para. 1.2; emphasis added). The suggestion was that the most genuine needs belonged to those people who were married or wished to marry in order to start a family. Instead, non-genuine single females became pregnant and in this way were able to take advantage of the perverse incentives offered by the homelessness legislation, which says 'more about demand than about need' (para. 2.5). Single females with children were regarded as having a non-genuine need, or less need than married couples. The White Paper in 1995 put the matter baldly: '*Allocation schemes should reflect the underlying values of our society. They should balance specific housing needs against the need to support married life, so that tomorrow's generation grows up in a stable home environment*' (DoE, 1995, p.36; emphasis added). The same point was made in a further consultation paper, which was linked to the 1995 White Paper (DoE, 1996a, para. 29). This provided the only justification (so far) for giving married families priority in an allocation scheme: 'the importance of a stable home environment to children's development'. Presumably single parents are unable to provide this and married couples are. The generality was breathtaking.

The third strand was slightly more subliminally placed in the consultation paper, but concerned reducing the numbers of homelessness applicants (note the way this was linked to the queue jumping rationale above). It is suggested that this was the dominant reason – the other two can be rejected fairly simply, as we will show in the next section. It was hardly surprising that this was the dominant rationale because even the DoE statements recognized that the context of the whole process was the rationing of supply. Indeed, the consultation paper attempted to justify this rationing by referring to the environmental crisis which would ensue as a result of building new homes: 'future generations may not thank us if we continue to devote scarce natural resources to producing ever more dwellings' (ibid., para. 2.3).

Reducing demand for this reason could be seen within the general rationale for the reforms by considering the role which the government perceived was legitimate for itself to adopt:

> The Government's aim is that a decent home should be within the reach of every family. This does not mean that everyone seeking rented accommodation should

expect the state to provide for them on demand. ... The role of government is ... to provide a safety net in time of crisis. Within this framework, individuals should be free to choose between the alternatives available, and should endeavour to meet their own housing needs. (Ibid., para. 1.2)

The twin towers of 'self-reliance' and 'personal responsibility' were as evident in the consultation paper as in other areas of welfare reform. This partly explained why the government devoted a paragraph of the paper to discussing home ownership and the private rented sector 'for those who cannot afford' home ownership (para. 2.1). It was the government's argument that, if one were to make the homelessness legislation needs-based, as opposed to being demand-led, the 'perverse incentive' of the homelessness legislation would be cancelled and fewer people would use it as a result.

Specific Proposals[1]

Briefly, the 1994 Consultation Paper proposed (in relation to the homelessness legislation) specifically that

1. the definition of homelessness would be changed so that it only encompassed the situation where an applicant had 'no accommodation of any sort available for occupation' (paras. 5.1, 8.4-8.5);
2. accommodation duties would not begin until entitlement had been established (para. 5.2);
3. no duties were to be owed to those 'asked to leave [accommodation] by family or friends' (paras. 8.1-8.3);
4. those entering the country on the basis that they are to have no recourse to public funds would not be entitled to accommodation;
5. no duties would be owed 'where there is other suitable accommodation available' (paras 9.1-9.5);
6. the 'full' housing duty, owed to those who still satisfied the relevant criteria, would be for a 'limited period' (paras 6.1-6.7) subsequently described as 'emergency assistance' (for example, para. 8.4);
7. accommodation agencies and advisory services should be used by local authorities in discharging their duties (paras. 7.2, 24-5);
8. those accepted as statutorily homeless were to lose their 'reasonable preference' on the waiting list.

All families, of whatever type, and all single people were to be equally affected by these suggestions. Single mothers were not penalized more than others and it followed that the second rationale was, in fact, irrelevant. While the reasonable preference was to be taken away from the statutory homeless, there was no sign that they would not still *effectively* receive this preference. That is, the proposals did not answer the point made in the 1989 Review that, on any needs-based system of housing allocation, the homeless would be expected to receive a high priority. It would be far better if these proposals were considered for what they were – extremely crude methods of reducing demand for housing.

There were two reasons why this reduction would have benefited the government. First, they could argue that the number of homeless people had actually been reduced by their reforms. This would have been because the definition of homelessness had been narrowed to only include roofless people (and not those having no accommodation, which it would have been reasonable to continue to occupy); to increase the breadth of intentional homelessness; to ensure that no person from abroad would be entitled to housing; and finally, and crucially, to remove the duties where other suitable accommodation (in the private sector) was available. The majority of applicants make use of the homelessness legislation after leaving accommodation occupied by their parent(s), other family or friends. Such people could be found intentionally homeless if they could have 'continue[d] to live together without undue strain' and somewhat bizarrely[2] the paper argued that a method of proving strain might be to require a possession order (ibid., para. 8.3). In other words, the method of collating the homelessness statistics was being manipulated by these proposals.

Second, the obvious reduction in the numbers of applicants successfully gaining access to public sector accommodation would have been reduced, which would provide further reasons for reducing public sector grants. Public sector provision of housing could be phased out in favour of the private sector. Here the consultation paper itself was slightly more willing to compromise:

> While local authorities and housing associations will remain the major providers of rented housing for the foreseeable future, the government believes that the private rented sector has an increasingly important role to play in ensuring the maximum range of opportunities for those relying on rented accommodation. (Ibid., para. 23.1)

Indeed, the 'other suitable accommodation' proposal would have made private sector 'fodder' out of most homeless people. Homeless people would have been directed to the private sector to take accommodation rather than offered accommodation in the public sector. Therefore there was some justification in the rumour that the state of homelessness was being privatized by the government.

Attacking the *Folklore*: Single Mothers and Queue Jumpers

Thatcher argued that 'there was a persistent tendency in polite circles to consider all the "roofless" as victims of middle-class society, rather than middle-class society as victims of the "roofless"' (Thatcher, 1993, pp.603-4). There remained a need for the government to legitimize their planned proposals both before and after publication of the consultation paper. They were able successfully to do this by building on the folk devils summed up in the phrases 'single mother' and 'queue jumpers'. There was also an explicit linking of these two elements in the suggestion that single females became pregnant in the first place to gain access to council housing. As has already been argued, the specific proposals in the consultation paper affected all homeless people, not just single mothers, and their true target was reducing demand for public sector housing, not to curb the practice of queue jumping. However, the government, as primary definers of their own policies, were able to manipulate the media so as to present a partial picture. In this section, it is my intention to demolish these justifications, which can be reduced to anecdotal folklore. The next section outlines how this folklore became manipulated by the media *to represent the law*.

Single Mothers

Young's speech to the Conservative Party conference in 1993 (part of which was quoted above) was part of the fervour aroused by the 'back to basics' message of that conference. This was a slightly different way of phrasing Thatcher's ideal of a return to 'Victorian values'. The 'back to basics' message was that the causes of single motherhood should be stamped out. All homeless people were to be penalized as a consequence of the fecklessness of this group. The analogies with the previous chapter's analysis are stark: the supposed rise of the supposed group of 'New Age' travellers heralded the penalization of squatters and travellers; the supposed rise of the supposed group of 'aggressive' beggars heralded possible legislation to criminalize begging further; the supposed rise of the supposed group of people who abused Britain's 'liberal' asylum laws led to those laws being tightened generally. Here, the supposed rise of the supposed group of single mothers or, as Murray put it, 'illegitimacy' was the cause of substantial reductions in the obligations to the homeless population.

Single motherhood was presented as a *genus*. It was assumed that all single mothers wished to abuse the system. In other words, they were feckless with a purpose. Single mothers were generally portrayed as being at the lower end of the wage scale. Indeed, one would be forgiven for believing that, for Murray, single motherhood only occurred within the lower-wage groups. A further important element was the concentration on *mother*hood and not fatherhood. Generally, although not completely, deprecatory newspaper commentary would refer to single mothers, whereas more positive commentary would refer to single *parents*. This genus was also meant to appeal to the popular perception that single mothers were largely teenagers, and so there was an implicit connection not only with youth but also with more general welfare abuse which is assumed to be done by young people.

Nevertheless, it is possible to attack this ideologue at its roots. There was no *genus* of single motherhood. Females became single mothers for a variety of reasons; for example, one of the results of 'domestic' violence or divorce would undoubtedly be the creation of a single parent family with a mother at its head. It would be a rare event for such people to be portrayed in the same way as the 'feckless teenager'. However, Clarke (1993) reports that, in early 1983, a letter to the *Daily Mail* recorded this view:

> In our part of the soft South-east we echo [the] beliefs that there are women about who set out deliberately to milk the State system. For instance, an unmarried mother of three children automatically gains more housing points than a married couple with one legitimate child. And the Homeless Persons Act gives a battered woman with children higher priority than a 'normal' family.
>
> C.R. Cheeseman (Secretary)
> Merton Women's Aid Ltd, London

Secondly, there was no evidence, other than purely anecdotal folklore, that females became pregnant to abuse the system. Indeed, all the evidence pointed to the opposite conclusion. Soon after publication of the government's consultation paper, the Institute of Housing (a body not noted for its radicalism or opposition to the government) issued an immediate rebuttal of the proposition, based upon a survey of local authority HPUs (IoH, 1994). A longitudinal study of the reasons why people make housing tenure decisions also provided a rebuttal of the government's proposition (Ermisch, 1996). Finally, a study based on census information found that a significant proportion of teenage single mothers actually lived with their parents and so it could not be said of these that they became pregnant to obtain local authority housing; furthermore, a larger proportion were economically inactive or unemployed and thus would naturally require some form of state assistance (Green & Hansbro, 1995, ch. 8).

The best that could have been argued was that the vast majority of people become homeless because they left their parental home, or houses occupied by friends or relatives. However, this was a long way from accepting that single females became pregnant to obtain accommodation. It was true that the government argued that such people should be found intentionally homeless but this was to 'reduce the abuse' (DoE, 1994a, para. 8.2) of the legislation and was phrased more generally. Pregnancy and having dependent children were reasons why a person might receive a priority need (one of the hurdles to be overcome under the homelessness legislation). It was also true that most successful applicants under the homelessness legislation had a priority need for those reasons. However, this was far from saying that single females became pregnant to obtain council accommodation. The deficit in the supply of accommodation meant that few single people could be accepted as having a priority need. Indeed, Chapters 2–6 have shown that single people – who have to show that they are 'vulnerable' for a particular reason – have particular problems in being accepted as having a priority need. In any event, if this were a rationale for reform, the government would surely have proposed reforming the priority need categories. They did not.

Queue Jumpers

The allegation usually applied to single mothers, but often used more widely, that successful homeless applicants were able to jump the housing queue, was more serious because a simplistic interpretation would suggest that there was an element of truth to it. The argument came down to the position that the *wrong* people were being allocated accommodation. So, if we return again to Young's conference speech, the essential point that he was making was that young single mothers had less (moral and political) need than young couples who have waited for appropriate accommodation from the waiting list before they have a child.

Section 22, Housing Act 1985 gave a 'reasonable preference' in the allocation of housing accommodation to specific groups of people, one of which was those 'persons towards whom the authority are subject to a duty under section 65 or 68' (s.22(d)), which were the statutorily homeless. Even though local authorities had never been required to have a waiting list, this was taken to mean a 'reasonable preference' on the waiting list. If the waiting list was the queue, then it appeared that persons to whom duties were owed under the homelessness legislation were able to jump that queue because of their entitlement to a 'reasonable preference'. If one accepted this argument, one still had to face the point that queues only develop when there is sufficient demand for a rationed resource. Use of the pejorative terminology (see Chapter 2 for its initial use), however, enabled the government to place *blame* on successful homeless applicants (the 'non-genuine' or too much 'demand' and not enough 'need') for exposing this 'loophole'.

Once again, it is possible to attack this piece of folklore at its roots. The first stage is the argument, based on the legislation, that a 'reasonable preference' does not entitle those within these groups to *priority*. This is to confuse their different meanings. That term was defined as involving some degree of preference but 'to deflate the preferred might be "reasonable", so long as there is some degree of preferential treatment' (*R.* v. *Newham L.B.C. ex parte Watkins* (1994) 26 H.L.R. 434, 451, *per* Sir Louis Blom-Cooper QC). In other words, the notion of 'reasonable preference' did not connote much of significance. Secondly, those fulfilling the criteria under the homelessness legislation were but one group of persons given preference. Yet no political capital was made of the other groups who, on this analysis, should also have been regarded as jumping the queue, even though many homeless people themselves would also fit within these categories. For example, another preference group was 'persons having large families' (s.22(b)) which was amply wide enough to include some single mother families, quite apart from the homelessness legislation. The other preference groups were wide enough to cover all types of homeless persons ('persons occupying insanitary or overcrowded houses' and 'persons living under unsatisfactory housing conditions'). Thirdly, as between various types of statutory homeless people, local authorities were entitled to establish priorities (*R.* v. *Brent L.B.C. ex parte Enekeme The Times* 11 April 1996[3]), making it possible to penalize single mothers and other more deviant groups in this way. Indeed, the courts had accepted for some time that authorities would need to provide temporary accommodation, often for quite significant periods, before they would be able to provide permanent accommodation (see, for example, *R.* v. *East Hertfordshire D.C. ex parte Hunt* (1985) 18 H.L.R. 51). Quite apart from enjoying an automatic priority, successful homeless applicants had to wait their turn on the list.

So, the Act did not give the homeless automatic priority over other groups. Still the government argued in their 1994 Consultation Paper that

> statutorily homeless households receive automatic priority over others on the waiting list in the allocation of tenancies. ... Nevertheless, it appears from the research that, of those who did manage to get re-housed, people using the waiting list route had to wait nearly twice as long (on average 1·2 years as against 0·7 years) as people re-housed under the homelessness legislation (who would be temporarily accommodated elsewhere by the local authority in the intervening period). (DoE, 1994a, para. 2.6)

This is apparently damning evidence, but the research on which the DoE based these comments (Prescott-Clarke *et al.*, 1994), as well as the use made of it by the DoE in the consultation paper, has been subjected to withering criticism. Ian Loveland has argued: 'The Prescott-Clarke study could not be described, even by the most charitable of observers, as an analytically sophisticated treatment of allocation trends. It offers a wealth of statistical data, but makes no serious attempt to unpack their wider implications' (Loveland, 1994, p.372). Furthermore, the DoE's use of the report appeared disingenuous. The study conducted by Prescott-Clarke *et al.* in fact suggested that only 29 per cent of homeless applicants were offered housing, compared to 52 per cent from the general waiting list. Of the London authorities in the study, only 43 per cent of homeless applicants were offered housing, compared to only 23 per cent from the general waiting list. However, in 20 per cent of cases no reasons were given, making it practically impossible to draw any conclusions (Prescott-Clarke *et al.*, 1994, Table 5.16). Yet the authors tried to do so:

> If the cases with missing information are assumed to be distributed in the same way as cases with information, then the proportion rehoused because of homelessness in London rises to 53% and if all those for whom no information was provided are assumed to have been homeless, the proportion rises to 63%. (Ibid., para 5.4.1)

One can make other criticisms of the report. For example, it was, as Loveland pointed out, bizarre to discuss allocation schemes *en masse* when there was no formal requirement on local authorities to have a waiting list (Loveland, 1994, p.372). Furthermore, it must be impossible to discuss allocation schemes generally when there are substantial variations between the priorities attached to the various groups. The report also obfuscated the issue of homelessness as a reason for allocation by drawing attention (and ascribing particular importance) to the tenants' own definitions of homelessness, as opposed to the correct legal definitions. Finally, the report paid no attention to the quality of accommodation offered to the homeless applicant, as opposed to that offered to waiting list applicants. However, it is well known that institutionalized discrimination operates between these groups (see, for example, Bonnerjea & Lawton, 1987; Commission for Racial Equality, 1987).

Media Reporting

The way in which the media reported the various arguments was critical to the success of the government's apparent policy of avoiding discussion of the supply deficit. It can be analysed into four distinct phases: the first phase was the use of the single mother myth (because we can now use that word to describe the notion that single mothers became pregnant in the first place to obtain housing) from the middle to the end of 1993; the second phase was from early January 1994 to the end of that month, coinciding with publication of the consultation paper; the third phase centred upon the announcement that the government were to go ahead with the majority of their reforms in mid-July 1994; the final phase lasted from that point until the Housing Bill was discussed in parliament and included discussion of the government's White Paper on housing.

My argument is that, in the first phase, the media was sensitized to the issue of single mothers becoming pregnant to jump the housing queue or, put even more simply, 'to get council housing', 'so that their surveillance procedures and journalistic categories are sharpened to capture similar subsequent events and give them considerable prominence' (Golding & Middleton, 1982, p.60). The second phase showed the media to have become so influenced by that process of sensitization that many were led to believe, or believed, that the 1994 Consultation Paper only affected single mothers. By the third phase, however, practically all newspapers reported the government's decision to go ahead with the main provisions in the consultation paper as attacking single mothers. In the final phase, however, the media concentrated on *other* aspects of the Housing White Paper and Housing Bill, including the quality of the environment on and around local authority estates. By that time, the issue had lost its edge.

Thus, throughout the debate, the government were able entirely to obscure and avoid the critical issue relating to the deficiency in the supply of low-cost accommodation. The debate assumed rationing was a *desirable* consequence of a rush of single mothers and not a signal of housing crisis. This was almost certainly because they paraded their proposed amendments to the homelessness legislation in this way. So it did not matter that David Curry, the housing minister from 1995, was able to divorce himself from the 'morality debate'. By that time, the media had lost interest.

Phase 1: Mid- to End-1993

'Single mothers' had for some time been the scourge of society. Sometimes this had been related to housing, although more often the relationship was with welfare benefits. However, from mid-1993 this emphasis changed. First, John Redwood, then secretary of state for Wales, delivered a speech in Cardiff in early July 1993 which alleged that one of the benefits of single motherhood was instant access to public housing and that many teenagers *used* this fact. Second, an influential BBC current affairs television programme, *Panorama*, followed up John Redwood's speech by interviewing teenage females on a Welsh council estate. These interviewees provided (anecdotal) *confirmation* that single mothers did, in fact, become pregnant to gain 'fast track' access to council housing. This programme was enormously important because, throughout the whole period, it provided the only (anecdotal) confirmation of the link. Sir George Young was able to argue in an opposition debate on housing and homelessness, soon after publication of the consultation paper: 'I did not suggest that young ladies became pregnant intentionally in order to secure a council house. The principal advocate for that case is the BBC, which devoted an entire "Panorama" programme to support for the proposition' (H.C. Debs, Vol. 236, col. 309 (26 January 1994)). This comment implied that the *Panorama* programme obtained a significance beyond that of the Conservative Party conference, the third sensitizing event during this period, which was the notorious 'back to basics' conference.

During that conference it was variously argued that there should be a return to basic or core Conservative values, which was interpreted by many of the speakers as an attack on single parents. In this context, Young announced that the DoE was in the process of conducting a review of the homelessness legislation. His comment that single parents often gained housing ahead of married couples (see above) was, in fact, innocuous in the context of that conference (Michael Howard outlined a 32-point plan for 'combating crime'; Peter Lilley, then Secretary of State for Social Security, outlined plans to halt 'benefit tourism': see Deans, 7 October 1993). However, the comment provided *legitimacy* to the claims that if single teenagers became pregnant they would be allocated accommodation more quickly than others. Furthermore, the day after the speech, it was reported that local authorities would not be allowed to allocate accommodation to single mothers (Wynn Davies, 8 October 1993) or single mothers were to lose their rights 'to leap [the] housing queue' (Bell, 8 October 1993; Johnston *et al.*, 8 October 1993; cf. Sherman, 8 October 1993, which faithfully reported in the same way but gave greater prominence to the views of the 'National Organisation of One Parent Families' and only granted the proposals a small column). An editorial in the *Daily Mail* argued:

> As things stand, unmarried teenage mothers can leap-frog married couples on council house waiting lists. This is not only unfair, it has been a key factor in encouraging the massive increase in young women having babies outside marriage, not to mention the irresponsible behaviour of their feckless partners. (*Daily Mail*, 8 October 1993)

Young's speech had not gone this far, but it had given sufficient reference to the single mother myth for it to be reported within that context as well as the spirit of the conference. This was not only a sensitizing event, it was also a *referential* event, for from this point the majority of media reporting of the homelessness proposals discussed them as an attack on single mothers *by reference to the 'back to basics' ideology.* Indeed, the post-conference ministerial resignations due to personal indiscretions (Tim Yeo, Earl Caithness and others) all served to heighten the atmosphere, rather than dampen it.

Phase 2: January 1994

On 8 January, *The Guardian* reported that the consultation paper was due to be published the following week. The article thought it unlikely that 'Sir George [Young] will endorse proposals by the right-wing Wandsworth council to bar single mothers aged under 21 from the homelessness measures. Wandsworth proposes that the young mother's family be given the duty to house' (Wintour, 8 January 1994). This was not a view shared by the front pages of other newspapers on the right wing, which believed that the government were going to back down over the consultation paper. It had apparently been recalled by either John Major or John Gummer 'amid fears that its content may further inflame the row over ministers' roles in promoting moral standards' (Helm & Wastell, 16 January 1994; Greig & Eastham, 17 January 1994; Hennessy, 17 January 1994, quoted 'Right wing Tory MP David Shaw' as saying 'it should be pursued on the grounds of commonsense, morality, and public expenditure').

On 18 January, Young gave an interview on the BBC radio *Today* programme during which he put forward the queue jumping argument as *the* rationale for reform. He argued that the government wanted a system 'that reinforces responsible behaviour and encourages people to stay together rather than promoting family disruption and eviction' (the 'perverse incentive' suggestion in the consultation paper). Finally, he suggested that many single mothers would, in fact, benefit from the reforms. This interview was faithfully recorded by *The Independent* (MacIntyre, 19 January 1994), but others which reported the interview portrayed a somewhat different scenario. Both placed the interview in the context of the single mother issue. The headline in *The Guardian* was 'Single mothers will lose council housing priority', although the subsequent story was more general (Wintour & Simmons, 19 January 1994). More blatantly, in the *Daily Express*, the front page headline 'Minister: we'll stop the queue jump mums' implied that this was what Young had argued in the interview. This article hinted at a slightly different rationale for the planned consultation paper:

> Controversial plans to stop single mothers jumping the council house queue will be announced tomorrow.
> Ministers are pushing the proposals through swiftly to counter claims that they have been forced into a major policy retreat by the Back to Basics row.

Under the plan, single mothers will lose their automatic right to council homes ahead of families and others on the waiting list. (Hennessy, 19 January 1994; see also Bell, 19 January 1994)

Whether the minister had actually made this point in private to Hennessy or this was 'the *newspaper's own version of the language of the public to whom it is principally addressed*' (Hall et al., 1978, p.61; original emphasis) or this was a blatant misreport designed to appeal to the newspaper's readership, these were all signs that the interpretation of the government's proposals was going to be placed in the context of the 'back to basics' campaign. A *Daily Mail* editorial the same day argued that any accommodation to be provided to single mothers 'at the taxpayer's expense should be functional rather than plush' so as to avoid encouraging teenagers to become pregnant (*Daily Mail*, 19 January 1994).

The day after the consultation paper was published, only *The Guardian* and *The Independent* concentrated on reporting the proposals themselves (Wintour & Simmons, 21 January 1994; Simmons, 21 January 1994; Whitfield & Brown, 21 January 1994). Editorials in both those newspapers referred to their belief that the proposals were fair but were a result of the housing crisis. For example, it was argued that 'the misery engendered by all [these results of the housing crisis] cannot be compared with injustices that may occur through queue jumping' (*The Independent*, 21 January 1994; *The Guardian*, 21 January 1994). However, both newspapers, in their editorials and articles, accepted the myth that the homelessness legislation created queue jumping.

All other newspapers reported the consultation paper through the single mother myth. Typical of this (mis-)reporting was the following on page two of *The Sun*:

Ban on single mums jumping housing queue
Single mothers will be banned from jumping the queue for council homes in a government crackdown announced yesterday.
Housing Minister Sir George Young claimed new rules would prevent girls from being 'rewarded' for getting pregnant.
... *In future they will wait the same length of time as married couples with children.* (Murphy, 21 January 1994; original emphasis)

That newspaper is well known for its exaggerated, hyperbolic style. However, similar reports were carried in *The Daily Telegraph* (Johnston & Grigsby, 21 January 1994) and *Daily Mail* (Bell, 21 January 1994). The latter also placed the proposals in the context of its earlier report with the suggestion that single mothers were to be housed in 'private homes of a higher standard'. *The Times* chose a slightly different angle in its suggestion that the consultation paper had exposed differences within the government on the lone mother issue (Sherman & Kelly, 21 January 1994).

Phase 3: July 1994

On 18 July 1994, Young announced that the government were going to pursue the majority of their proposals. At this stage, they dropped their proposals to change the definition of homelessness to rooflessness and that local authorities should remain under a duty to continue to accommodate applicants pending their enquiries (DoE, 1994b). Young dismissed the majority of the 10 000 negative responses to the consultation paper as not addressing 'the actual proposals, but responding to misleading claims by lobby organisations. Others wrote in about the hypothetical effects of our policy' (H.C. Debs, Vol. 247, col. 21 (18 July 1994)). This was a difficult claim to sustain in fact (see, for example, CNHC, 1994; Perry, 6 May 1994) but, as the consultation paper had been publicized within the 'back to basics' context, this was a sustainable position. Young made the further point that 'It is not and has never been our intention that families and other vulnerable people should be left to live on the streets or in unsatisfactory accommodation – as some of the more alarmist propaganda from our opponents has suggested' (H.C. Debs, Vol. 247, col. 21 (18 July 1994)).

The newspaper reports of Young's Commons statement were in sharp contrast. With the sole exception of *The Guardian*, each newspaper gave prominence to the single mother and queue jumping rationales, often joining them together. *The Guardian* chose to rely exclusively on the 'suitable alternative accommodation' proposal. The report closely followed Young's statement, with particular reference to the queue jumping rationale and to a press conference at which Young had apparently admitted that the policy would push more people into private sector accommodation, at a higher price to the housing benefit bill (Simmons & Bates, 19 July 1994, p.2). The tabloids reported the announcement as, for example, a 'crackdown on single mums' (Bradshaw, 19 July 1994). The *Daily Mail* cited an actual example of a single female who had become pregnant, and remained single, in order to take advantage of the welfare system, including the homelessness legislation (Hughes, 19 July 1994). An editorial in that newspaper made the following comment:

> This long-deliberated and carefully balanced policy shift should deter foreigners from dossing down here at the expense of British taxpayers. It should at least make some single girls think twice before producing babies and becoming dependent on the state. ... Sir George Young's announcement was greeted by

Pavlovian sneers and jibes from the opposition party. (*Daily Mail*, 19 July 1994)

The broadsheets were equally misleading. *The Independent* reported the Commons statement in the following way on page 5 (Brown, 19 July 1994):

Bill to ban 'queue-jumping' by homeless
New laws will end duty to provide homes for single mothers

While it kept the two rationales separate, this headline implied that one followed from the other. It is even more surprising, then, that the rest of the report was *accurate* but did not report the problem of the lack of supply of accommodation. That was left to the editorial which, in welcoming the reforms because they would put a stop to queue jumping, argued:

> The root of the housing problem lies not in queue-jumping but in the lack of affordable property. ... Sir George's action in tackling injustices in the allocation of council property is a welcome development. But applause should be muted. His initiative represents no more than a positive footnote in the history of the Government's failure to combat the misery felt by the many with inadequate housing or with no homes at all. (*The Independent*, 19 July 1994)

During the whole debate, this was the only commentary which referred to the key failure of supply.

The Times front page (Sherman & Prynn, 19 July 1994) made the following assertions:

Lone mothers lose priority in council housing queue
The Government yesterday went ahead with plans to stop pregnant teenagers jumping council housing queues despite widespread opposition to the scheme. ... Sir George caused a public outcry when he trailed the plans at the Tory conference last October and published a consultation document earlier this year. His action came after comments by right-wing ministers, including Peter Lilley [Secretary of State for Social Security], that the 'fast track' to housing had prompted young women to start a family. Government figures show that 43 per cent of the homeless are lone parents.

The opening sentence appeared to be completely out of line with Young's statement, while the final sentence in the quote contained a misleading,[4] albeit accurate, general statistic which was carried by most other newspapers as well. The reporting of such trite, 'obvious' morality enabled the newspaper to avoid any in-depth coverage of the rationale(s) of the proposals. The *Daily Telegraph* pursued a similar line (Grigsby & Kirkbride, 19 July 1994) but with the added suggestion that the system was being abused:

Abuse of system has delayed genuine cases, says minister
Single mothers lose automatic right to housing

The abuse apparently arose because 'people who were legally regarded as homeless had taken precedence over those who had been on the waiting list for years'. In other words, the abuse was caused by people taking advantage of a legal loophole. The newspaper, however, also gave prominence to the views of Julian Brazier MP, who argued that the homelessness legislation 'had been the origin of an "unparalleled explosion of illegitimacy and the breakdown of family life"'. Given these references, there were no comments about the availability of low-cost accommodation.

As this was the last period in which issues of *access* to housing, as opposed to the environment of housing, were discussed in the media, the lack of serious debate meant that the government were able to pursue their proposals because of the belief, without foundation, that the homelessness legislation allowed successful applicants to queue jump. The media had been persuaded or had persuaded themselves that the proposals were an attack on single mothers, a belief which was equally flawed. That latter argument could be easily sidestepped by the government in defending their proposals. Two further propositions follow from the media concentration on single mothers. First, it seems that the media were anxious and able to keep the single mother myth alive as an appeal to their readership's consensus. Having created the suggestion, they needed to legitimate it. Second, the more Draconian propositions in the consultation paper could be portrayed as having a *narrower* effect. In other words, the context was made to fit *their* preoccupation as opposed to the reality. In turn, this (misin)formed public opinion and enabled a subsequent housing minister to appear more 'reasonable' when he discounted any lingering beliefs that he sought to punish single mothers (Meikle, 20 March 1996).

Phase 4: August 1994–January 1996

During this phase, media concentration largely turned from issues of access to housing through the homelessness legislation to the environment of housing and, finally, to the privatization of estates and housing association tenancies. Issues surrounding the environment of housing were raised when John Major, in the course of a speech to the right-wing Social Market Foundation on 26 April 1995, suggested that local authority estates in inner city areas were 'grey, sullen, concrete wastelands, set apart from the rest of the community, robbing people of ambition and self-respect' (see Meikle &

Wintour, 27 April 1995). While this backfired on Major, who it transpired had been responsible for one such block of housing, this speech signalled the start of wider discussion about the poverty of local authority management, compared to the relative privilege of other social housing and home ownership. In other words, Major's call was not for increased public subsidy but increased *private* finance and involved an explicit move towards privatization (Adonis, 27 April 1995). This new sensitizing event meant that subsequent discussions concentrated on privatization and not on access to housing.

The White Paper, *Our Future Homes*, was published on 27 June 1995. John Gummer, Secretary of State for the Environment, stressed in the preface that the document embodied three key themes: choice, opportunity and responsibility. He argued that 'public provision cannot and should not be all-pervading and ... we need to empower people to make their own decisions and to accept individual responsibility for the choices they make' (DoE, 1995, p.3). The paper largely concerned privatization: giving rights to housing association tenants to buy their homes and making local authorities more exposed to private sector disciplines such as through the highlighting of compulsory competitive tendering of housing management. Access was dealt with in a page and a half (ibid., 1995, pp.36-7). The proposals, once again, were based upon the beliefs that the homelessness legislation encouraged queue jumping, that allocation should be to 'responsible' people, mainly married couples, and that the government would *'maintain the safety net'* (see above).

These access proposals were ignored by the media in their headlines, which concentrated on the proposal to enable housing association tenants to buy their own properties: 'More tenants will be helped to buy their homes' (Murray, 28 June 1995); 'Gummer launches push to extend home ownership' (Meikle, 28 June 1995); 'Door slams on council house era' (Bentham, 28 June 1995). By this stage, the homelessness proposals were reported by reference to past events, as *old news*, and were therefore marginalized. The *Daily Express* referred to the 'changes to stop single mothers jumping the queue for council homes'; *The Times* referred to Gummer's resolve to change the homelessness legislation; whereas *The Guardian* referred to the homelessness changes as 'a sop to the right of the [Conservative] party, who have been worried by the appearance that single mothers have been given preference'. Each newspaper therefore reported the changes according to its own particular slant, but without giving too much space to discussing the issues. The access proposals had been superseded. When *The Guardian* reported publication of the consultation paper on access to local authority accommodation, which was linked to the White Paper, it did so under the banner of 'Tories soften line on single mothers', which reflected the position that newspaper had adopted on the White Paper (Meikle, 9 January 1996).

The Apotheosis of the Reactionary Judiciary

The judiciary have always accepted that the homelessness legislation enabled successful applicants to jump ahead of others who equally had a genuine need for housing (see Chapter 2), whether or not this was an accurate proposition. This reason alone was often given for reactionary decisions, which usually provided conclusions diametrically opposed to the original policy of the legislation (see, generally, Loveland, 1995, ch. 3; 1996). However, such an appreciation could not have prepared one for the (quite frankly) amazing judgment of the House of Lords in *R. v. Brent L.B.C. ex parte Awua* [1996] 1 A.C. 55. Rather than representing the policy of the original legislation, the rationale of the decision as well as many of the comments made by Lord Hoffmann (who gave the only reasoned judgment) bore a far closer resemblance to the specific changes to the homelessness legislation outlined in the 1994 Consultation Paper. Such was the virulence of the judgment that a leading practitioner in the field questioned the wisdom of bringing the case and, further, suggested that there was little point in the government introducing a new Housing Bill to amend the existing homelesness law.[5] It seemed as if the House of Lords were collaborating in producing a dramatic and controversial limitation on the rights of the homeless which removed the necessity for government legislation. Searching through the judgment, it is possible to find evidence of each particular rationale for the government's 1994 Consultation Paper (discussed above).

Lord Hoffmann thought that the case called upon the House of Lords to consider the meaning of the word 'accommodation' in the 1985 Act – almost exactly the same issue as had been considered in *Puhlhofer*. In giving his judgment, it became clear that Lord Hoffmann had come under the 'baleful influence' (Hoath, 1988) of *Puhlhofer*. Elsewhere, it has been argued that the word 'accommodation' was used in totally different senses in different parts of the Act, partly as a result of the reforms which *Puhlhofer* itself caused in the Housing and Planning Act 1986 (Cowan, 1997). 'Accommodation' in the homelessness definition partly relates to the 'inherent quality of the accommodation' but the same word in the intentional homelessness clause does not (as had been accepted by Lord Brightman in *Puhlhofer* [1986] A.C. 484, 516). Lord Hoffmann's decision was that this word meant the same thing in each part of the Act and, in this way, ran totally contrary to the Act's policy. One consequence of Hoffmann's interpretation was that

> A local housing authority could take the view that a family like the Puhlhofers,

> put into a single cramped and squalid bedroom, can be expected to make do for a limited period. On the other hand, there will come a time at which it is no longer reasonable to expect them to continue to occupy such accommodation. ([1996] 1 A.C. 55, 68)

Throughout his speech, Lord Hoffmann seemed particularly concerned by the fact that an applicant could be living in perfectly pleasant accommodation, albeit temporarily, but could nevertheless be considered homeless. He did not consider this desirable, particularly with the current housing shortage. This appeared to be closer to the government's proposed change to the definition of homelessness in their 1994 Consultation Paper than to the original policy of the act.

This intepretation clearly would have been bad enough, but Hoffmann did not stop there. He went on to challenge the basic assumption lying behind the homelessness legislation: those who satisfy the various criteria of homelessness, priority need and intentional homelessness are entitled to permanent accommodation. As Stephen Ross MP had argued in opening the second reading of his private member's bill in the House of Commons:

> In 1948 it was believed that a short stay in some kind of temporary accommodation would be adequate to tide people over until they could make arrangements for somewhere permanent to live. That may have been so then, but the nature of homelessness today is certainly not like that ... *The need of most homeless people is a permanent solution to their problem which they have been unable to arrange for themselves.* (H.C. Debs, Vol. 926, col. 898 (18 February 1977); my emphasis)

Even though the bill was significantly amended in its tortuous progress through its parliamentary stages, there was no comment upon this primary statement of principle.

Hoffmann adopted a novel interpretation of the provisions which create the duty. He prefaced his comments with the following observation:

> Take, for example, the pregnant woman and her partner, who are unintentionally homeless and in priority need under section 59(1)(a). They are found temporary accommodation by the local housing authority. The child is born and placed for adoption. They have no other children [sufficient to give them a priority need]. Is the council still under a duty to find them permanent accommodation, in priority to others on its waiting list? Is the council still under a duty to provide them with accommodation at all? Why should their earlier homelessness and need give them a priority over others? ([1996] 1 A.C. 55, 71)

Other than the moralistic overtones of such a comment, such a statement rewrote the enquiry duties upon local authorities by suggesting that local authorities must continue to assess applicants after accommodation has been provided to them (in line with the Housing Act 1996, Part VII - the reformed homelessness legislation). It was unclear from the judgment after how long these (intrusive) enquiries should cease. Hoffmann then went on to quote Lord Brightman's heavily criticized comments – essentially referring to the assumed fact that the homelessness legislation was a 'lifeline of last resort' and that those accepted as homeless needed to be considered alongside the 'legitimate aspirations' of those on the waiting list – as 'true and perceptive as they were in 1986' ([1996] 1 A.C. 55, 71). These statements suggested that Hoffmann was persuaded by the negative image of successful homelessness applicants (the 'genuine' rationale) and that the homelessness legislation enabled people to queue jump.

Having prefaced his remarks in this way, Hoffmann was able to deliver the killing blow to the efficacy of the homelessness legislation. He asserted that, so long as the local authority provided accommodation for more than 28 days, 'it seems to me that the term for which the accommodation is provided is a matter for the council to decide' ([1996] 1 A.C. 55, 72). He said that some cases, involving the old, mentally ill or handicapped (covered by priority need in s.59(1)(c)) might reasonably be provided with permanent accommodation. This meant that in most cases, practically, there was no or little temporal distinction between duties owed to the intentionally homeless on the one hand and duties owed to the unintentionally homeless on the other. This was very far from the original parliamentary intention. It was, though, on the same lines as the government's consultation paper, even though Hoffmann's construction was probably even harsher.

Given the impact of the cases considered in the previous chapter and the resonance given to them by the media, it might appear surprising that the media did not actually report the outrageous *Awua* decision. It was left to David Curry, appointed housing minister after Sir George Young, to argue that the government's reforms in the Housing Bill were required to correct some of the uncertainties created by *Awua*. Furthermore, he was able to argue that the Housing Bill was *more benevolent* than this interpretation of the 1985 Act (Curry, 1996).

Conclusion

In their 1994 Consultation Paper, the government's rationales for reforming the homelessness legislation were that many people in genuine housing need were not being allocated accommodation because there was too much demand for housing through the homelessness legislation. The proposals, however, affected all applicants who came through the homelessness route, whether or not they had as much genuine housing need as others. They would not stop queue jumping because, as the government themselves admitted, in any rational system of housing allocation according to need the homeless would receive priority. The proposals themselves therefore more closely reflected the third proposition, which did not appear explicitly in the document but which was, it has been argued, *the* critical proposition. The requirement on local authorities to redirect successful homelessness applicants to private sector accommodation represented both the *creation of demand* for private sector tenancies (and therefore an internal market) and private sector landlords, as well as the *denial of the public sector*. As such, it was a brilliant solution to the 'problem' of homelessness.

On the other hand, the media representation of the consultation paper and subsequent events concentrated upon the notion of the single mother 'getting pregnant to get a council house'. This derived from the 'back to basics' campaign of 1993. The government was therefore able to avoid discussion of the central issue of the deficit of low-cost accommodation. Even when the Housing Bill was discussed in depth in Parliamentary Standing Committee, the housing minister was able to sidestep this issue by saying that what was required was a *fair* system (see H.C. Standing Committee G, Fifteenth Sitting, cols 587-9; Eighteenth Sitting, cols 690-91). Indeed, the judiciary's concentration upon the non-genuine and queue jumping myths enabled the government to appear 'reasonable' at a time when they were proposing cutbacks on obligations to the homeless that were unthinkable even to Thatcher just five years earlier.

Notes

1. For detailed criticism of the proposals and their ethos, see Cowan & Fionda (1994a) and Loveland (1994, 1995, pp.323-48).
2. Some local authorities' initial interpretations of the 1977 Act had required court orders in these circumstances. The 1991 edition of the Code had suggested that this was not acceptable practice (para. 5.5). In this sense, the re-evaluation might be regarded as bizarre. However, if the aim is to keep family units together, requiring adversarial litigation could only break families further apart.
3. This case also contained the suggestion that local authorities need not allocate any accommodation at all to a particular preference group. So the 1985 Act contained ample scope for local authorities to ignore the needs of the homeless.
4. In the context of the rest of the article, this statistic placed the suggestion that 43 per cent of successful applicants were teenage females seeking to take advantage of the legislation. As such it was misleading.
5. The case immediately generated considerable adverse comment from Arden (1995a), a response from the solicitor and a barrister in the case (Gellner & Gallivan, 1995) and a riposte from Arden (1995b).

9 Defining *in*appropriateness

The fulfilment of the Major government's moral and ideological crusade on homelessness – Parts VI and VII of the Housing Act 1996 – took effect in early 1997 (1 April and 20 January, respectively). During 1996, it became much clearer that the central focus of the crusade was to reduce the numbers of people found homeless as well as providing a steady market for the private and quasi-private housing sectors. So, for example, certain people became ineligible for consideration as homeless so that, even if they had no accommodation at all in England and Wales, they would still not enter the central statistics. Local government was forced to withdraw its assumed responsibility to these people. The Act almost raised a presumption that most people will be housed in the private sector. In the same way as there are no more 'jobs for life', no longer is there to be 'housing for life' (see Morgan, 1996). The Housing Act 1996 provides an organized, formal means of enabling, or empowering, those requiring (re-)housing to have the ability to exit from local authority tenure (sometimes before there has been entry into that tenure) and into the private sector. After the privatization of the bricks and mortar, the category of persons known as homeless people were to be privatized. The scheme was high-risk because it assumed that the private rental market would adequately accept its increased role.

During 1996, it was apparent that the government had withdrawn almost entirely from the 'back to basics' morality that characterized the presentation and discussion of the 1994 Consultation Paper. Rather, the government concentrated its attack on the queue jumping rationale and argued that there should be one single waiting list which identified 'housing need'. One of the principal causes of this retreat was a realization that the government's majority in the House of Commons was on a knife-edge. Within the Standing Committee which discussed the detail of the bill, the government's majority was similarly slim. This was proved when discussion in that Committee turned to whether gay people should be allowed to succeed to statutory tenancies. David Ashby, a Conservative MP, voted with Labour to inflict a defeat on the government which further emphasized this tension (Ashby was subsequently deselected by his constituency party). Few of the debates were characterized by the personal morality emphases of the Housing (Homeless Persons) Bill in 1977.

David Curry, Housing Minister during this period, was therefore forced to adopt a 'reasonable' approach to the discussions and made a number of significant concessions to the opposition parties. Indeed, when he was forced to draft a list of these people who were most in 'housing need' and who were therefore to gain preference on the housing waiting list, it is significant that this essentially only differed from the Labour Party's list by discounting homeless persons (Standing Committee G, Seventeenth Sitting, col. 649 (Nick Raynsford)). Furthermore, at an early stage in the parliamentary proceedings the government conceded that homeless people with 'enough or nearly enough priority' on the waiting list would be entitled to be allocated accommodation ahead of others in the queue. In subsequent debates, this was referred to as 'the layered protocol' (H.L. Debs, Vol. 573, cols 329-30). In other words, the form had been changed but the substance may well have been almost unaltered. Political expediency seemed to demand these concessions, which in turn suggested that many Conservative MPs had not been persuaded by the government's case.

This chapter provides a critique of the new provisions through a consideration of whether they put into practice the government's rationales for reforming the homelessness legislation as stated in the 1994 Consultation Paper (DoE, 1994a). It will be argued, first, that even though a sop was provided to those who believed that the homeless were non-genuine the government did not pursue that particular belief in any depth. Single mothers are not penalized on the face of the Act. Furthermore, the reality of the 1996 Act is that *more* people, not fewer, are allowed to jump the housing queue and this will include many homeless people. In this way, the government's comment in their 1989 review of the homelessness legislation that, in any rational allocation system, the homeless will have preference, has proved true. Reducing demand is far more apparent in both the Act and the new Code of Guidance. This will be discussed under three headings: denial, deterrence and privatization. If the homelessness legislation was ever about need, the introduction of eligibility criteria will surely now lift that cloud.

The focus of the chapter then changes to consider how far the reforms made in the 1996 Act will assist homeless applicants who have community care needs, who fall within the scope of the Children Act, have suffered from racial harassment, and are female and have suffered from male violence. In other words, how will the 1996 Act affect future discussions of the issues considered in Chapters 3-6? In those chapters, I have argued that government created expectations of the homelessness legislation which the administrators of that legislation were unable to fulfil (if they had wanted to). There were a number of reasons given for this failure which were largely

Defining in*appropriateness* 189

generated by the original legislation, such as elements of administrative gatekeeping, which were considered in Chapter 2. My argument here is that the Act itself has generally worsened matters for each group, although there are some specific, positive provisions. As for partnership between agencies, a matter given some prominence in Chapters 2-6, it will be argued that the 1996 Act has significantly worsened the position. This suggests a further aim in the new Act, which is an attempt to discredit local government even though far more control can be exerted by central government within the bounds of the 1996 Act.

Each section within this chapter is also infused with details of the new Code of Guidance (DoE, 1996b). This significantly expanded upon the Act, both ideologically and practically. This was particularly true because, as it required no parliamentary approval, it was not distilled other than through a consultation process that was short and limited, and which did not include many of the central parts of the guidance (see the version produced in October 1996, many sections of which had the legend 'to follow' in parenthesis). A further context is that, after the 1996 Act, much of the regulation is to be found in *statutory instruments* which are introduced where relevant.

The Housing Act 1996[1]

The basic scheme of the 1996 Act is that the homelessness legislation should provide for *short-term* needs. All *long-term* allocations should be made through the local authority's housing waiting list (now known as the housing register). The latter, on this analysis, therefore becomes a register supposedly of long-term housing need on which the homeless are given no greater priority than others because (apparently) homelessness is not a *symptom* of such long-term need. The new homelessness legislation builds on the old so that the enquiries required to be made by the HPU only differ from those of the 1985 Act in a few respects. However, the duties owed to successful applicants, including the way those duties are to be satisfied, are radically altered. Furthermore, the housing register provisions involve a number of changes that are commensurate with a move away from local to more centralized control through the now firmly established legislative mechanism of quasi-legislation, guidance and codes of practice.

Changes to the Homelessness Enquiry Duties

1 There is a slight change to the definition of homelessness, so that it only encompasses applicants who have no accommodation anywhere in the

world (as opposed to accommodation in the UK): s.175(1).[2]
2 Certain people are made ineligible for housing, whether or not they are homeless (s.185). This category embraces asylum seekers and immigrants caught by the provisions of the Asylum and Immigration Act 1996; illegal entrants; those overstaying their visa requirements or only given temporary admission to the UK; EU nationals in breach of residence directives; those whose visa gives them no recourse to public funds; those not habitually resident in the UK; and asylum seekers not entitled to housing benefit (see S.I. 1996/2754).
3 The definition of domestic violence has been significantly altered so that the within/outside the home dichotomy (see Chapter 6) has been discarded. Instead, domestic violence takes its definition from the Family Law Reform Act 1996, so that it is defined by reference to the applicant's relationship with the perpetrator of the violence or threats of violence. If the perpetrator does not fit within the relevant category, then the applicant must rely on the HPU's interpretation of the 'reasonable to continue to occupy' test within the definition of homelessness (s.178).
4 In determining whether it would be reasonable for a person to continue to occupy accommodation, a statutory instrument sets out certain matters, relating to income and expenditure, which must be taken into account. That is, 'reasonableness' is explicitly related to, amongst other matters, affordability (S.I. 1996/3204).
5 The final significant alteration is that the intentional homelessness criterion has been beefed up to catch two further situations: first, where there has been an arrangement under which the applicant leaves accommodation in order to take advantage of the munificence of the legislation; second, where the applicant fails to secure accommodation in the private sector after being provided with an appropriate level of advice and assistance to enable the applicant to occupy such accommodation (s.191(4)). This provision is extraordinarily convoluted.

Changes to the Homelessness Accommodation Duties

There are three significant alterations to the accommodation duties owed by local authorities to those who satisfy the relevant criteria. First, where there is *other suitable accommodation* available for the applicant in the authority's area, the only duty on the authority is to provide the appropriate level of advice and assistance to enable the applicant to secure that accommodation (s.197(1)-(2)). Here 'suitable' is related non-exclusively to affordability (S.I. 1996/3204). Second, if there is no such suitable accommodation available, the authority must provide the applicant with accommodation for *a minimum period of two years* (s.192). Third, *the authority itself can only provide this accommodation for two years*, after which the authority must seek alternative sources (s.207).

Gaining access to Permanent Accommodation: the Housing Register

The 1985 Act contained no duties on authorities to have a stock of accommodation, let alone a waiting list governing access to any such accommodation. It did, however, contain the requirement that, in any allocation, a reasonable preference was to be given to four categories, including the homeless. As we saw in the previous chapter, one of the principal charges levelled against the 1985 Act's scheme was that it enabled the homeless to 'queue jump'. Whilst that charge could be refuted, either by way of association with the other categories or statistically, the 1996 Act's scheme has departed quite radically from that scheme.

First, the 1996 Act *requires* authorities to have a housing register, which can be run in common with other persons or organizations such as housing associations or private sector landlords. Second, certain persons are not entitled to appear on the register (including those groups centrally prescribed as well as those whom the authority itself decides should not be entitled to appear: S.I. 1996/2753). Third, most allocations can only be made through the register (there are certain exceptions). Fourth, the list of categories to whom the authority must grant a 'reasonable preference' is larger, and additional preference is to be given to one of these categories (s.167(2)). The importance of these new categories cannot be overstated:

1. people occupying insanitary or overcrowded housing or otherwise living in unsatisfactory housing conditions;
2. people occupying accommodation which is temporary or occupied on insecure terms;
3. families with dependent children;
4. households consisting of or including someone who is expecting a child;
5. households consisting of or including someone with a particular need for settled accommodation on medical or welfare grounds;
6. households whose social or economic circumstances are such that they have difficulty in securing settled accommodation.[3]

Those in the fourth category are entitled to additional preference where the individual 'cannot reasonably be expected to find settled accommodation for themselves in the foreseeable future'. These six categories therefore are the government's version of the characteristics of persons in most long-term housing need.

A Critique

In their 1994 Consultation Paper, the government argued that the homelessness legislation required radical reform because homeless applicants without genuine housing need were able to jump the housing queue, which contained others with more genuine housing need, and thus caused there to be too much demand for accommodation. In the previous chapter, it was argued that the only significant rationale was that there was too much demand for accommodation.

In this section, I wish to dissect the new provisions to argue that the government itself destroyed the apparently dominant rationales in the new legislation (that applicants, including single mothers, were non-genuine and jumped over others in the queue with greater housing need). Of far greater importance have been the methods used in the 1996 Act to *deny* an applicant's housing need and *deter* applicants from using the homelessness legislation, in particular through the tightening of the criteria, and the *privatization* ethos of the new act. In these ways, the government has reduced demand for public sector housing stock. The government continually referred to the homelessness legislation as a 'safety net', but, as many people will not be able to use it, this will be a net with gaping holes. Before commencing this analysis, one argument needs to be disposed of: that the new Act returns us to the position under the National Assistance Act, 1948 (see, for example, Shelter, 1995; H.C. Standing Committee G, cols 575-85, *per* Nick Raynsford MP and Clive Betts MP).

Back to the Future?

The argument that the 1996 Act returns us to the position under the National Assistance Act, 1948 is unsustainable. For example, the quality of accommodation that is required to be provided to homeless people under Part VII has, in fact, been strengthened by the increased use of the word 'suitable' in the new Act. That word never appeared in the 1948 Act. Secondly, one of the original premises of the homelessness legislation of 1977 - that families should, wherever possible, be housed together - has been retained. While it might be possible to argue that the minimum duty to house successful applicants for two years suggests that the government adopted a median line between the temporary duties in the 1948 Act and the apparently permanent duties in the 1977 Act (or, as Morgan would have it, towards a 'casualization of housing': 1996, pp.448-50), this would only be telling part of the story. It was the government's belief that most successful homeless applicants who are the subjects of the new housing duty will, before that two year period ends, reach the top of the local authority's housing register and be entitled to permanent housing. There are even provisions in the Act which allow local authorities to seek the secretary of state's consent to continue providing accommodation in their own accommodation for longer than two years. So, where certain groups could not expect to be allocated accommodation by the authority within the two year period, the authority can obtain dispensation to continue to provide accommodation.

On the other hand, there are significant linguistic overlaps between the new assessment criteria for allocation through the housing register under the 1996 Act and the 1948 Act. In order to gain temporary accommodation under s.21(1)(b) of the 1948 Act, an applicant was required to show that (a) they had an urgent need for accommodation *and* (b) that need could not reasonably have been foreseen, or (c) that need could arise when the authority itself so deemed it. In order to gain additional preference on the housing register, the 1996 Act requires the applicant to show (a) a particular need for settled accommodation *and* (b) that need arises because of medical or welfare grounds *and* (c) the applicant could not reasonably have been expected to find settled accommodation in the foreseeable future. However, the most that can be said is that this is a linguistic overlap.

What is Genuine Housing Need?

It might be argued that the government's rationale has been well served by the move to a central housing register on which every person will be assessed according to the same principles. However, this assumes that all the new categories of persons to whom a 'reasonable preference' is to be given have a genuine housing need. The government appeared to believe that these categories reflected *long-term housing need* as opposed to the short-term housing need implied by the status of being homeless. Even if it were accepted that homelessness only requires a short-term solution in the majority of cases, a careful reading of the new categories suggests that many people within them will only have a short-term housing need.

In other words, there is no qualitative distinction between the needs of homeless people and the needs of others in the statutory categories. For example, those who fall within the first and second categories outlined above only have a short-term need *until they have been provided with accommodation*. It is difficult to argue that the presence or expectation of a child suggests a long-term *housing* need in most cases. For example, where a pregnant female occupies insanitary accommodation or where the accommodation occupied is too small for a family, once the female or that family are moved, the need is satisfied. It is thus only short-term as well. The only categories which suggest need which will continue at least until after allocation are the last two. Looked at in this way, the philosophy behind the new Act appears unsound. Indeed, whether a person is homeless, has a low income or is pregnant does not matter: each has a housing need.

Having destroyed the basis of the new allocation scheme in this way, it may well be possible to reconstruct it by arguing that the priority need categories contained in the old homelessness legislation are largely retained in the reasonable preference categories. Thus families with dependent children and pregnancy are priority need categories (s.59(1)(a) & (b)). The Code makes this point plain because it recognizes 'the importance of a stable home environment to a child's development' (DoE, 1996b, para. 5.17; cf. the short-term duties to successful homelessness applicants). Many of those who would have received priority need owing to 'vulnerability' (s.59(1)(c), 1985 Act) would fall within the final two categories and the same could be said for some who would have had a priority need on the grounds of 'emergency' (s.59(1)(d), 1985 Act) although that is somewhat more strained. In other words, many of those who would have qualified for priority need should also be accorded a 'reasonable preference' under the new system and, because the new categories are cumulative, may receive greater preference than before. Furthermore, many of those who would be in priority need owing to 'vulnerability' should also be accorded 'additional preference' on medical or welfare grounds:

> The provision is aimed at individuals who are particularly vulnerable, *for example as a result of old age, physical or mental illness, and/or because of a learning disability.* These are people who could live independently with the necessary support, but who could not be expected to secure accommodation on their own initiative. (DoE, 1996b, para. 5.10; emphasis added)

At least three factors militate against complete acceptance of this line of argument. The first is technical and concerns whether the reasonable preference category due to 'families with dependent children' *excludes* single parent families. This category should be contrasted with that which gives preference to 'households' containing a pregnant female. It is, as the government accepted, perfectly possible for a household to include just one person, for 'otherwise, a single person would never be housed' (H.L. Debs, Vol. 573, col. 398 (19 June 1996)). The difficulty is whether the word 'family' refers to a nuclear family only or includes a one parent family. Presumably the word 'household' was used because an application might include only one person who is pregnant, although if that was the case the corresponding priority need category, 'a person with whom dependent children reside' (s.189(1)(c)), would be out of kilter. On balance, though, it would probably be better to regard the 'families' category as including single parent families.

The second point leads on from that, for the way this part of the Act is to be interpreted is entirely within the local authority's discretion. For example, if the authority decides to allocate accommodation on a points system, it may allocate more points to one category than another. Even more than that, the authority may allocate more points to individual groups within the same category. For example, it would probably be lawful for an authority to grant more points to a two parent family that falls within the last category than a single parent family which falls within that category. Allocation schemes therefore become hostages to political fortune.

The third point raises the concern that, even though single mothers are probably not penalized on the face of the Act, the Code of Guidance makes it perfectly plain that the government's approach favoured two parent families:

> Discretion rests with the authority, as it did previously ... *The Secretaries of State would encourage local authorities to exercise this discretion to ensure that first priority should be the provision of housing for married couples with children, and for vulnerable individuals, who are living in unsuitable accommodation.* (DoE, 1996b, para. 5.21; my emphasis)

This should be read with the consultation paper which was linked to the bill which provided a similar rationale:

> The remaining three categories [broadly approximating to categories (3), (5) and (6) above] reflect the underlying social characteristics of households whom the government believes warrant preference for settled accommodation over other households living in similar conditions. Recognizing the importance of a stable home environment to children's development, the Government believes that local authorities should give priority to ensuring that families, *particularly married couples*, with dependent children ... have access to settled accommodation. *Consideration should also be given to the needs of those who have delayed starting a family because of their accommodation.* (DoE, 1996a, para. 29; my emphasis)

The code is only exhortatory, as local authorities are only required to 'have regard' to it (s.169(1)) but both statements suggest that local authorities may justifiably penalize single parent families – or allow two parent families to jump above them in the housing queue – and also that judicial decisions may well interpret the provisions of Part VI with such statements as their guide.

Finally, if we were really dealing with 'genuine need', would we really exclude some people altogether from that consideration (see below)?

Queue Jumping

One the arguments that we used in the previous chapter to justify discarding this as a real rationale with any justification was that there were other groups to whom only a reasonable preference was given under the old law. It was never suggested that people in those categories jumped the housing queue. The 1996 Act enhances that argument because it provides not only a greater number of categories of supposed queue jumpers but also enables those in one category to jump even those other queue jumpers. Consequently, it can be argued with some justification that this rationale has been undermined by the legislation that the government itself has brought forward.

Neither is it possible for government to argue that *homeless people* are not able to jump the housing queue for, as was suggested in the last section, most homeless people will fit into these categories anyway. If a 'reasonable preference' is equated with queue jumping, then this argument holds true now as it did before. In addition, some homeless people will truly be entitled to jump the queue by virtue of what was described as the 'layered protocol'. Where a homeless person has 'enough or nearly enough priority', it was argued by the government that there was sufficient discretion within the new act to enable the authority to house that person through the housing register at the point of being found homeless. It is probably fair to say that this is a narrow category, which the code suggests is activated in the following circumstances:

> It would be open to an authority to establish, as part of their allocation scheme, a procedure for dealing with special cases on an exceptional basis. For example if a household on the register *has* a reasonable expectation of being offered accommodation within three months but suddenly *lose their* existing home as a result of a disaster, it would be open to the authority to make an immediate offer of accommodation through the register. (DoE, 1996b, para. 5.8)

Even so, this exception destroys the government's queue jumping rationale.

Reducing Demand

There are three methods used by the government to reduce demand for public sector housing: denial, deterrence and privatization. All of these appear on the face of the legislation and suggest that this was what the government had in mind when pushing and cajoling its reforms through parliament. The methods of denial and deterrence mean that the homelessness legislation reflects need less than before because the category of *inappropriate* applicants under the homelessness legislation has grown.

Privatization enables authorities to divert applicants into the private sector. As Curry argued in a moment of pique

> Let us [the members of the Standing Committee] get one thing clear. The Bill will not change the supply of social housing so the proposals will have no effect on the number of families allocated to social housing in a given year. What may change are the households that get the accommodation. (H.C. Standing Committee G, Twentieth Sitting, col. 785)

Denial Denial occurs when certain people claim to be entitled to seek assistance under the legislation but the administrators (still the HPU) are forced to refuse that assistance because of the terms of the legislation or, as in this case, the statutory instrument. The homelessness legislation contains three categories of people who are 'ineligible for assistance': 'a person from abroad' (s.185(1)); 'a person who is subject to immigration control under the Asylum and Immigration Act 1996 ... unless he is of a class prescribed by regulations made by the Secretary of State' (s.185(2)); and even if an asylum-seeker (or that person's dependent) can make it through these strict rules, 'if he has any accommodation in the United Kingdom, however temporary, available for his occupation' he is also ineligible. As the code says, 'an asylum seeker living in a temporary hostel or bed and breakfast hotel would not be eligible for assistance' (para. 12.32). The intention was to bring the homelessness legislation into line with housing benefit regulations and so included in the ineligible categories are those who are not habitually resident in the 'Common Travel Area', with some limited exceptions (S.I. 1996/2754, reg. 4(a); for criticism of the test in the housing benefit context, see NACAB, 1996), as well as those EU residents who are required to leave the UK (ibid., reg. 4(b): see also *R. v. Westminster C.C. ex parte Castelli* (1996) 28 H.L.R. 616)). So, if you are not able to pay for accommodation, you cannot be homeless. The habitual residence test was described by David Curry, the Housing Minister in the following way: 'The test, which looks at a person's settled pattern of residence over the last few years, his future intentions, and the focus of his main interests and ties, applies equally to British citizens, European Union citizens and settled immigrants' (H.C. Standing Committee G, Nineteenth Sitting, col. 740). The leading social security textbook suggests that '"Habitually" implies that the residence should be adopted both voluntarily and for settled purposes, for example education, business employment or health, but it does not require an intention to live in a place permanently or indefinitely' (Ogus *et al.*, 1995, p.401).

The only difference between the denial in the new homelessness legislation and the denial that disentitles certain people from even appearing on the housing register is that in the latter case asylum seekers, *who are entitled to benefits*, will not be entitled to appear on the register as qualifying persons (s.161(2)-(3); S.I. 1996/2753). This is because the government believed that 'we do not know whether they will have a long-term need' at that point (H.L. Debs, Vol. 573, col. 338 (19 June 1996)). In other words, if their claim for asylum was rejected, they would not be entitled to appear on the housing register; if the claim was accepted, then only at that point would the person be entitled to appear on the register. The central consequence of all of this is that HPU and allocations officers will be required to become *immigration officers* in order to *police* the type of people who slip through the narrowly opened gate to housing (see DoE, 1996b, paras 12.34-12.42). At the time of writing it appears that there will be a way of circumventing these provisions through the community care legislation (see Chapter 7 and, especially, discussion of *R.* v. *Hammersmith & Fulham L.B.C. ex parte M* (*The Times* 10 October 1996)).

In addition to the statutorily ineligible, the local authority is also given power to specify certain other people who will not be entitled to appear on their housing register (s.161(4)). The code suggests that local authorities can exclude

> people with a history of anti-social behaviour, people who have attacked housing department staff, or tenants with a record of rent arrears. Authorities could impose other qualifications, such as those related to residency in the authority's district or ownership of a property, although they may wish to consider the implications of excluding all members of such groups, e.g. elderly owner-occupiers. (DoE, 1996b, para. 4.27)

The regulations prescribe that successful applicants under the homelessness part, who are *over 18*, must be placed on the register (S.I. 1996/2753, reg. 5). Thus intentionally homeless applicants, or those without a priority need, may be excluded from the register. If that register were ever intended to be a register of housing need in the local authority's area, these exclusions surely deny that title. At the time of writing, it appears that local authorities who wish to exclude those who have a criminal record may well be able to do so, particularly where that person has been convicted of a paedophile offence. Furthermore, those seeking judicial review of the decision to exclude certain groups will be unsuccessful if the authority has room to manoeuvre in exceptional cases.

Deterrence In Chapters 2-6 of this book, discussion was partly centred around the methods used by local authority HPUs to '*deter* people from defining themselves as homeless' (Carlen, 1994, p.19). The 1996 Act also gives local authorities greater room to manoeuvre in deterring people from defining themselves as homeless. First, the definition of homelessness has been expanded so that, if applicants have accommodation *anywhere in the world*, they will not be homeless (s.175(1)). This was introduced into the bill at a later stage as a result of the adverse publicity given (on the front page of the *Daily Mail*) to the correct first instance decision in *R. v. Camden L.B.C. ex parte Aranda* (1996) 28 H.L.R. 672 (see Doran, 19 February 1996).

Secondly, the intentional homelessness provision was bolstered so that it covered the following circumstance:

> (a) he enters into an arrangement under which he is required to cease to continue to occupy accommodation which it would have been reasonable to continue to occupy, and
> (b) the purpose of the arrangement is to enable him to become entitled to assistance under this part,
> and there is no other good reason why he is homeless. (Section 191)

This provision aims to stamp out collusion between applicants and other occupiers/owners of accommodation in which they lived. As a response to the supposed problem of fraudulent applications which were not genuine, one might accept it as a reasonable proposition whilst nevertheless doubting its basis. However, somewhat bizarrely, Curry justified this provision in the following terms:

> *The government do not believe that there is a massive or intractable problem ... local authorities can probably sort out problems almost intuitively. ... We do not intend to impose a new draconian power but local authorities may need a little extra support to sort out new problems.* (H.C. Standing Committee G, Twentieth Sitting, col. 768; my emphasis)

The government's first rationale, which was in any event discarded above, looks even more unrealistic. The minister said that the guidance would provide examples, although there was general concern that an Act of Parliament might say one thing 'and guidance will say that something a little more sympathetic[ally]' (ibid., *per* Andrew Bennett MP). However, there is a darker side to this provision. Most people make their homelessness application after leaving, or while in the process of leaving, other accommodation. When the Housing (Homeless Persons) Act 1977 first came into force, many local authorities forced parents to seek eviction orders against their children before an application would be accepted from the latter; or required applicants to wait until an eviction order was made before an application would be accepted. The third edition of the Code suggested that authorities should not allow this to happen (DoE, 1991), a suggestion which must be exaggerated now that court fees are so excessive. However, no similar provision appears in the new Code (see DoE, 1996b, para. 15.10). Authorities may well seek to use this provision to deter applicants through requiring court orders (for a parallel deterrent, see Chapters 5 and 6).

The final deterrent overlaps with the privatization element but, one might well ask, what would be the point in making a homelessness application if the authority were going to divert you into the private sector anyway? It would be far easier and less stressful for both the authority and the applicant to seek that accommodation without making an application. So there must be concern that authorities' gatekeeping devices (in the traditional use of that phrase) will ensure that homeless people will be directed towards the private sector without an application having been accepted. In other words, the anticipation is that authorities will categorize a significant portion of the potential client group as 'no homeless'.

Privatization[4] Privatization was probably the dominant reason for the reforms in the 1996 Act. It is evident in three different ways. First, where there is other suitable accommodation available in the area, the authority's duty towards successful homelessness applicants is to provide the requisite 'advice and assistance' to enable those applicants to secure that accommodation (s.197). The authority is required to consider the state of the local housing market and the applicant's circumstances (s.197(4)). Presumably, this accommodation can be either a private sector assured shorthold tenancy or the equivalent from a housing association (renamed in the Act, 'registered social landlords', hereafter 'RSLs') (s.209).

Secondly, if the authority house the applicant themselves for the minimum two year period and are considering whether to continue providing that accommodation, one of the matters to which the local authority should have regard is 'the efforts the household have made themselves during the period to secure their own accommodation' (DoE, 1996b, para. 20.28). The government's argument was that this reliance on the private sector 'requires the individual to take some responsibility for arranging his own accommodation' except where that person is unable to do so (H.C. Standing Committee G, Twenty-first Sitting, col. 799 (for example)). The new Code, however, emphasizes that the authority's own stock is for long-term allocations and not for the homeless (para. 21.20).

Thirdly, authorities are given powers to set up and maintain their housing registers in conjunction with RSLs and private landlords (s.162(3)). RSLs are required to cooperate with the authority 'to such extent as is reasonable in the circumstances in offering accommodation to people with priority on the authority's housing register' (s.170). Where accommodation is provided by an RSL, the person is entitled to exit from their management by exercising the new right to *acquire* (as opposed to the right to buy) in Part I of the 1996

Act. In other words, complete exit from state provision can occur in this way.

These duties and powers expose the government's identification of public sector housing as a residual and *marginal* rump. Only those incapable of accepting a private sector or housing association tenancy will end up in the public sector. Usually, this will be those who either cannot *afford* the rent or would be unable to accept private sector accommodation because, for example, there is no such accommodation which has (say) wheelchair access. For the others, though, Parts VI and VII effectively *create* a market for the private sector, which raises difficult questions about whether that sector wishes to have this supply or, indeed, is able to meet the demand.

The government's answer would, no doubt, be that their deregulation and decontrol of the private sector market has stopped the historic decline in that sector and has also led to a modest increase in the availability of those properties. As Part III of the 1996 Act has further deregulated the private sector market, this should also lead to an increase in the availability of those properties. However, there is no evidence to justify this assertion. Indeed, all the available evidence suggests that other socio-economic characteristics, such as recession, negative equity and mortgage repossession, have caused the increase in this sector: see Crook & Kemp, 1996. Deregulation and decontrol provided the perfect opportunity to see through the rough storm of recession. However, once the housing market regalvanizes itself, a significant number of these properties will presumably be sold on.

Furthermore, there are many suggestions in the available research that few landlords wish to rent to people who are in receipt of housing benefit (Crook *et al.*, 1995; Bevan *et al.*, 1995). Bevan *et al.* noted that landlords in their study were generally wary of renting to homeless people. Ironically, the government's stigmatization of homeless households had had an impact on the landlords' decisions about whether to let their property to such households:

> A number of landlords had negative perceptions of people who were homeless. Some landlords felt that it would not be fair on other tenants or neighbours to accept homeless households. One landlord went so far as to suggest that a separate building would have to be provided which was specially sound-proofed ... many landlords prefer not to let to families with children. Some landlords tended to be dismissive of the idea of providing accommodation for homeless households in general, because they felt that the accommodation they were providing was not suitable for families. ... A number of landlords considered that they would only let to homeless households as a last resort, if they could not find 'preferred' tenants. (Bevan *et al.*, 1995, p.58)

As regards the RSL movement, there must be considerable doubt about its future involvement, if that involvement is to be substantial. In announcing a further Green Paper on housing (DoE, 1996c), Gummer suggested that 4·4 million new units of accommodation will be needed over the next 20 years. He also pointed out that '[this] is one million more [households] than is currently being planned for' (Nuttall, 26 November 1996). However, the following day, the Chancellor of the Exchequer announced large cuts to the Housing Corporation's budget (as well as the local authority housing budget, *The Guardian*'s calculation being *a loss of about a quarter* from the housing investment budget: Smithers & Meikle, 28 November 1996). It has been suggested that this will mean that the number of homes produced over the next year will miss the government's target 'by a wide margin' (Coulter, 4 December 1996)[5]:

> Ken Clarke's 'prudent' budget has set the housing world reeling. Slicing well over a third off the cash for affordable homes is anything but sensible. Politically expedient in the short term perhaps, but in the long term the results will be disastrous. No wonder people in the social housing world are outraged. (Ibid.)

Applying the New Provisions

In this section, the point of concern switches from the general effect of the provisions to a consideration of the ways in which they may or will have an impact upon the categories considered in Chapters 3-6. It was observed in those chapters that the government created expectations of the homelessness legislation but those expectations were, at that time and under that legislative system, incapable of being fulfilled. This was particularly the case because, while the general direction of policy was towards 'a seamless service' or 'partnership' or 'multi-agency working' (all basically meaning the same), the old homelessness legislation did not encourage or facilitate these relationships. In the context of the Children Act and community care, furthermore, it was shown that precisely the same problems existed in both unitary and non-unitary authorities. The key question in this section is whether the government has, in fact, responded to some of the problems which were encountered by the HPUs in our study. I begin by examining whether the new legislation encourages the HPU to participate with other bodies in making assessments.

Participation

The 1996 Act provided the perfect opportunity for the government to redress the difficulties HPUs were having with the lack of participation and interagency working. On the face of it, this opportunity has not been taken. Indeed, bearing in mind both that the new legislation has moved even further from being a needs-based test for housing and the complexity of a person's entitlement to housing under the 1996 Act, the Children Act and community care legislation appear now to be *even more distinct* from it. It became apparent throughout the debates in the House of Lords that the government would not create further *duties* on housing authorities to work with other agencies when assessing individuals (compare the exhortation to set up joint waiting lists, use the private sector and so on in terms of *provision*). This was the case even though the government accepted that *many assessments could not be made by housing authorities*. While many of the reasonable preference categories and the additional preference category require housing authorities to make assessments which appear to be outside their expertise, Part VI of the Act imposes no requirement on the housing authority to seek the assistance of those other agencies and no duties on those other agencies to assist in the assessment. Lord Mackay, then Social Security Minister, argued against the imposition of these duties at length:

> I agree that local housing authorities should work closely with social services departments in addressing the needs of community care clients and vulnerable people. However, *co-operation is a matter of good practice; it is not achieved simply by prescription*. I am mindful of the remarks of the noble Lord, Lord Templeman, in the *Northavon* case, who observed that the law is not the way to obtain co-operation. Co-operation is, by definition, a two-way process. ...
> We would not expect local housing authorities to carry out [reasonable and additional preference] assessments in isolation. *Where special needs are thought to exist the assessment is best shared with social service authorities, which have the expertise in this area*. We will be advising authorities on the type of arrangements that may be appropriate in the circumstances.
> There is guidance. I have it in my hand. It is a fairly detailed document ... It was prepared in 1991, before the present Children Act came into being and before the care in the community legislation took effect. *So we have to look again at the question of the guidance for co-operation between housing and social services that is issued. We shall therefore issue fresh statutory guidance that will cover this matter before the legislation is commenced.* (H.L. Debs, Vol. 573, col. 353 (19 June 1996); my emphasis)

This misses the point. If the legislation does not fulfil the policy aim, then guidance is hardly likely to assist. In fact, the increased negative emphasis of the homelessness legislation is so far removed from the approach advocated by the government for all the categories considered in Chapters 3-6 that it is difficult to see how guidance will assist. In any event, the new Code of Guidance does not even refer to the supposed multi-agency response to domestic violence or racial harassment. Clearly, the government's concern in those areas is to be seen to be doing something but without providing any extra resources or support.

204 *Homelessness*

Even if guidance will assist, that provided seems hardly adequate for the mountainous task ahead. So, for example, the guidance often simply repeats the provisions of the Children Act and community care legislation with the occasionally bland assertion that agencies 'should liaise over the best solution for each client, recognising, for example, that the provision of more appropriate housing may assist in the delivery of social services' (para. 2.16); or suggesting that 'a joint approach should be agreed' between departments (para. 2.15); or 'Research has shown that provision of suitable, stable housing is essential if community care is to be a reality for this vulnerable group of clients' (para. 2.17). It is difficult to imagine the exhortatory effect of simply repeating almost verbatim the provisions of s.27 of the Children Act (para. 2.21).

Furthermore, there are infelicitous comments in the new Code of Guidance which *deny* or *marginalize* the housing authorities' assessment expertise. For example, 'housing authorities are unlikely to be able to reach a decision on the level of priority [on the housing register] to accord [to a child in need] without taking into account the views of the social services authority' (para. 5.15). When considering whether a person with a 'physical disability or long-term acute illness' is in priority need, the code recommends that advice should be sought from health or social services staff *if necessary* (para. 14.8). In Chapter 4, we saw how written agreements on the Children Act were largely useless and caused more confusion than they solved. The new Code of Guidance, on the other hand, suggests, in a paragraph on whether children have a priority need, that:

> Effective collaborative working is best facilitated by corporate policies and clear departmental procedures between social services and housing departments. Such procedures should make it clear who takes responsibility in cases where there is any room for dispute. Agreements will be most useful if they cover not only assessment, but also planning for and delivery of provision. (Para. 14.14)

Such comments will have little effect if the HPU deny responsibility in these cases because a child or person requiring community care services is not vulnerable.

Community Care

Other than the general points made above and in the previous section, specific provisions of the Act suggest that some members of the community care client group will be better served by the 1996 Act. The principal beneficial section is that which grants reasonable preference on the housing register to 'households consisting of or including someone with a particular

Defining in*appropriateness* 205

need for settled accommodation on medical or welfare grounds' and additional preference to the same category of people 'who cannot reasonably be expected to find settled accommodation for themselves in the foreseeable future' (s.167(2)). One does not, perhaps, need to look too far for the reasons for this benevolence. There is a wide belief that community care has failed and that failure was associated with the Major government. *The Daily Telegraph*, a newspaper strongly associated with the Conservative Party, has run a campaign against community care for a number of years (see, for example, Fletcher, 25 August 1995) and adverse comment pours out of every newspaper every time a 'schizophrenic' kills.

In addition to the concerns that arise from the possibility that many might be excluded from appearing on the housing register, the Code of Guidance actually *legitimates* the practice which we found in our study HPUs of not accepting a rehousing obligation under the old homelessness legislation:

> The provision is aimed at individuals ... who could live independently with the necessary support, but who could not be expected to secure accommodation on their own initiative. ... *An authority should take into account: the availability of suitable accommodation, whether a package of care and support services is required in order to take up an offer of accommodation, as well as decisions by social services or health agencies about how the applicant's support, care or health needs should be met.* (Paras 5.9-5.10; my emphasis)

This, in fact, follows a suggestion made by Lord Mackay in the parliamentary debates because otherwise

> It could lead to many problems for a housing authority if it housed someone who perhaps had a history of mental illness which led him (or her) sometimes to be a difficult neighbour, should there not be a proper care package in place from social services in order to try to deal with the difficulty that the person had so that it would not spill over to the neighbours. (H.L. Debs, Vol. 573, col. 354 (19 June 1996))

So, this is a relevant consideration because otherwise estate management problems will result. Allocation of accommodation, in other words, is to be guided by the effect of allocation and not by entitlement. If a person is entitled to additional preference, it is bizarre to argue that an allocation cannot be made because no care plan is available or in practice.

As regards the homelessness provisions themselves, the 1996 Act makes no positive changes. Attempts were made, fairly consistently throughout the bill's parliamentary passage, to widen the priority need categories to include those with a housing need as assessed under the NHS and Community Care Act 1990. These calls were rejected partly because the new Code of

Guidance was promised to deal with these issues in more depth than previously and partly because the minister does not appear to have believed that a clear case had been made out for their inclusion (Standing Committee G, Twentieth Sitting, cols 759-60). Nevertheless, the new code does not pay significantly greater attention in relation to priority need (see, for example, paras 14.7-14.8) although the earlier parts of the guidance do give details of the provisions of the community care legislation.

Children

The regulations entitling all those accepted under Part VII to appear on the housing register apply *only* to those applicants over 18 (S.I. 1996/2753, reg. 4). It may well be that an authority, however benevolent it wishes to be, will attempt to restrict demand by refusing to place applicants under 18 on the housing register (even if they fulfil the criteria under Part VII). Where this is the case, it is likely that further problems will arise between the housing and social services departments under the Children Act 1989. One might therefore be forgiven for postulating that fewer people will be assessed by the latter as being in need of accommodation under the 1989 Act or that the latter will approach the housing department. The government provided two reasons for this exclusion: first, youth 'is not in itself an indication of a need for an independent tenancy'; second, the law of property creates difficulties when tenancies are granted to under-18s (as they cannot hold a legal estate in land) and there is no way of enforcing rent obligations against an under-18.

Both of these justifications are open to considerable doubt. First, while youth may not itself be an indication of housing need, the government has always accepted that certain categories of youth *do* have such a need. The Code of Guidance under the homelessness legislation has always suggested (even when this legislation was thought to create a duty to provide a long-term tenancy) that 'children at risk' should be found to be in priority need and this has not changed in the 1996 Act Guidance. Indeed, the new guidance appears to have enhanced the importance of housing this group under Part VII (see paras 14.10-14.17). This should at least provide a cogent rationale for not automatically excluding children from the housing register, subject to exceptional cases.

The second justification, that children cannot take a legal estate in land, caused technical problems for property lawyers because children would take the accommodation under a strict settlement by virtue of the Settled Land Act, 1925. However, the admittedly significant problems of strict settlements have now been resolved by the Trusts of Land and Appointment of Trustees Act 1996 (see, further, Hopkins, 1996). In any event, it was usually the case that authorities were able to circumvent the (dubious) legal problem that children were not legally obliged to pay rent by, for example, making the SSD become a guarantor of the tenancy. Certain persons who will be entitled to appear on the housing register and given a reasonable preference raise similar rent problems within the law of restitution. For example, certain 'mentally incapacitated' persons are in the same position as children (see Goff & Jones, 1995, ch. 23).

The true rationale seems to be the belief that children should not leave their parental home until they are over 25 (see Thatcher, 1993, p.603). Indeed, this would mesh with the recent changes to housing benefit entitlement which similarly give a disincentive to leaving home before that age (because housing benefit is much less in those cases). This once again marginalizes those who do not live in the Conservatives' idyll.

In similar vein, despite calls for a widening of the priority need categories in the homelessness part of the new Act to include all children under 18, no such widening occurred. The rationale for this was that some children were covered by the priority need provisions in the old guidance and, furthermore, there are duties within the Children Act which can be passed over to the HPU under s.27 (see, for example, H.L. Debs, Vol. 574, cols 117-8 (8 July 1996) and above). The only changes to the homelessness part which might affect applications from children is that which entitles authorities to find applicants intentionally homeless where there has been collusion (see above and, for possible effect of requiring checks to be made with parent(s) or carer(s), Chapter 4).

Racial Harassment

Neither the Act nor the Code of Guidance has positively affected the way in which those who have suffered racial harassment might gain access to accommodation. No doubt, the government would adopt the paternalistic justification that it is always better to deal with the perpetrator than move the so-called 'victim(s)'. However, this surely does not respond to what the person who has suffered racial harassment actually wants (compare the ill-fated 'victim-centred' approach discussed in Chapter 5). Furthermore, if the authority excludes those people who have built up rent arrears from appearing on the housing register, a person who leaves their accommodation as a result of racial harassment and does not pay any rent after that time will be excluded (unless there is some exception for these situations).

Violence to Women

I take the view that the single achievement of the 1996 Act is to rid from the statute books the outrageous distinction that had operated since 1977 which allowed authorities to discriminate between applicants who have had to suffer violence, or threats of violence, from within and outside their home. In line with the Family Law Reform Act 1996, violence is no longer related to *where* it happens; rather, it is defined by reference to the *person* who causes it to occur (s.177(1)). That person, known in the Act as an 'associated person', must either have been in a relationship with, or be related to, the applicant (s.178). The provision will thus rarely apply to racial harassment cases. Where the aggressor is not 'associated' with the applicant, the violence or threats are not 'domestic' within the Act and so, once again, the applicant must show that it is not reasonable for them to continue to occupy the accommodation. On the other hand, the Code of Guidance has not taken a bolder line on the (lack of) usefulness of injunctions in violence cases (para. 13.10) and there is a suggestion in the code that accommodation in a refuge may count as a complete discharge of duty in certain circumstances for the two year period (para. 21.17(j)).

Single females fleeing violence tended to fit, or be fitted, into a category of priority need, and were thus subject to the old homelessness obligations. Significantly, in the new Act, unless single females in this situation have 'social or economic circumstances ... such that they have difficulty in securing settled accommodation', they will not receive a reasonable preference on the housing register. Their only potential entitlement will be to short-term housing. Guidance on the housing register provisions does not refer to violence to women other than making the following general comment:

> Many authorities have in the past made arrangements that effectively set aside a quota of anticipated allocations for groups with particular characteristics [such as those fleeing violence] and in some cases allocate the accommodation on the basis of referrals from social services department, welfare bodies or specialised agencies [such as Women's Aid]
> ...
> The Secretaries of State would encourage authorities to ensure that the wider objectives of delivering social housing in support of a range of social policies can continue to be met, for example by maintaining or establishing quota arrangements. (Paras 5.22-5.23; examples in square brackets are my own)

This lack of reasonable preference is a huge omission. As has been suggested time and time again, the needs of a female fleeing violence are permanent housing. The availability of accommodation is a crucial determinant in whether or not a female decides to leave a violence situation (Dobash & Dobash, 1992; Hague & Malos, 1993). If nothing else has exposed the government's reforms as a sham based on an ideological preference for the private sector, then this surely has.

Conclusion

The 1996 Act was supposedly required because too many homelessness applicants were jumping the housing queue and there were others in the housing queue who had greater needs. Here it has been argued that *reducing demand* for public sector accommodation was the only rationale which appeared on the face of the Act. This was effected through denying that a person is homeless, deterring authorities from accepting applications and privatizing the duties. While the Act does create a requirement to have a single waiting list, it enables many others to jump the queue through widening the 'reasonable preference' categories, as well as creating a true band of queue jumpers through the creation of an 'additional preference' category. Provisions were created to stop apparently non-genuine homelessness applicants but even the government did not suggest that there was 'a massive or intractable problem'. The effect of the 'back to basics' ideology, so prominent in the period preceding the bill in both the media and the government's justifications (see Chapter 8), has only been felt in the accompanying Code of Guidance to which local authorities are required 'to have regard'. As a result of this, when considering the potential specific applications of the new Act, the only positive aspect (that the domestic violence provisions have discarded the old inside/outside the home dichotomy) has stacked against it so much that is negative. For some time, researchers have been suggesting that the effect of an individual tenant's right to buy is the residualization and marginalization of the public housing sector. It is crystal clear that the Housing Act 1996 has further propagated that view.

Notes

1 The following does no more than analyse some of the provisions in the new Act as they may affect the issues considered in the previous chapters of this book. For a more general analysis of the new Act, see Cowan (1996).
2 This was to counter the problems caused by the fact that a person could have accommodation in (say) Italy, but be homeless because they had no accommodation in the UK: see, for example, *R.* v. *Camden L.B.C. ex parte Aranda* (1996) 28 H.L.R. 672, as reported on the front page of the *Daily Mail*: Doran, 19 February 1996.
3 Large families', given reasonable preference under the 1985 Act, do not retain such preference. Burnet explains this exclusion thus:
> This is probably not the thin end of the wedge of some eugenics policy, but explicable by the fact that adequate consideration can presumably be given to such families under one of the new categories, such as families with dependent children. However, against their exclusion it has been argued that they are disadvantaged in the public sector through lack of suitable housing stock, and bound to struggle in the private sector because of shortages and landlords' reluctance to let to families with many children. (Burnet, 1996, p.120)

Furthermore, as the categories are cumulative, greater priority would have been given if this category had been retained.
4   I am not going to discuss the (many) issues whch derive from the new powers to contract out homelessness and housing register functions: S.I. 1996/3205. These are outside the scope of this book.
5   The author is chief executive of the National Housing Federation, which represents the various RSLs.

10 Conclusion

The old homelessness legislation did not provide the relevant criteria for determining housing need in individual cases because it required the applicant's past, present and potential conduct to be assessed in the light of the availability of accommodation in the area. The new system which has been devised to allocate housing to those who supposedly have the 'greatest long-term housing need' is fundamentally flawed because, in building upon the old scheme, the central concern was not about how such need might be defined but about reducing demand on the public sector through denial, deterrence and privatization. Neither the old nor the new legislation required lines to be drawn between the deserving and the undeserving, for the line could only be drawn between the more deserving and the less deserving. What was true before will remain true in the future in this respect.

The main thrust of this book has involved reconsidering these dividing lines at both an operational and a policy level. The deserving/undeserving debate, which has been raging for centuries, has always proved sterile but nevertheless has enabled politicians and others to draw conclusions about a person's need from their previous conduct and to use that conduct to make dubious points of 'morality'. The transition made in 1977 was only symbolic and organizational. These policy motivations evident in earlier schemes are just as evident in the old and new homelessness legislation. The foregoing chapters have argued that one result of government policies has been to require that the boundaries between the more deserving and the less deserving be redrawn. In many cases our fieldwork suggested that those boundaries were drawn by reference to an expectation of the applicant's potential conduct in offered property as well as the availability of services to assist the applicant.

While others have argued that the central context of the homelessness legislation has been the rationing of supply of accommodation (a proposition from which I would not dissent), it may well be that similar judgments would have been made even had the supply of accommodation been plentiful. Thus, for example, the HPUs in this study were generally concerned with stemming the tide of applicants, but at the same time they were making judgments about how well the applicant would (be able to) use the accommodation. The homelessness legislation itself often played second fiddle to these concerns. So, for example, if the HPU decision maker(s) believed that relevant community care services would not be provided, accommodation might not be offered; if the HPU decision maker(s) believed that a person under 18 would not make the best use of the property, it might not be offered; if the HPU decision maker(s) believed that the applicant should have remained living in a violent or near violent situation (because their property was, for example, in the private sector), or that the applicant would return to that situation after being offered accommodation, attempts might be made to bypass the offer of accommodation. The relationship between agencies, whether statutory or voluntary, therefore provided a context within which the decision-making process operated. In certain situations, it might have been *the* determinative context.

It makes sense that these relationships are important. In a comprehensive, cogent social welfare system, serving complete individual requirements must be important. When de Friend argued that, if the homelessness legislation were to fail, it would do so because it did not recognize the complexity of the reasons why people become homeless, he was not far from the truth (de Friend, 1978). It was one reason. Statutory overlays, which came into force in the early 1990s, as well as the general direction of welfare policy, further directed this train of thought, for they were all merging towards the same ideal, albeit often expressed differently (as 'partnership', 'multi-agency working', providing 'the seamless service' and so on). So government appears to have recognized the importance of this policy premise. It also appears to have recognized the problem, for reliance on the 'corporate approach' required a strengthening of the power base of local government social services, or at the least not the weakening of that base which central government wished. The backdrop was declining available resources, privatization and negative publicity.

Furthermore, I have argued that the homelessness legislation itself proved inadequate for the task. The critical element of the (re-)provision of housing did not really appear in the consultation papers and the legislation. It was quietly forgotten, mainly because the public sector could not provide it. Thus the implications of community care and the Children Act surely required a reconsideration at the least of the homelessness legislation. Only the homelessness guidance was upgraded to take into account the Children Act but this, almost mesmerically, repeated the provisions of the Children Act without providing guidance on how the two Acts should work together. The guidance on 'domestic' violence and racial harassment did not and still does not play any part in the homelessness legislation; nor does the new guidance. In earlier chapters, the reader's attention was drawn to the belief of some homelessness officers that certain people were 'set up to fail' by the SSD. A central theme of this book is that the whole scheme was 'set up to fail' by the government.

This is not simply conspiracy theory bred out of paranoia, as I have attempted to show. Consider further the following example. As I have written, guidance was not updated to take the crucial new community care legislation into account (even in the 1991 edition after the Children Act and community care legislation had been given royal assent) or to publicize the multi-agency approach that was increasingly being required by other agencies, including the police (in the context of the need for a joint response to the needs of people who are HIV-positive; see Goss, 1994). Guidance underplayed the genuine fears about the Children Act. On the other hand, when the courts decided that certain 'illegal immigrants' were *ineligible for housing* through the homelessness legislation and the government themselves had passed their *restrictive legislation* covering asylum seekers in 1993, it did not take them too long to update their guidance to local authorities (DoE, 1994c).

This also suggested the *new* context of homelessness. While one could justifiably argue that both the individual and the government's housing failure (however that is expressed) was the critical element of the old homelessness legislation, the new context is *housing exclusion*. This context is not a matter of developing principles and policies designed to avoid people being excluded from housing. The new principles and policies are *designed to exclude*. The policy discussion has centred, not around the most deserving/less deserving divide, but around who is the *most undeserving*. It has been argued above that central government concentrated the discussion in this way because of its concern to avoid the central question of the mid-1990s. It was trying to avoid the fact that the financial constraints on the provision of more low-cost housing would have to dominate that discussion. It became a simple impracticality to argue for more housing in the public sector; rather, it became necessary to argue that certain people did not deserve public housing. The developing private sector, subject to market principles, therefore became the governing ideology.

No longer was it necessary to ask how to provide a comprehensive, cogent social welfare system. The brief period in which that thesis asserted its control has ended. The thesis is already an anachronism. The real question came down to how to reduce demand for a declining supply of accommodation. This was eventually completed, through a process of subterfuge, by excluding certain groups from any form of assistance, whatever their experience and whatever their needs. It was not without some significance that the government suggested that the housing parts of the Asylum and Immigration Appeals Act 1993 (which concerned the *exclusion* of certain people from the ambit of the homelessness legislation) 'were in many ways a precursor to the proposals' set out in the 1994 Consultation Paper (DoE, 1994a, para. 14.4).

In the panic to exclude, ideology overcame principles espoused before and concurrently with the reforms. At the time of writing, the DoH and the DoE are attempting to compile a new joint statement of appropriate methods of enabling housing and social services departments jointly to assess a person's need. Given that the backdrop is exclusion and the new system is unable to cater for a person's need, this development must be one of the most futile attempts at policy making.

Homelessness policy has now been closely aligned with policy towards crime control. At breakneck speed, homelessness policy collided with Michael Howard's form of criminology. In this form, the causes of homelessness are equated with a reduction in the 'penalties for fecklessness': more punishment and less provision. This may well be only temporary and fortuitous, for it enabled the government to avoid discussion of the housing deficit. However, this context provides an instant justification for a failure by central government to provide sufficient resources. If Jack Straw and 'new' Labour is to be believed (see, generally, Birch, 1996), the future may well involve slightly increased resources (through local authorities' ability to spend the receipts from the right to buy) *together with* policies towards housing exclusion. So, even when there are more resources available to begin meeting the supply deficit, the context will nevertheless *remain* exclusion.

Even those *included* are affected because their exclusion is often only a matter of time. So, for example, in the new local authority 'introductory tenancies' scheme, even once a person is housed, the local authority can evict its tenants if they 'misbehave' within the first year of their allocation. Eviction and subsequent exclusion can apparently be executed on the say-so of other tenants. This is not the protection of the community from nuisance tenants, but the exclusion of those who *do not fit in*. The homeless rarely fit in. In a study of the way resistance to central government policy was exercised in a part of Tower Hamlets, the resistance movement did not refer to the homeless or to racial divisions because it was anticipated such references would lead to divisions in the movement (Woodward, 1990). This was not because the homeless were perceived as queue jumpers – that has been an easy excuse for central government's policy development. It was because homelessness was still perceived as a reflection of personal inadequacy.

The current criminological vogue, exemplified by the Howard and Straw battle for the *moral* high ground in criminal policy, favours the 'eliminative ideal' (Rutherford, 1996). The political lurch to the right, partly as a result of focus group politics, has had an impact upon policy as homelessness is no longer regarded as a *housing issue* and responsibility of the DoE but is becoming a *crime control issue* and thus the responsibility of the Home Office. The causes of homelessness are not the housing crisis but the fact that a portion of the population are feckless and do not take responsibility for their own housing. The government's position was a toned-down version of Sir William Rees-Davies' contribution to the debates about the 1977 homelessness legislation. This tendency has recently been exemplified in the response to 'vagrancy' and 'aggressive' begging which is now regarded primarily as a crime control matter. The response to homelessness, and particularly street homelessness, now forms part of the movement towards the 'broken windows' thesis.

It has recently been suggested that the main foci of opposition to the government have been the judiciary and the House of Lords. As I have endeavoured to show, the judiciary have almost anticipated the government's homelessness policy. They have certainly based much of the homelessness jurisprudence upon the government's rationales, so that they have been collaborators and fellow pursuers of the eliminative ideal. From introducing an eligibility test in homelessness applications (see Cowan & Fionda, 1993; also *R.* v. *Secretary of State for the Environment ex parte Tower Hamlets L.B.C.* (1993) 25 H.L.R. 524) to misapplying the policy of the homelessness legislation (Loveland, 1995, 1996) to putting the final nail in its coffin (Cowan, 1997), the judiciary have done their utmost to endorse the government's reforms for similar reasons to those of the government. The House of Lords has proved a thorn in the government's flesh – by, for example, attempting to soften the blow of the Asylum and Immigration Act 1996 – but this thorn is easily extracted. Opposition parties in the House of Commons voted against the Housing Act 1996 and there are commitments from Labour to reintroduce the 1977 homelessness legislation's fault-based system of allocating housing to homeless families (Birch, 1996, p.77) but, to use Loveland's expressive phrase, in the context of the supply deficit that Act had become 'an exercise in legislative deceit' (1995, p.331). Furthermore, allocation on the 'less fault' basis is precisely the penalizing approach which excludes.

However, *the speed* with which government and opposition have developed their proposals is also frightening. In 1994, when Cowan and Fionda considered the local authority HPU response to the housing of ex-offenders, both authors believed that those views which linked crime with the response to homelessness (that is, a person who intentionally committed a crime was intentionally homeless) were marginal and unnecessary (Cowan & Fionda, 1994c). The rush to penalize, however, has probably made our position out of date already. Neither of us could be described as 'New Left idealists' – people can become homeless through their own fault – but the system conspires against so many people. Penalizing those people and excluding others is the response of the politically arrogant.

Appendix 1
Study authorities' action under the homelessness provisions of the Housing Act 1985

Table A1.1 Study authorities' action under the homelessness provisions of the Housing Act 1985: 1992

Local authority	Approx. total applications recorded	Decisions under s.64 issued during year			
		Found not to be homeless (%)	Non-priority homeless (%)	Intentionally homeless (%)	Successful (%)
LA1	2 900	13	38.5	0.5	32
LA2	x	17.5	26.5	i	16.5
LA3	150	43	27	2.5	19.5
LA4	150	26	17.5	7.5	49.5
LA5	450	12	6.5	1.5	64
LA6	1 050	23	40	i	37
LA7	700	40	2	2.5	17
LA8	1 000	6	41	i	18.5
LA9	950	17	6	i	41.5
LA10	1 450	30.5	51	1	33
LB1	2 150	11	31.5	1.5	46
LB2	1 050	3.5	0.5	1	33
LB3	900	51	6	1	42
LB4	2 150	3	1.5	i	32
LB5	n	n	n	n	n

Notes:
i = insufficient numbers.
LB5 statistics incomplete; LB's statistics affected by reorganization.
Variations partly reflect different methods of recording numbers of applicants and decisions made and different policies.
Source: DoE statistics.

Table A1.2 Study authorities' action under the homelessness provisions of the Housing Act 1985: 1993

Local authority	Approx. total applications recorded	Decisions under s.64 issued during year			
		Found not to be homeless (%)	Non-priority homeless (%)	Intentionally homeless (%)	Successful (%)
LA1	4 050	29	32.5	i	38.5
LA2	3 900	15	35	i	27
LA3	600	44	20	6	20.5
LA4	250	22.5	22.5	5	46
LA5	650	12.5	7	1.5	47
LA6	700	47	20.5	0.5	49.5
LA7	2 050	8	1.5	0.5	6.5
LA8	700	10	41	1	39
LA9	1 450	43.5	15	i	29.5
LA10	1 400	34.5	38	1.5	31
LB1	1 950	6	27	i	45
LB2	1 050	47	i	5	75
LB3	1 600	35	39	1	20
LB4	3 050	9	6	0.5	50
LB5	n	n	n	n	n

Notes:
i = insufficient numbers.
LB5 statistics incomplete; LB2's statistics affected by reorganization.
Variations partly reflect different methods of recording numbers of applicants and decisions made and different policies.
Source: DoE statistics.

Table A1.3 Study authorities' action under the homelessness provisions of the Housing Act 1985: 1994

Local authority	Approx. total applications recorded	Decisions under s.64 issued during year			
		Found not to be homeless (%)	Non-priority homeless (%)	Intentionally homeless (%)	Successful (%)
LA1	3 700	41	30.5	i	30.5
LA2	2 700	27.5	28	0.5	33
LA3	600	46	22.5	2.5	14.5
LA4	250	33	23	i	38
LA5	550	3.5	3.5	i	43
LA6	600	35.5	13.5	0.5	54
LA7	2 500	2	1	1	4
LA8	650	9	37	0.5	25.5
LA9	1 500	42	14	i	31
LA10	1 500	27.5	28.5	0.5	33
LB1	2 050	5.5	25.5	1	52
LB2	950	34	4	4	48.5
LB3	1 350	44	33	0.5	20
LB4	2 200	15.5	8.5	1	70.5
LB5	n	n	n	n	n

Notes:
i = insufficient numbers.
LB5 statistics incomplete.
Variations partly reflect different methods of recording numbers of applicants and decisions made and different policies.
Source: DoE statistics.

Appendix 2
Housing tenure in study areas

Table A2.1 Housing tenure in study areas

Area	Owner-occupier (%)	Private rent (%)	Housing assoc. (%)	Local authority (%)
LA1	52	8.5	5.5	32.5
LA2	57.5	8.5	5.5	27
LA3	63	3	2	30
LA4	71	7	2	14
LA5	78	12.5	2	6.5
LA6	69	5	1	22
LA7	74	10	1.5	11
LA8	77	4.5	1.5	16
LA9	69	4.5	3.5	22
LA10	68	2	1.5	27.5
LB1	73.5	8	1.5	15.5
LB2	78	9	1.5	10.5
LB3	75	6	3	14.5
LB4	49.5	17.5	6.5	25
LB5	36.5	15	10	37

Source: OPCS (1993).

Appendix 3
Housebuilding in study authorities

Table A3.1 Housebuilding in study authorities: 1992

Local authority	Dwellings started			
	Private sector	Housing assoc.	Local authority	All
LA1	224	189	23	436
LA2	192	339	0	531
LA3	93	24	0	117
LA4	197	31	8	236
LA5	187	0	0	187
LA6	218	3	0	221
LA7	103	0	0	103
LA8	371	0	0	371
LA9	1 133	841	56	2 030
LA10	515	138	0	653
LB1	618	173	0	791
LB2	331	213	0	544
LB3	316	12	0	328
LB4	341	402	0	743
LB5	12	156	0	168

Source: DoE statistics.

Table A3.2 Housebuilding in study authorities: 1993

Local authority	Dwellings started			
	Private sector	Housing assoc.	Local authority	All
LA1	425	368	21	814
LA2	129	99	0	228
LA3 (xmths)	120	22	0	142
LA4	277	31	0	308
LA5	205	179	0	384
LA6	254	11	0	265
LA7	–	–	–	–
LA8	600	0	0	600
LA9	1 086	479	3	1 568
LA10	751	379	0	1 130
LB1	854	340	0	1 194
LB2	323	228	0	551
LB3	460	142	0	602
LB4	96	260	0	356
LB5	99	193	0	292

Source: DoE statistics.

Table A3.3 Housebuilding in study authorities: 1994

Local authority	Dwellings started			
	Private sector	Housing assoc.	Local authority	All
LA1	136	179	21	336
LA2	297	215	0	512
LA3	148	4	0	152
LA4	309	31	0	340
LA5	314	13	0	327
LA6	510	52	0	562
LA7	–	–	–	–
LA8	341	129	0	470
LA9	1 341	470	1	1 812
LA10	912	201	0	1 113
LB1	823	162	0	985
LB2	673	10	0	683
LB3	405	336	2	743
LB4	83	314	0	397
LB5 (9 mths)	50	321	0	371

Source: DoE statistics.

Appendix 4
Study authorities' acceptances issued under right to buy

Table A4.1 Study authorities' acceptances issued under right to buy

	1991/2	1992/3	1993/4
n	85 447	77 468	82 188
LA1	n/a	900	900
LA2	550	400	400
LA3	n/a	n/a	n/a
LA4	85	112	181
LA5	89	71	78
LA6	210	339	396
LA7	99	86	120
LA8	180	249	201
LA9	119	263	351
LA10	165	122	248
LB1	528	391	309
LB2	n/a	n/a	n/a
LB3	261	219	278
LB4	n/a	n/a	439
LB5	980	676	541

Note: n = England.
Source: DoE statistics.

Bibliography

Adonis, A. (1995), 'Stirring up the council stock', *Financial Times*, 27 April.
Anderson, B. (1995). 'No one has a right to asylum', *The Times*, 8 December.
Arden, A. (1995a), 'Homelessness: a step backwards', *Legal Action*, August, 22.
Arden, A. (1995b), 'Homelessness litigation', *Legal Action*, October, 27.
Arnold, P. and Page, D. (1992), *Housing and Community Care: Bricks and Mortar or Foundation for Action?*, Hull: School for Social and Professional Studies, Humberside Polytechnic.
Arnold, P., Bochel, H., Brodhurst, S. and Page, D. (1993), *Community Care: The Housing Dimension*, York: Joseph Rowntree Foundation.
Association of Local Authorities (1989), *Community Care: Before and After the Griffiths Report*, London: ALA.
Association of Metropolitan Authorities (1987), *Racial Harassment*, London: AMA.
Audit Commission (1986), *Making a Reality out of Community Care*, London: HMSO.
Audit Commission (1992), *The Community Revolution: Personal Social Services and Community Care*, London: HMSO.
Bailey, R. (1973), *The Squatters*, London: Penguin.
Bailey, R. (1976), *Blunt Powers, Sharp Practices*, London: Shelter.
Bailey, R. and Ruddock, J. (1972), *The Grief Report*, London: Shelter.
Baldwin, J., Wikeley, N. and Young, R. (1992), *Judging Social Security*, Oxford: OUP.
Ball, J. (1994), *Stitching the Patchwork*, London: Homeless Network.
Barnett, H. (1995), 'The end of the road for gypsies', *Anglo-American Law Review*, **24**, 133.
Barron, J. (1990), *Not Worth the Paper..?*, Women's Aid Federation England.
Barron, J. and Harwin, N. (1992), *Written Evidence to the House of Commons Home Affairs Committee Inquiry into Domestic Violence*, Women's Aid Federation England.
BASW (British Association of Social Workers) (1986), *Housing – Its Effect*

on *Child Care Policies and Practice*, Birmingham: BASW.
Bayley, R. (1973), *Mental Handicap and Community Care*, London: Routledge.
Beale, A. and Geary, R. (1994a), 'Gypsies, judges and the state: a review of the Caravan Sites Act 1968', *Cambrian Law Review*, 89.
Beale, A. and Geary, R. (1994b), 'Abolition of an unenforced duty', *New Law Journal*, **145**, 47.
Becker, H. (1963), *The Outsiders*, New York: The Free Press.
Bell, C. (1993), 'Single mothers lose right to leap housing queue', *Daily Mail*, 8 October.
Bell, C. (1994a), 'Back in the queue: action on single mothers reinstated', *Daily Mail*, 19 January.
Bell, C. (1994b), 'Unsold homes for single mothers', *Daily Mail*, 21 January.
Bentham, M. (1995), 'Door slams on council house era', *Daily Express*, 28 June.
Bevan, M., Kemp, P. and Rhodes, D. (1995), *Private Landlords and Housing Benefit*, York: Centre for Housing Policy, University of York.
Binney, V., Harkell, G. and Nixon, J. (1981), *Leaving Violent Men*, Women's Aid Federation England.
Birch, J. (1996), *Votes for Homes: The Roof Guide to British Housing Politics*, London: Roof.
Birkinshaw, P. (1982), 'Homelessness and the law - the effects and response to legislation', *Urban Law and Policy*, **5**, 255.
Blom-Cooper, L., Hally, H. and Murphy, E. (1995), *The Falling Shadow: One Patient's Mental Health Care 1978-1993*, London: Duckworth.
Bonnerjea, L. and Lawton, J. (1987), *Homelessness in Brent*, London: Policy Studies Institute.
Bradshaw, D. (1994), 'Tory crackdown on single mums', *Daily Mirror*, 19 July.
Brewer, C. and Lait, J. (1980), *Can Social Work Survive?*, London: Temple Smith.
Bridges, L. and Forbes, D. (1990), *Making the Law Work Against Racial Harassment*, London: Legal Action Group.
Brindle, D. (1996), 'Britons hit by "tourist benefit" cut', *The Guardian*, 14 February.
Brooke, C. (1996), 'Bailiffs evict the squatter estate agency', *Daily Mail*, 29 February.
Brown, C. (1994), 'Bill to ban "queue jumping" by homeless - new laws will end duty to provide homes for single mothers', *The Independent*, 19 July.
Bull, J. (1994), *The Housing Consequences of Relationship Breakdown*, London: HMSO.

Burkeman, S. (1976), '"We Go by the Law Here"', in M. Adler and A. Bradley (eds), *Justice, Discretion and Poverty*, London: Professional Books Ltd.
Burnet, D. (1996), *An Introduction to Housing Law*, London: Cavendish.
Carlen, P. (1994), 'The governance of homelessness: legality, lore and lexicon in the agency-maintenance of youth homelessness', *Critical Social Policy*, **41**, 18.
Carnwath, R. (1978), *A Guide to the Housing (Homeless Persons) Act 1977*, London: Charles Knight & Co.
Carter, M. and Ginsburg, N. (1994), 'New government housing policies', *Critical Social Policy*, **41**, 100.
Central Housing Advisory Committee (1969), *Council Housing Purposes, Procedures and Priorities*, London: HMSO.
Challis, L. *et al.* (1988), *Joint Approaches to Social Policy*, Cambridge: CUP.
Charles, N. (1994), 'Domestic violence, homelessness and housing: the response of housing providers in Wales', *Critical Social Policy*, **41**, 36.
Chaudhary, V. and Bowcott, O. (1995), 'Forgotten homeless "victimised" by everyone', *The Guardian*, 7 September.
Clarke, A. (1993), 'Prejudice, ignorance and panic! Popular politics in a land fit for scroungers', in M. Loney, D. Boswell and J. Clarke (eds), *Social Policy and Social Welfare*, Milton Keynes: Open University Press.
Clarke, J. (1996), 'After social work', in N. Parton (ed.), *Social Theory, Social Change and Social Work*, London: Routledge.
Clarke, J., Cochrane, A. and Smart, C. (1987), *Ideologies of Welfare*, London: Routledge.
CNHC (Churches National Housing Coalition) (1994), *Families Need Homes*, Manchester: CNHC.
Cochrane, A. (1993), 'Challenges from the Centre', in J. Clarke (ed.), *A Crisis in Care? Challenges to Social Work*, London: Sage.
Cohen, S. (1972), *Folk Devils and Moral Panics*, London: Macgibbon & Kee.
Cohen, S. and Young, J. (eds) (1973), *The Manufacture of News, Deviance, Social Problems and the Mass Media*, London: Constable.
Cole, I. and Furbey, R. (1994), *The Eclipse of Council Housing*, London: Routledge.
Colton, M., Drury, C. and Williams, M. (1995), 'Children in need: definition, identification and support', *British Journal of Social Work*, **25**, 711.
Commission for Racial Equality (1986), *Race and Housing in Liverpool*, London: CRE.
Commission for Racial Equality (1987), *Living in Terror: A Report on Racial Violence and Harassment in Housing*, London: CRE.

Commission for Racial Equality (1989), *Racial Discrimination in Liverpool City Council: Report of a Formal Investigation into the Housing Department*, London: CRE.

Conan Doyle, Sir Arthur (1994), 'The man with the twisted lip', in *The Adventures of Sherlock Holmes*, London: Penguin.

Cook, D. (1989), *Rich Law, Poor Law: Different Responses to Tax and Supplementary Benefit Fraud*, Milton Keynes: Open University Press.

Cooper, J. and Qureshi, T. (1994), 'Violence, racial harassment and council tenants', *Housing Studies*, **8**, 241.

Copley, D. (1995), 'Tory's advice for pregnant girls: have an abortion', *Daily Telegraph*, 19 February.

Coulter, J. (1996), 'Empty promises', *The Guardian*, 4 December.

Cowan, D. (1995a), 'HIV and Homelessness: Intervention and Backlash in Local Authority Policy', in National AIDS Trust (ed.), *Socio-Economic Implications of AIDS in Europe*, London: Cassells.

Cowan, D. (1995b), 'Accommodating community care', *Journal of Law and Society*, **22**, 212.

Cowan, D. (ed.) (1996), *Housing Act 1996 – A Practical Guide*, Bristol: Jordans.

Cowan, D. (1997), 'Doing the government's work', *Modern Law Review*, **60**, 275.

Cowan, D. (forthcoming), 'Homelessness internal appeals mechanisms: serving the administrative process', *Anglo-American Law Review*, Pt I & Pt II.

Cowan, D. and Fionda, J. (1993), 'New angles on homelessness', *Journal of Social Welfare and Family Law*, **15**, 403.

Cowan, D. and Fionda, J. (1994a), 'Back to basics: the government's homelessness proposals', *Modern Law Review*, **57**, 610.

Cowan, D. and Fionda, J. (1994b), 'Usurping the Housing Act', *Cambridge Law Journal*, 19.

Cowan, D. and Fionda, J. (1994c), 'Meeting the need: the response of local housing authorities to the housing of ex-offenders', *British Journal of Criminology*, 444.

Cowan, D. and Fionda, J. (1995), 'Housing homeless families – an update', *Child and Family Law Quarterly*, **7**, 66.

Cranston, R. (1985), *Legal Foundations of the Welfare State*, London: Weidenfeld & Nicolson.

Crook, A. (1992), 'Private Rented Housing and the Impact of Deregulation', in J. Birchall (ed.), *Housing Policy in the 1990s*, London: Routledge.

Crook, A. and Kemp, P. (1996), 'The revival of private rented housing in Britain', *Housing Studies*, **11**, 51.

Crook, A., Hughes, J. and Kemp, P. (1995), *The Supply of Privately Rented*

Homes, York: Joseph Rowntree Foundation.
Curry, D. (1996), 'The government's response', *The Guardian*, 7 February.
Daily Express (1994), Single mothers join queue', *Daily Express*, 19 July.
Daily Mail (1993), 'Give two-parent families a chance', *Daily Mail*, 8 October.
Daily Mail (1994), 'Editorial', *Daily Mail*, 19 January.
Daily Mail (1994), 'Common sense and common sneers', *Daily Mail*, 19 July.
Daily Mail (1996), 'Bringing some sanity to the asylum laws', *Daily Mail*, 12 December.
Daily Mail reporter (1996), 'Paul, the estate agent to the squatting classes', 27 February.
Daily Mail reporter (1996), 'Old law mops up squeegee menace', 23 May.
Darke, J. (1994), 'Women and the Meaning of Home' in R. Gilroy and R. Woods (eds), *Housing Women*, London: Routledge.
de Friend, R. (1978), 'The Housing (Homeless Persons) Act 1977', *Modern Law Review*, **41**, 173.
Deans, J. (1993), 'Lilley halts crooks' tours for spongers', *Daily Mail*, 7 October.
Deans, J. (1994), 'Door to be slammed on queue jumpers', *Daily Mail*, 18 July.
Deans, J. (1996), 'Carry on claiming', *Daily Mail*, 22 June.
Deans, J. (1997), 'Ever changing views of Blair beggar belief, says Major', *Daily Mail*, 8 January.
Denny, C. and Ryle, S. (1996), 'Disillusioned homeowners back council house revival', *The Guardian*, 10 December.
Department of Environment (1987), *Housing: The Government's Proposals*, London: HMSO.
Department of Environment (1989a), *The Government's Review of the Homelessness Legislation*, London: DoE.
Department of Environment (1989b), *Tackling Racial Violence and Harassment in Local Authority Housing: A Guide to Good Practice for Local Authorities*, London: HMSO.
Department of Environment (1991a), *Homelessness Code of Practice for Local Authorities*, London: HMSO.
Department of Environment (1991b), *The Structure of Local Government in England: A Consultation Paper*, London: HMSO.
Department of Environment (1992), *Gypsy Site Policy and Illegal Camping*, London: DoE.
Department of Environment (1993), *Local Housing Statistics*, London: HMSO.
Department of Environment (1994a), *Access to Local Authority and Housing*

Association Tenancies, London: HMSO.
Department of Environment (1994b), 'Government proposes fairer access to social housing', Press Release No. 421.
Department of Environment (1994c), *Homelessness Code of Practice for Local Authorities*, London: HMSO.
Department of Environment (1994d), *Racial Incidents in Council Housing: The Local Authority Response*, London: HMSO.
Department of Environment (1995), *Our Future Homes: Opportunity, Choice, Responsibility*, London: HMSO.
Department of Environment (1996a), *Allocation of Housing Accommodation by Local Authorities - Consultation Paper Linked to the Housing Bill*, London: DoE.
Department of Environment (1996b), *Code of Guidance on Parts VI and VII of the Housing Act 1996*, London: DoE.
Department of Environment (1996c), *Household Growth: Where Shall we Live?*, London: HMSO.
Department of Environment (1996d), *Housing and Construction Statistics 1984-1994*, London: HMSO.
Department of Health (1989), *Caring for People: Community Care in the Next Decade and Beyond*, London: HMSO.
Department of Health (1990a), *Caring for People: Community Care in the Next Decade and Beyond*, Policy Guidance, London: HMSO.
Department of Health (1990b), *The Children Act 1989 Guidance and Regulations*, Volume 2: *Family Support, Day Care and Educational Provision for Young Children*, London: HMSO.
Department of Health (1990c), *The Children Act 1989 Guidance and Regulations*, Volume 3: *Family Placements*, London: HMSO.
Department of Health (1994), *Implementing Caring for People: Housing and Homelessness*, Lancashire: Health Publications Unit.
Department of Health/Department of the Environment (1992), 'Housing and community care', Circular 10/92, London: DoH.
Department of Health and Social Security (1981), *Growing Older*, London: HMSO.
Dobash, R.E. and Dobash, R. (1980), *Violence against Wives*, London: Open Books.
Dobash, R.E. and Dobash, R. (1992), *Women, Violence and Social Change*, London: Routledge.
Doran, A. (1996a), 'Tenant's £20,000 worth of cheek', *Daily Mail*, 19 February.
Doran, A. (1996b), 'The illegal immigrant who can't be evicted', *Daily Mail*, 24 April.
Doran, A. (1996c), 'Asylum flood halved', *Daily Mail*, 3 July.

Doran, A. (1996d), 'Asylum-seekers have a right to life, says judge', *Daily Mail*, 9 October.
Doughty, S. (1995), 'Travellers' charter', *Daily Mail*, 7 November.
Doughty, S. (1996), 'How asylum judges opened the floodgates', *Daily Mail*, 16 August.
Doyal, L. and Gough, I. (1991), *A Theory of Human Need*, Basingstoke: Macmillan.
Dummett, A. and Nicol, A. (1990), *Subjects, Citizens, Aliens and Others*, London: Weidenfeld & Nicolson.
Dwelly, T. (1990), 'Statute tory framework', January/February, *Roof*, 27.
Eastham, P. (1996a), 'Judge's threat to asylum cash clamps', *Daily Mail*, 6 February.
Eastham, P. (1996b), 'The bomber's friend', *Daily Mail*, 28 June.
Ermisch, J. (1996), *Household Formation and Housing Tenure Decisions of Young People*, Essex: University of Essex.
Evandrou, M., Falkingham, J. and Glennerster, H. (1990), 'The Personal Social Services: "Everyone's Poor Relation but Nobody's Baby"', in J. Hills (ed.), *The State of Welfare*, Oxford: OUP.
Fish, S. (1994), 'Being interdisplinary is so very hard to do', *There's no Such Thing as Free Speech and it's a Good Thing, too*, Oxford: OUP.
Fisher, K. and Collins, J. (eds) (1993), *Homelessness, Health Care and Welfare Provision*, London: Routledge.
Fitzgerald, M. (1989), 'Legal approaches to racial harassment in council housing: the case for reassessment', *New Community*, 16, 93.
Fletcher, D. (1995), 'Care of mentally ill "in state of turmoil"', *The Daily Telegraph*, 25 August.
Ford, J. (1996), 'High-wire recovery', July/August, *Roof*, 24.
Ford, R. (1995), 'Rid our streets of the beggars and addicts, says Straw', *The Times*, 6 September.
Ford, R. (1996), 'Judges condemn Lilley for asylum benefit cuts', *The Times*, 22 June.
Ford, R. and Sherman, J. (1996), 'Defiant Lilley presses ahead with asylum cuts', *The Times*, 12 January.
Forrest, R. and Murie, A. (1989), 'The right to buy', in C. Grant (ed.), *Built to Last*, London: Roof.
Forrest, R. and Murie, A. (1991), *Selling the Welfare State - The Privatisation of Public Housing*, London: Routledge.
Fowler, R. (1991), *Language in the News: Discourse and Ideology in the Press*, London: Routledge.
Frost, B. (1996), 'Victorian bylaw could clean squeegee boys off Brighton streets', *The Times*, 23 May.
Garland, D. (1996), 'The limits of the sovereign state', *British Journal of*

Criminology, **36**, 445.

Geary, R. and O'Shea, C. (1995), 'Defining the traveller: from legal theory to practical action', *Journal of Social Welfare and Family Law*, **17**, 167.

Gellner, D. and Gallivan, T. (1995), 'Homelessness: a response', *Legal Action*, September, 22.

Gibb, F. (1996), 'High Court rules that asylum seekers may claim benefit', *The Times*, 9 October.

Gilroy, R. (1994), 'Women and Owner Occupation in Britain: First the Prince, then the Palace?', in R. Gilroy and R. Woods (eds), *Housing Women*, London: Routledge.

Gilroy, R. and Woods, R. (eds) (1994), *Housing Women*, London: Routledge.

Ginsburg, N. (1992), 'Racism and Housing: Concepts and Reality', in P. Braham, A. Rattansi and R. Skellington (eds), *Racism and Antiracism: Inequalities, Opportunities and Policies*, London: Sage.

Ginsburg, N. and Watson, S. (1992), 'Issues of Race and Gender Facing Housing Policy', in J. Birchall (ed.), *Housing Policy in the 1990s*, London: Routledge.

Glastonbury, B. (1971), *Homeless Near a Thousand Homes*, London: Allen & Unwin.

Goff, Lord Robert and Jones, G. (1995), *The Law of Restitution*, London: Sweet & Maxwell.

Golding, P. and Middleton, S. (1982), *Images of Welfare*, Oxford: Basil Blackwell.

Goodrich, P. (1994), '*Jani Anglorum*: signs, symptoms, slips and interpretation in law', in C. Douzinas, P. Goodrich and Y. Hachamovitch (eds), *Politics, Postmodernity and Critical Legal Studies*, London: Routledge.

Goss, S. (1994), *The Housing Aspects of AIDS and HIV Infection*, London: DoE.

Grace, S. (1995), *Policing Domestic Violence in the 1990s*, Home Office Research Study 139, London: HMSO.

Green, H. and Hansbro, J. (1995), *Housing in England 1993/94*, London: HMSO.

Greig, G. and Eastham, P. (1994), 'Retreat over lone mothers', *Daily Mail*, 17 January.

Greve, J., Page, D. and Greve, S. (1971), *Homelessness in London*, Edinburgh: Scottish Academic Press.

Griffith, J. (1966), *Central Departments and Local Authorities*, London: Allen & Unwin.

Griffith, J. (1991), *The Politics of the Judiciary*, London: Penguin.

Griffiths, R. (1988), *Community Care: Agenda for Action*, London: HMSO.

Grigsby, J. and Kirkbride, J. (1994), 'Single mothers lose automatic right to

housing', *Daily Telegraph*, 19 July.
The Guardian (1994), 'A policy where the roof leaks', *The Guardian*, 21 January.
Hadfield, G. (1996), 'Judges' blow to war on benefit tourists', *Daily Mail*, 22 February.
Hague, G. and Malos, E. (1993), *Domestic Violence: Action for Change*, Cheltenham: New Clarion Press.
Hague, G., Malos, E. and Dear, W. (1995), *Against Domestic Violence: Inter-Agency Initiatives*, Bristol: The Policy Press.
Hague, G., Malos, E. and Dear, W. (1996), *Multi-Agency Work and Domestic Violence*, Bristol: The Policy Press.
Hall, S., Critcher, C., Jefferson, T., Clarke, J. and Roberts, B. (1978), *Policing the Crisis: Mugging, the State, and Law and Order*, Basingstoke: Macmillan.
Hallett, C. (1991), 'The Children Act 1989 and community care: comparisons and contrasts', *Policy and Politics*, **19**, 283.
Harrison, J. (1992), *Housing Associations after the Housing Act 1988*, Bristol: School for Advanced Urban Studies, University of Bristol.
Hawes, D. (1991), 'Gypsy site policy: a failure of both carrot and stick', *Policy & Politics*, **19**, 49.
Hawes, D. and Perez, B. (1995), *The Gypsy and the State*, Bristol: The Policy Press.
Heffer, S. (1997), 'Should the workhouse come back for people like this?', *Daily Mail*, 8 January.
Helm, T. and Wastell, D. (1994), 'Tories back down over lone mothers', *The Sunday Telegraph*, 16 January.
Henderson, C. (1996), 'Off limits for beggars', *The Mail on Sunday*, 1 December.
Henderson, J. and Karn, V. (1987), *Race, Class and State Housing*, Aldershot: Gower.
Henderson, P. and Gallagher, T. (1995), 'Such a soft touch', *Daily Mail*, 28 November.
Hennessy, P. (1994a), 'Single mother homes rethink', *Daily Express*, 17 January.
Hennessy, P. (1994b), 'Minister: we'll stop the queue jump mums', *Daily Express*, 19 January.
Hills, J. (1991), *Unravelling Housing Finance*, Oxford: Clarendon.
Hoath, D. (1983), *Homelessness*, London: Sweet & Maxwell.
Hoath, D. (1986), '*R. v. London Borough of Hillingdon ex parte Puhlhofer*', *Journal of Social Welfare Law*, 305.
Hoath, D. (1988), 'Homelessness law after the Housing and Planning Act 1986: the '"Puhlhofer" amendments', *Journal of Social Welfare Law*, 39.

Hoath, D. (1990a), 'The review of the homelessness legislation - a missed opportunity', *New Law Journal*, **140**, 412.
Hoath, D. (1990b), 'Homelessness law: first aid in need of intensive care?' in M. Freeman (ed.), *Critical Issues in Welfare Law*, London: Stevens.
Home Office (1989), *The Response to Racial Attacks and Harassment: Guidance for the Statutory Agencies*, London: Home Office.
Home Office (1990), *Domestic Violence*, Circular 60/1990, London: Home Office.
Home Office (1991a), *The Response to Racial Attacks: Sustaining the Momentum*, London: Home Office.
Home Office (1991b), *Squatting - A Home Office Consultation Paper*, London: Home Office.
Home Office (1995), *Inter-Agency Circular*, London: Home Office.
Hopkins, N. (1996), 'The Trusts of Land and Appointment of Trustees Act 1996', *The Conveyancer*, 411.
House of Commons Home Affairs Committee (1992), *Domestic Violence*, London: HMSO.
House of Commons Home Affairs Committee (1994), *Racial Attacks and Harassment*, London: HMSO.
Hoyes, L. and Means, R. (1991), *Implementing the White Paper on Community Care*, Bristol: School for Advanced Urban Studies, University of Bristol.
Hoyes, L., Lart, R., Means, R. and Taylor, M. (1994), *Community Care in Transition*, York: Joseph Rowntree Foundation.
Hudson, B. (1987), 'Collaboration in social welfare: a framework for analysis', *Policy and Politics*, **15**, 175.
Hughes, D. (1994), 'Single mothers to join homes queue', *Daily Mail*, 19 July.
Hunter, C. and McGrath, S. (1992; supp. 1995), *Homeless Persons*, London: Legal Action.
The Independent (1994a), 'Rough justice for homeless families', *The Independent*, 21 January.
The Independent (1994b), 'A footnote to housing misery', 19 July.
IoH (Institute of Housing) (1994), *One Parent Families - Are they Jumping the Housing Queue?*, London: IoH.
Jacobs, K. and Manzi, T. (1996), 'Discourse and policy change: the significance of language for housing research', *Housing Studies*, **11**, 543.
James, D. (1974), 'Homelessness: can the courts contribute?', *British Journal of Law and Society*, **1**, 195.
Jeffers, S. and Hoggett, P. (1995), 'Like counting deckchairs on the Titanic: a study of institutional racism and housing allocations in Haringey and Lambeth', *Housing Studies*, **10**, 325.

Johnston, L. (1996), 'Attacked, robbed, pelted, abused: Big Issue sellers run the gauntlet', *The Observer*, 3 November.
Johnston, P. and Grigsby, J. (1994), 'Housing list "attack" on lone parents', *The Daily Telegraph*, 21 January.
Johnston, P. *et al.* (1993), 'Single mothers must queue', *The Daily Telegraph*, 8 October.
Jury, L. (1995), 'Travellers' victory puts evictions in doubt', *The Independent*, 2 September.
Kaganas, F. (1995), 'Partnership under the Children Act 1989 – an overview', in F. Kaganas, M. King and C. Piper (eds), *Legislating for Harmony*, London: Jessica Kingsley.
Karn, V. (1993), 'Remodelling a HAT: The implementation of the Housing Action Trust legislation 1987-92', in P. Malpass and R. Means (eds), *Implementing Housing Policy*, Buckingham: Open University Press.
Kay, H. (1994), *Conflicting Priorities: Homeless 16- and 17-year-olds – A Changing Agenda for Housing Authorities?*, London: CHAR.
Kemp, P. (1993), 'Rebuilding the private rented sector?', in P. Malpass and R. Means (eds), *Implementing Housing Policy*, Buckingham: Open University Press.
Kewley, A. (1994), *The Inter-Agency Response to Domestic Violence in Hull*, Hull: Humbercare.
Langan, M. (1993), 'New directions in social work', in J. Clarke (ed.), *A Crisis in Care? Challenges to Social Work*, London: Sage.
Laurie, L. (1991), *Building our Lives*, London: Shelter.
Leach, R. (1994), 'Restructuring local government', *Local Government Studies*, **20**, 345.
Lewis, J. (1994), 'Choice, needs and enabling: the new community care', in A. Oakley and S. Williams (eds), *The Politics of the Welfare State*, London: UCL Press.
Lewis, J. (1995), 'Mothers, wives or workers? Policy prescriptions for lone mother families in twentieth century Britain', paper presented at European Forum Conference, European University Institute, 24 and 25 March, Italy: European University Institute, Florence.
Lewis, J. and Glennerster, H. (1996), *The Implementation of the New Community Care*, Buckingham: Open University Press.
Lidstone, P. (1994), 'Rationing housing to the homeless applicant', *Housing Studies*, **9**, 459.
Linton, M. and Meikle, J. (1995), 'Comfort for Straw in poll on begging', *The Guardian*, 11 October.
Littlejohn, R. (1996), 'Safe as houses? Not with Blair's barmy brainwave', *Daily Mail*, 7 March.
Lloyd, L. (1993), 'Proposed reform of the 1968 Caravan Sites Act:

producing a problem to suit a solution?', *Critical Social Policy*, **38**, 77.
London Race and Housing Forum (1981), *Racial Harassment on Local Authority Housing Estates*, London: CRE.
London Research Centre (1993), *Harassment in London*, London: London Research Centre.
Loughlin, M. (1986), *Local Government in the Modern State*, London: Sweet & Maxwell.
Loughlin, M. (1994), 'The Restructuring of Central-Local Government Relations' in J. Jowell and D. Oliver (eds), *The Changing Constitution*, Oxford: OUP.
Loveland, I. (1987), 'Welfare benefits, administrative discretion and the politics of the "new urban left"', *Journal of Law and Society*, **14**, 474.
Loveland, I. (1988), 'Housing benefit: administrative law and administrative practice', *Public Administration*, **66**, 57.
Loveland, I. (1989), 'Policing welfare', *Journal of Law and Society*, **16**, 187.
Loveland, I. (1991a), 'Legal rights and political realities: governmental responses to homelessness in Britain', *Law and Social Inquiry*, **18**, 249.
Loveland, I. (1991b), 'Administrative law, administrative processes, and the housing of homeless persons', *Journal of Social Welfare and Family Law*, **13**, 4.
Loveland, I. (1993), 'The politics, law and practice of "intentional homelessness"', *Journal of Social Welfare and Family Law*, **15**, 113 (Pt I), 185 (Pt II).
Loveland, I. (1994), 'Cathy sod off! The end of the homlessness legislation', *Journal of Social Welfare and Family Law*, **16**, 367.
Loveland, I. (1995), *Housing Homeless Persons*, Oxford: OUP.
Loveland, I. (1996), 'The status of children as applicants under the homelessness legislation – judicial subversion of legislative intent', *Child and Family Law Quarterly*, **8**, 89.
Lyon, C. (1995), 'Working Together – An Analysis of Collaborative Inter-Agency Responses to "The Problem of Domestic Violence"', in J. Bridgeman and S. Millns (eds), *Law and Body Politics*, Hampshire: Dartmouth.
MacEwen, M. (1991), *Housing, Race and the Law*, London: Routledge.
MacIntyre, D. (1994), 'Tory dampens housing row', *The Independent*, 19 January.
Maguire, S. (1988), 'Sorry love: violence against women in the home and the state response', *Critical Social Policy*, **23**, 35.
Malone, A. (1996), 'Saudi exile wants Rushdie whipped', *The Sunday Times*, 21 April.
Malpass, P. and Murie, A. (1994), *Housing Policy and Practice*, Basingstoke: Macmillan.
McCluskey, J. (1993), *Reassessing Priorities: The Children Act 1989 – A*

New Agenda for Young Homeless People?, London: CHAR.
McCluskey, J. (1994), *Acting in Isolation: An Evaluation of the Effectiveness of the Children Act for Young Homeless People*, London: CHAR.
McHardy, A. (1995a), 'Government tries again with Council's review', *The Guardian*, 3 March.
McHardy, A. (1995b), 'Gummer gives 15 towns new deal', *The Guardian*, 22 March.
McRae, S. (1995), 'The Cost of being a Mother, the cost of being a Father', paper presented to the European Forum Conference 1994–5, Gender and the Use of Time.
Means, R. and Smith, R. (1994), *Community Care: Policy and Practice*, Basingstoke: Macmillan.
Meikle, J. (1995a), 'Gummer launches push to extend home ownership', *The Guardian*, 28 June.
Meikle, J. (1995b), 'Police to "clear beggars from streets"', *The Guardian*, 3 October.
Meikle, J. (1995c), 'Police fears help block beggar plan', *The Guardian*, 11 December.
Meikle, J. (1996a), 'Tories soften line on single mothers', *The Guardian*, 9 January.
Meikle, J. (1996b), 'Blair champions the homeowner', *The Guardian*, 6 March.
Meikle, J. (1996c), 'Building a fine reputation', *The Guardian*, 20 March.
Meikle, J. and Travis, A. (1995), 'Scorn and doubts greet begging review', *The Guardian*, 4 October.
Meikle, J. and Wintour, P. (1995), 'The house that John built', *The Guardian*, 27 April.
Mental Health Task Force (1994), *Priorities for Action*, London: DoH.
Millar, J. (1992), 'Lone Mothers and Poverty' in C. Glendinning and J. Millar (eds), *Women and Poverty in Britain: the 1990s*, London: Routledge.
Molnar, J. and Rogers, D. (1979), 'A comparative model of interorganisational conflict', *Administrative Science Quarterly*, **24**.
Morgan, J. (1996), 'The casualization of housing', *Journal of Social Welfare and Family Law*, **18**, 445.
MORI (1993), *Attitudes to Housing and Homelessness*, London: Shelter.
Morley, R. and Mullender, A. (1994), *Preventing Domestic Violence to Women*, Crime Prevention Unit Series Paper 48, London: Home Office.
Morris, J. (1990), *Our Homes, Our Rights*, London: Shelter.
Morris, J. (1993), *Community Care or Independent Living?*, York: Joseph Rowntree Foundation.
Morris, J. (1994), 'Community care or independent living?', *Critical Social*

Policy, **40**, 24.
Mullins, D., Niner, P. and Riseborough, M. (1993), 'Large scale voluntary transfers', in P. Malpass and R. Means (eds), *Implementing Housing Policy*, Buckingham: Open University Press.
Murphy, J. (1994), 'Ban on single mums jumping housing queue', *The Sun*, 21 January.
Murray, C. (1990), *The Emerging British Underclass*, London: Institute for Economic Affairs.
Murray, C. (1994), *Underclass: The Crisis Deepens*, London: Institute for Economic Affairs.
Murray, I. (1995), 'More tenants will be helped to buy their own homes', *The Times*, 28 June.
Murray, I. (1996), 'HIV foreigners win housing battle', *The Times*, 22 February.
NACAB (National Association of Citizens' Advice Bureaux) (1996), *Failing the Test*, London: NACAB.
National Federation of Housing Associations/Mind (1989), *Housing: The Foundation of Community Care*, London: NFHA.
National Inter-Agency Working Party (1992), *Domestic Violence*, London: Victim Support.
Nevin, C. (1997), 'The mail order biz', *The Guardian*, 12 February.
Niner, P. (1989), *Homelessness in Nine Local Authorities*, London: HMSO.
Nuttall, N. (1996), 'Gummer urged to stem the tide of urban sprawl', *The Times*, 26 November.
Ogus, A., Barendt, E. and Wikeley, N. (1995), *The Law of Social Security*, London: Butterworths.
Oldman, C. (1988), 'More than bricks and mortar', *Housing*, June/July, 13.
Oliver, M. (1995), *Understanding Disability*, Basingstoke: Macmillan.
OPCS (1993), *County Report*, London: HMSO.
Otway, O. (1996), 'Social Work with Children and Families: from Child Welfare to Child Protection', in N. Parton (ed.), *Social Theory, Social Change and Social Work*, London: Routledge.
Pahl, J. (ed.) (1985), *Private Violence and Public Policy*, London: Routledge.
Partington, M. (1990), 'Rethinking British Housing Law: the Failure of the Housing Act 1988', in M. Freeman (ed.), *Critical Issues in Welfare Law*, London: Stevens & Sons.
Parton, N. (1996), 'Social Work, Risk and the "Blaming System"' in N. Parton (ed.), *Social Theory, Social Change and Social Work*, London: Routledge.
Peach, C. (1986), 'Patterns of Afro-Caribbean Migration and Settlement in Great Britain: 1945-1981', in C. Brock (ed.), *The Caribbean in Europe*,

London: Cass.
Peach, C. and Byron, M. (1994), 'Council house sales, residualisation and Afro-Caribbean tenants', *Journal of Social Policy*, **23**, 363.
Penal Affairs Consortium (1994), 'Squatters, travellers, ravers, protesters and the criminal law', London: NACRO.
Perry, J. (1994), 'Why did the government have to backtrack on its plans for the homeless?', *The Guardian*, 6 May.
Pollock, F. and Wright, R. (1888), *An Essay on Possession in the Common Law*, Oxford: OUP.
Prescott-Clarke, P., Clemens, S. and Park, A. (1994), *Routes into Local Authority Housing*, London: HMSO.
Preston-Shoot, M. (1996), 'Contesting the contradictions: needs, resources and community care decisions', *Journal of Social Welfare and Family Law*, **18**, 307.
Prichard, M. (1981), *Squatting*, London: Sweet & Maxwell.
Pyatt, J. (1996), 'The big earner', *The Sun*, 28 October.
Pycroft, C. (1995), 'Restructuring local government: the Banham Commission's failed historic enterprise', *Public Policy and Administration*, **10**, 49.
Randolph, B. (1993), 'The re-privatization of housing associations', in P. Malpass and R. Means (eds), *Implementing Housing Policy*, Buckingham: Open University Press.
Ritchie, J., Dick, D. and Lingham, R. (1994), *The Report of the Inquiry into the Care and Treatment of Christopher Clunis*, London: HMSO.
Robson, P. and Poustie, M. (1996), *Homeless People and the Law*, London: Butterworths.
Rutherford, A. (1996), 'Criminal policy and the eliminative ideal', Southampton: Institute of Criminal Justice, University of Southampton.
Sampson, A., Stubbs, P., Smith, D., Pearson, G. and Blagg, H. (1988), 'Crime, localities and the multi-agency approach', *British Journal of Criminology*, **28**, 478.
Sanders, A. (1988), 'Personal violence and public order: the prosecution of "domestic" violence in England and Wales', *International Journal of the Sociology of Law*, **16**, 359.
Sandland, R. (1996), 'The real, the simulacrum and the construction of "gypsy" in law', *Journal of Law and Society*, **23**, 383.
Sarre, P., Phillips, D. and Skellington, R. (1989), *Ethnic Minority Housing: Explanations and Policies*, Aldershot: Avebury.
Schwehr, B. (1995), 'The legal relevance of resources - or a lack of resources - in community care', *Journal of Social Welfare and Family Law*, **17**, 179.
Seebohm, F. (1968), *Report of the Committee on Local Authority and Allied*

Personal Social Services, Cmnd 3703, London: HMSO.
Seebohm, F. (1994), *Seebohm - 25 Years on*, London: Policy Studies Institute.
Shelter (1995), *Shelter's Response to the White Paper*, London: Shelter.
Sherman, J. (1993), 'Reforms attacked', *The Times*, 8 October.
Sherman, J. (1996), 'Blair presents labour as the homeowner's saviour', *The Times*, 6 March.
Sherman, J. and Kelly, R. (1994), 'Housing reforms reveal Tory split over lone mothers', *The Times*, 21 January.
Sherman, J. and Prynn, J. (1994), 'Lone mothers lose priority in council housing queue', *The Times*, 19 July.
Simmons, M. (1994), 'Homeless to join the queue', *The Guardian*, 21 January.
Simmons, M. (1995), 'Banham Commission "near mutiny" over sacking', *The Guardian*, 25 March.
Simmons, M. and Bates, S. (1994), 'Homeless face local authority suitability test', *The Guardian*, 19 July.
Smith, D. (1992), 'Taking the lead', *Housing*.
Smith, R., Glaster, L., Harrison, L., Martin, L., Means, R. and Thistlethwaite, P. (1993), *Working Together for Better Community Care*, Bristol: School for Advanced Urban Studies, University of Bristol.
Smith, S. (1996), *The Politics of 'Race' and Residence*, Oxford: Polity.
Smithers, R. and Meikle, J. (1996), 'Council tax may rise by 6%', *The Guardian*, 28 November.
Social Services Committee (1985), *Community Care with Special Reference to Adult Mentally Ill and Mentally Handicapped People*, London: HMSO.
Social Services Inspectorate (1994), *Children In Need: Report of Issues Arising from Regional Social Services Inspectorate Workshops, January-March 1994*, Lancashire: DoH.
Solomon, R. (1995), 'Tri-Partnership: Statutory, Voluntary and Private Partnerships', in F. Kaganas, M. King and C. Piper (eds), *Legislating for Harmony - Partnership under the Children Act 1989*, London: Jessica Kingsley.
Spicker, P. (1993), *Housing and Community Care in Scotland*, Edinburgh: Shelter.
Stewart, A. (1996), *Rethinking Housing Law*, London: Sweet & Maxwell.
Stewart, G. and Stewart, J. (1993), *Social Work and Housing*, Basingstoke: Macmillan.
Straw, J. (1995a), 'Letter to The Guardian', *The Guardian*, 6 September.
Straw, J. (1995b), 'Straw defiant on begging', *The Guardian*, 9 September.
Straw, J. (1995c), 'Straw and order', *New Statesman*, 15 September, p.18.

Straw, J. (1995d), 'Put the heart back into communities', *The Times*, 8 November.
Thatcher, M. (1993), *The Downing Street Years*, London: HarperCollins.
Thomas, P. and Campbell, S. (1992), *Housing Gypsies*, Cardiff: Cardiff Law School, University of Wales.
Thornton, R. (1988), 'Homelessness through relationship breakdown', *Journal of Social Welfare Law*, 10, 67.
Thornton, R. (1990), *The New Homeless*, London: SHAC.
Tomas, A. and Dittmar, H. (1995), 'The experience of homeless women: an exploration of housing histories and the meaning of home', *Housing Studies*, 10, 493.
Torode, J. (1996a), 'Why do we give this bigot houseroom?', *Daily Mail*, 19 April.
Torode, J. (1996b), 'The madness of letting this racist remain in Britain', *Daily Mail*, 18 June.
Travis, A. (1995), Straw takes on "addicts and winos"', *The Guardian*, 5 September.
Travis, A. (1996), Court undermines benefits ruling', *The Guardian*, 22 February.
Travis, A. and Meikle, J. (1997), Parties squabble over street cred', *The Guardian*, 8 January.
Tunnard, J. (1991), 'Setting the scene for partnership', in Family Rights Group (eds), *The Children Act 1989: Working in Partnership with Families: Reader J*, London: HMSO.
Tunstill, J. (1985), 'Aiming to prevent misunderstanding', *Social Work Today*, 17 May.
Vincent-Jones, P. (1995), 'Squatting and the Recriminalisation of Trespass', in I. Loveland (ed.), *Frontiers of Criminality*, London: Sweet & Maxwell.
Walker, A. (ed.) (1982), *Community Care: The Family, the State and Social Policy*, Oxford: Blackwell/Robertson.
Walker, A. (1989), 'Community Care', in M. McCarthy (ed.), *The New Politics of Welfare*, Basingstoke: Macmillan.
Warner, N. (1992), 'Housing discontent', *Community Care*, 4 June.
Warner, N. (1994), 'Making sure that who cares wins', *The Guardian*, 5 June.
Watchman, P. (1988), 'Heartbreak hotel', *Journal of Social Welfare Law*, 147.
Watchman, P. and Robson, P. (1981), 'The homeless persons' obstacle race', *Journal of Social Welfare Law*, 1 (Pt I), 65 (Pt II).
Watson, S. (1985), 'Definitions of homelessness: a feminist perspective', *Critical Social Policy*, ii, 60.
Watson, S. (1988), *Accommodating Inequality: Gender and Housing*,

Sydney: Allen & Unwin.
Weale, S. (1995), 'Travellers' win "makes Criminal Justice law unworkable"', *The Guardian*, 1 September.
Webb, A. (1991), 'Coordination: a problem in public sector management', *Policy and Politics*, **19**, 229.
Whitfield, M. and Brown, C. (1994), 'Homeless set to lose housing rights', *The Independent*, 21 January.
Williams, D. (1996), 'Record numbers of asylum seekers flood into Britain', *Daily Mail*, 17 January.
Wintour, P. (1994a), 'Homelessness paper due soon', *The Guardian*, 8 January.
Wintour, P. (1994b), 'Portillo lays into yobbos and feckless', *The Guardian*, 23 April.
Wintour, P. and Simmons, M. (1994a), 'Single mothers will lose council housing priority', *The Guardian*, 19 January.
Wintour, P. and Simmons, M. (1994b), 'Families "must sleep rough to be seen as homeless"', *The Guardian*, 21 January.
Wistow, G. (1994), 'Community Care Futures: Inter-agency Relationships - Stability or Continuing Change?', in M. Titterton (ed.), *Caring for People in the Community: The New Welfare*, London: Jessica Kingsley.
Woods, R. (1996), 'Women and Housing', in C. Hallett (ed.), *Women & Social Policy*, Hertfordshire: Harvester Wheatsheaf.
Woodward, R. (1990), 'Mobilising opposition: the campaign against Housing Action Trusts in Tower Hamlets', *Housing Studies*, **6**, 44.
Wynn Davies, P. (1993), 'Lone mothers face council housing bar', *The Independent*, 8 October.
Young, Sir George (1993), 'Speech at LSE housing', London: DoE.

General index

accommodation, definition of 183
'additional preference' 191, 194, 203, 209
administrative reorganization 53, 59-61
advice centres 59, 64
al-Masari, Mohammed 155
alcohol problems 75, 153
appeals against decisions on homelessness 36-7
'appropriate applicants' 22-3, 27, 30-3, 39-41, 44, 50-1, 58, 63, 67, 70, 76, 82, 85, 94, 103, 111, 116, 119, 126, 138
Armstrong, Ernest 32
Ashby, David 187
assessment of applicants 9-10, 13, 43, 47-9, 56-7, 64-6, 203-4, 214
'associated persons' 208
Association of Chief Police Officers in England 102
Association of District Councils 49, 150
Association of Metropolitan Authorities 101
assured shorthold tenancies 93, 200
Asylum and Immigration Act (1996) 154, 190, 197, 215
Asylum and Immigration Appeals Act (1993) 154, 156, 213
asylum seekers 17-9, 142-3, 154-60, 170, 190, 198, 213
Awua case 30, 185

'back to basics' campaign 170, 176-9, 186-7, 209
Banham, John 19
battered women 117, 120, 125; *see also* violence
bed and breakfast accommodation 39, 62-3, 92, 132
begging, 'aggressive' 17-8, 143, 150-3, 160, 170, 215

behavioural problems 92
'benefit tourism' 159-60, 176
Big Issue, the 153
Blair, Tony 151, 153-4
Blom-Cooper, Louis 173
'bottom-up' policies 40
boundaries of council areas 53
Bowers case 34, 158
Brazier, Julian 159, 181
Brightman, Lord 33-4, 183, 185
Brooke J 156
Broxbourne judgment 135
buck-passing 51
Byas case 81, 95

Caithness, Earl of 177
Caravan Sites Act (1968) 148
Caravan Sites and Development Act (1960) 148
care *by* the community 45-6; *see also* community care
care managers 48-9
care orders 76
care packages 64, 66-7, 82, 205
case conferences 56, 66
case law 42; *see also Awua*; *Bowers*; *Broxbourne*; *Byas*; *Dyson*; *Northavon*; *Puhlhofer*; *Smith*
case loads 52-3
Cathy Come Home 21-2, 24
Channon, Paul 27
CHAR (pressure group) 74
child abuse 71, 74, 91-2, 95
Child Care Act (1980) 69-71, 80
children
    provision for 69-94
    rent payments by 206-7
Children Act (1989) 8-11, 31, 37-8, 70-95

passim, 150, 160, 202-7 *passim*, 212-13
Church of England 157
Circular LAC 18/74 26-7, 32, 148
Circular LAC 18/94 150
Clarke, Kenneth 202
Code of Guidance on homelessness 9, 12, 31, 39-40, 49, 76-7, 103, 108, 111, 114, 119-23, 127-8, 134-9, 160, 186, 188-9
collaborative links 14
Collins J 158
Commission for Racial Equality 98
community care 8, 11, 31, 38, 43-68, 202-5, 212-3
 definitions of 45
 HPUs experience of 50
 planning of 53-5
comparative properties approach 13-4
compulsory competitive tendering 5, 182
conflict, structural and organizational 14; *see also* inter-agency tensions
Conservative Party 205
 Central Office 142, 149
 housing policies 3-7, 10, 116, 163
conspiracy theory 12-3, 213
contracting out of council services 5, 182
'contracts' for provision of care 57, 66
council house sales 4-5
councillors, influence of 112, 114-5, 128, 163
Court of Appeal 81, 156-9
covenants against racial harassment 98
Criminal Justice and Public Order Act (1994) 18, 101, 145-50 *passim*
criminal records, applicants with 198
criminology 2-3, 141, 214
Cullingworth Committee report (1969) 25-6
Curry, David 5, 152, 175, 185, 188, 197, 199

Daily Express 177, 182
Daily Mail 145, 150, 153-7, 159-60, 171, 176, 178-80, 199, 209
Daily Telegraph 178, 180, 205
David, Baroness 30, 76
definition of homelessness 7, 29
demonization of certain groups 3
dependency 143
deregulation of private sector 201

deserving and undeserving 1-2, 21-2, 40, 44, 146-7, 211, 213
difficult cases 51, 91-2, 198
disablement 65, 72, 204
discretion of local authorities 195
doctors, registration with 62
domain consensus 13-4
domestic violence 123-4, 137, 190, 203, 208, 212
domestic violence units (DVUs) 125-6, 135
Doyle, Arthur Conan 152
drug problems 51, 75
Dyson case 33-4

Ellenborough, Lord CJ 161
empowerment of users 43, 48-50, 62, 77, 182
entitlement to assistance 205
estate management 106, 108-9, 112, 131, 205
ethnic minorities 104-5; *see also* racial harassment
European Court of Human Rights 160
evictions 24, 98, 101, 109, 214
 of children 199
 of travellers 150
exclusion 2, 17, 213-4

Fabricant, Michael 156
Family Law Reform Act (1996) 190, 208
'fast track' into social housing 166-7, 180; *see also* queue jumping
fecklessness, supposed 142, 160, 164, 170, 176, 214-5
floodgates, opening of 157; *see also* 'gatekeeping'
foreseeability test 24

'gatekeeping' 35, 41, 61, 77, 92, 100, 107, 111, 119, 124, 126, 189, 200
gender inequities 118
ghettoization 116
Griffith, Sir Roy 46
Griffiths Lord 78
groups, labelling of 143
The Guardian 145, 150, 152-3, 159, 177-9, 182, 202
guidance on homelessness legislation *see* Code of Guidance
Gummer, John 177, 182, 202

General index

'gut feelings' of homelessness staff 127, 131
gypsies 148-50

'habitual residence' test 159-60, 197
Hackney 155
Hastings, Somerville 25
Heseltine, Michael 163
High Court 158
hippies 148
HIV 36, 159, 213
Hoffmann LJ 183-5
Home Affairs Committee (House of Commons) 139
Home Office 146-7, 153, 215
home ownership, promotion of 4
Homeless Persons Act 171
homeless persons units (HPUs) 8
homelessness, definition of 168-9, 179, 184, 189, 199
'Homelessness Briefing Pack' 142
hospital discharges 52, 64
House of Lords 215
housebuilding 6
Housing Act (1985) 8, 29-30, 52, 76, 80-2, 85, 94, 102, 119-20, 158, 166, 172, 183-6, 189, 191
Housing Act (1996) 5, 19, 24, 116, 185-209 *passim*, 215
Housing Action Trust 143
housing associations 4-7, 55, 181-2, 200-201
housing benefit 197, 207
Housing Corporation 6, 139, 202
Housing (Homeless Persons) Act (1977) 22, 27, 29, 69, 148, 186, 188, 192, 199
housing register 189, 192, 196, 198, 200, 206-8
Housing for Wales 139
Howard, Michael 151-2, 154, 159, 176, 214
HPUs *see* homeless persons units

ideology of housing policy 13, 23, 187, 213-4; *see also* Conservative Party housing policies
immigrants 143, 154-5, 160, 190; *see also* asylum seekers
Immigration Service Union 159
'in-laws' 28-9
independent living, clients' capability for 57, 63-4, 66, 86, 88, 91, 212

The Independent 150, 177-8, 180
'Independent Living' group 45
ineligibility for housing assistance 197-8
injunctions against domestic violence 128-30, 208
Institute of Housing 171
intentional homelessness 27-30, 33-7, 41, 53, 58, 62, 64, 69, 76-83, 93-5, 101, 114, 117, 121, 137-8, 169, 172, 184-5, 190, 198-9, 207
inter-agency tensions and conflict 43-4, 51-6, 59-60, 82-3, 89
'introductory tenancies' 214
Irving, Charles 32

Jessel, Toby 27
Joint Council for the Welfare of Immigrants 156-7
judicial decision-making 18, 22-3, 33, 80-1, 87, 95, 144, 146, 150, 156-7, 160, 183-5, 215

Labour Party 188
landlords' perceptions of the homeless 201
large families 173, 209
large-scale voluntary transfers 19, 55
'last settled accommodation' 33-4
'law and order' debate 151
'layered protocol' 188, 196
Legal Action Group 98
legal advice services 128
legislation 2-3, 12, 212
  reviews of 163-70, 177-81
  staff knowledge of 52, 83-4, 91
  see also individual statutes
Lester, Anthony 79
Lilley, Peter 69, 154-5, 157, 176, 180
local authorities
  included in present study 15-6
  housing stock, reduction in 5, 142-3
Local Authority Social Services Act (1970) 23
local connection 28-9, 66, 120
Local Government Commission 16, 19, 45, 81
local housing market, state of 29-31, 41, 141
London Research Centre 97
low-cost accommodation, supply of 6, 141-2, 165, 175, 180-1, 186, 213

Mackay, Lord 203, 205
The Mail on Sunday 153
Major, John 151, 153-4, 157, 163, 165, 177, 181-2, 187
management ethos 13
manuals *see* policy manuals
marginalization of certain groups 12-3
married couples, preference for 195
media, the 144-5, 150, 152-60, 164, 171, 174-83, 199, 202, 205, 209
mental assessment panels 58-9, 62-4, 91

methodology of present study 15
Millett J 147
'mixed economy of care' 48, 71-2
Moraes, Claude 157
moral blameworthiness and moral judgments 21-4, 28-35, 41, 50, 75, 77, 141, 188, 211, 214
multi-agency approach *see* partnership between agencies
Murray, Charles 164

National Assistance Act (1948) 21, 23-5, 27, 148, 158, 192-3
National Assistance Board 23
National Housing Federation 210
National Organisation of One Parent Families 176
needs for housing 21, 28, 30, 35, 191, 196, 198
 definition of 76-7
 identification of 48
needs-based approaches 35, 38-40, 67-8, 163, 168-9, 203
negative equity 7, 201
Neill LJ 156
network awareness 13-4
networking 125
'New Age' travellers 148-50, 170
New Right ideology 70-71
Newham 99
news stories, presentation of *see* media
NHS and Community Care Act (1990) 46-52, 65, 205
'no crime' situations *see* unprosecutable cases
Nolan, Lord 80
Northavon case 78-9, 81-2, 85, 87, 89, 95, 203

Our Future Homes (1995 White Paper) 182
owner-occupiers 7, 35, 131, 201

paedophiles 198
Panorama 69, 145, 175-6
partnership
 'benevolent' and 'conspiratorial' models of 12-3
 between agencies 31-2, 74, 99, 108-9, 189, 202, 212
 between local authorities and parents 71, 77
 concept of 2, 8-9, 18
 definition of 9-11, 19
 inherent difficulties with 14
 see also social services departments relations with HPUs
patriarchal attitudes 117
Patten, John 71
penalization of certain groups 17-8, 215-6
points systems 195
police action 109, 113, 122, 125-7, 153
policy manuals 39-40, 90, 111, 129, 136-7
Poor Law 21, 23-5, 154
Popplewell J 158
Portillo, Michael 1
Princess of Wales 153
prioritization *see* rationing
priority need 27, 30, 62, 64, 66, 76-7, 92, 95, 111, 113-4, 121, 123, 137, 172, 184-5, 194, 198, 204-8 *passim*
private renting 7, 48, 106, 131, 142-3, 169, 186-7, 197, 200-201, 212
privatization 5, 10, 48, 192, 200, 208-9
 of council and housing association tenancies 181-2
 of homelessness 169, 187, 192
Prys-Davies, Lord 76
public expenditure on housing 2
Public Order Act (1986) 148
Puhlhofer case 29-30, 33, 120, 183
purchaser-provider relationship 48, 71

quality of accommodation offered 174
queue jumping 18, 25, 27-8, 33, 41, 69, 80, 86, 145, 147, 165-86 *passim*, 187-8, 191-2, 195-6, 209, 214

Race Relations Act (1976) 97
race workers 107, 115

racial discrimination in housing policies 98-9
racial harassment 8, 40, 97-116, 135-6, 203, 207, 212
  definition of 101-2
  extent of 97, 99-100
  legal remedies for 98, 111, 114
  panels to deal with 109-10
  perceptions of 101-2
  statistics of 97, 104-6
rationing 35-7, 48, 74, 167, 172, 175, 211
'reasonable preference' 191-6 *passim*, 203-4, 208-9
reasons for becoming homeless 21, 31, 88, 119, 212
recession, impact of 7, 201
Redwood, John 175
Rees-Davies, Sir William 28-9, 33, 42, 215
refuges, womens' 122-5, 131-4, 208
refusal to accept referrals, HPUs' 85, 87, 205
'registered social landlords' 200-201
rent arrears 198, 207
rent deposits 87-8
rent increases 143
repossessions 7, 201
resource constraints 37-8, 65, 92; see also rationing
'responsibilization' 141
'revolving door' syndrome 36, 53, 86
right to acquire 200
right to buy 4-5, 104, 142, 209
  use of receipts from 214
rooflessness 75
Ross, Stephen 22, 27, 32, 42, 117, 120-21, 184
Rossi, Hugh 27
Runnymede Trust 122
'safety net' provision 143, 166, 168, 182, 192
scapegoating 17
Scott, Nicholas 27
scroungerphobia 142-3, 147
'seamless service' *see* partnership between agencies
Sedley J 150
Seebohm Committee report (1968) 25-6
'selfness' and 'otherness', concepts of 3
Settled Land Act (1925) 206

Shaw, David 177
Shelter 78-9
sheltered accommodation for young people 73
Shepherd, William 24-5
short-term and long-term needs 189, 193-4
Silverman, Julius 27
Simon Brown LJ 156, 158, 160
single mothers 18, 69, 142, 164-82 *passim*, 186, 188, 192-5
single people 51, 65, 113, 137
social exclusion *see* exclusion
Social Market Foundation 181
social need 25-6
Social Security Advisory Committee 161
Social Services Committee (House of Commons) 46
social services departments
  'professional' ethic of 70
  relations with HPUs 8, 44, 49-67, 70, 73-7, 80-84, 88-91, 94, 203-6, 214
  staffs' knowledge of homelessness law 83-4, 91
social workers, role of 32, 48-9
solicitors, local firms of
  involvement in referrals 86-7
  provision of lists of 128
'special needs' housing 46
specialisms of homelessness staff 60, 90, 124
squatters 143, 145-8, 160, 170
statistics of homelessness 7-8, 59
Straw, Jack 151-2, 214
strict settlements 206
The Sun 178
Sunday Times 155, 164
supply of accommodation *see* local housing market

Templeman Lord, 80, 95, 203
temporary accommodation 36, 41-2, 57, 66, 94-5, 173, 184, 193
  for asylum seekers 154
  for victims of harassment 107-14 *passim*
  for women at risk of violence 128, 131-4, 137
Thatcher, Margaret 3, 142-3, 151, 163, 170, 186
thought processes of homelessness officers 17

The Times 153, 155, 157-9, 179-80, 182
Today programme 177
Tower Hamlets 214
training of homelessness staff 52, 93, 95
travellers 17-8, 143-50 *passim*, 160, 170
Trusts of Land and Appointment of Trustees Act (1996) 206

'underclass' theory 41, 164
unhouseable people 36
unitary authorities 16, 19, 44-7, 58-9, 62, 67, 70, 75, 81, 89, 93, 202
unprosecutable cases 138-9

vagrancy 150, 152, 215
value systems and goals 13-4, 167
'victim', definition of 116
victim-centred approaches 101-3, 106, 109-16 *passim*, 129, 133, 207
Victim Support 122
violence towards women 8, 99, 117-39
  degrees of 134
  evidence of 121, 133-5, 138
  legal remedies for 127-9
  policy on 40, 124, 131
  research on 117, 123
  statistics of 126, 137
  threats of 120
  within and outside the home 103, 110, 120-21, 128-30, 135-9, 190, 208
vulnerability 34, 36, 51-2, 62-6, 76, 88, 90, 94, 113, 123, 137, 158, 172, 194, 204

Waite LJ 156
waiting lists 172, 191, 209; *see also* queue jumping
Wandsworth 163, 177
welfare benefits 154-5, 175
Westminster (borough) 164
Winchester 153
'winter lets' 28, 33-4
Womens Aid 122, 124-5, 208
womens fora 123-4

Yeo, Tim 177
Young, Baroness 32
Young, Sir George 139, 166, 170, 172, 176-7, 179-80, 185
young people 35-6, 69-70; *see also* children

Index of authors cited

Arden, A. 186
Arnold, P. 43, 45, 53
   et al 43
Association of Local Authorities 43
Audit Commission 46, 48

Bailey, R. 24, 27, 146
Baldwin, J. et al 37
Ball, J. 43
Barendt, E. see Ogus, A. et al
Barnett, H. 148
Barron, J. 101, 125, 127
Bates, S. 179
Bayley, R. 45
Beale, A. 148
Becker, H. 144
Bell, C. 176, 178
Bentham, M. 182
Bevan, M. et al 7, 201
Binney, V. et al 117, 131
Birch, J. 214-5
Birkinshaw, P. 33
Blagg, H. see Sampson, A. et al
Blom-Cooper, L. et al 44
Bochel, H. see Arnold, P. et al
Bonnerjea, L. 174
Bowcott, O. 152
Bradshaw, D. 179
Brewer, C. 71
Bridges, L. 98
Brindle, D. 160
Brodhurst S. see Arnold, P. et al
Brown, C. 178, 180
Bull, J. 118
Burkeman, S. 40
Burnet, D. 209
Byron, M. 104

Campbell, S. 148-9
Carlen, P. 12, 57, 198
Challis, L. et al 9
Charles, N. 139
Chaudhary, V. 152
Clarke, A. 142, 171
Clarke, J. 71, 74
   et al 1
   see also Hall, S. et al
Clemens, S. see Prescott-Clarke, P. et al
Cochrane, A. 48, 71; see also Clarke, J. et al
Cohen, S. 144-5
Cole, I. 3, 146
Collins, J. 68
Colton, M. et al 74
Commission for Racial Equality 98, 100, 174
Cook, D. 142, 145
Cooper, J. 98-9, 113
Copley, D. 69
Coulter, J. 7, 202
Cowan, D. 33, 36-7, 67, 70, 72, 78-80, 164, 183, 186, 209, 215
Cranston, R. 1, 21, 58, 151
Critcher, C. see Hall, S. et al
Crook, A. 7, 201
   et al 201

Darke, J. 118
de Friend, R. 212
Deans, J. 154, 157, 176
Dear, W. see Hague et al
Denny, C. 7
Dick, D. see Ritchie, J. et al
Dittmar, H. 118
Dobash, R.E. and R. 118, 122, 132, 208
Doran, A. 155, 159, 199, 209
Doughty, S. 157

Doyal, L. 21
Drury, C. *see* Colton, M. *et al*
Dummett, A. 154, 159

Eastham, P. 155, 177
Ermisch, J. 69, 171
Evandrou, M. *et al* 48

Falkingham, J. *see* Evandrou, M. *et al*
Fionda, J. 33, 70, 72, 78-80, 164, 186, 215
Fish, S. 11
Fisher, K. 68
Fitzgerald, M. 101-2
Fletcher, D. 205
Forbes, D. 98
Ford, R. 155, 157
Forrest, R. 5, 37, 69, 104, 118
Fowler, R. 144
Furbey, R. 3, 146

Gallagher, T. 155
Gallivan, T. 186
Garland, D. 2-3, 141
Geary, R. 148-9
Gellner, D. 186
Gibb, F. 158
Gilroy, R. 12, 69
Ginsburg, N. 98, 142
Glaster, L. *see* Smith, R. *et al*
Glastonbury, B. 26
Glennerster, H. 48-9; *see also* Evandrou, M. *et al*
Goff, Lord Robert 207
Golding, P. 142-5, 175
Goodrich, P. 143, 154
Goss, S. 213
Gough, I. 21
Grace, S. 139
Green, H. 171
Greig, G. 177
Greve, J. and S. *et al* 24, 26
Griffith, J. 24, 33
Griffiths, R. 48
Grigsby, J. 178, 180

Hadfield, G. 159
Hague, G. 111, 117-8, 122, 128, 208
  et al 9, 12, 119, 122-3, 125
Hall, S. *et al* 144, 178
Hallet, C. 74

Hally, H. *see* Blom-Cooper, L. *et al*
Hansbro, J. 171
Harkell, G. *see* Binney, V. *et al*
Harrison, J. 6
Harrison, L. *see* Smith, R. *et al*
Harwin, N. 127
Hawes, D. 148-9
Heffer, S. 154
Helm, T. 176
Henderson, C. 153
Henderson, J. 98
Henderson, P. 155
Hennessy, P. 177-8
Hills, J. 5, 142
Hoath, D. 24, 30, 33, 164, 183
Hoggett, P. 98
Hopkins, N. 206
Hoyes, L. 43
  et al 48
Hudson, B. 13-4
Hughes, D. 179
Hughes, J. *see* Crook, A. *et al*
Hunter, C. 42

Jacob, K. 143
James, D. 33
Jeffers, S. 98
Jefferson, T. *see* Hall, S. *et al*
Johnston, L. 152-3
Johnston, P. 178
  et al 176
Jones, G. 207

Kaganas, F. 9, 19
Karn, V. 98, 143
Kay, H. 74
Kelly, R. 179
Kemp, P. 7, 201; *see also* Bevan, M. *et al*; Crook, A. *et al*
Kewley, A. 123
Kirkbride, J. 180

Lait, J. 71
Langan, M. 11, 49, 74
Lart, R. *see* Hoyes, L. *et al*
Laurie, L. 46
Lawton, J. 174
Leach, R. 19, 58
Lewis, J. 48-9, 69
Lidstone, P. 35

Index of authors cited

Lingham, R. *see* Ritchie, J. *et al*
Linton, M. 152
Littlejohn, R. 151
Lloyd, L. 149
London Race and Housing Forum 100
Loughlin, M. 5, 24
Loveland, Ian 10, 17, 21-2, 27, 30, 33, 41-2, 117, 141, 173-4, 183, 186, 215
Lyon, C. 123

McCluskey, J. 74-5
MacEwan, M. 12
McGrath, S. 42
McHardy, A. 19
MacIntyre, D. 177
McRae, S. 118
Maguire, S. 118
Malone, A. 155
Malos, E. 111, 117-8, 122, 128, 208; *see also* Hague *et al*
Manzi, T. 143
Martin, L. *see* Smith, R. *et al*
Means, R. 43-4, 60; *see also* Hoyes, L. *et al*; Smith, R. *et al*
Meikle, J. 151-3, 181-3, 202
Mental Health Task Force 43
Merton Womens Aid Ltd 171
Middleton, S. 142-5, 175
Millar, J. 69
Mind 43, 45
Molnar, J. 13
Morgan, J. 192
Morley, R. 139
Morris, J. 12, 43, 45-6
Mullender, A. 139
Mullins, D. *et al* 19, 143
Murie, A. 5, 37, 69, 104, 118
Murphy, E. *see* Blom-Cooper, L. *et al*
Murray, C. 41, 69, 165
Murray, I. 159, 182

National Federation of Housing Associations (NFHA) 43, 45
Nevin, C. 145
Nicol, A. 154, 159
Niner, P. 117; *see also* Mullins, D. *et al*
Nixon, J. *see* Binney, V. *et al*
Nuttall, N. 202

Ogus, A. *et al* 197

Oldman, C. 43
Oliver, M. 12-3, 45
OShea, C. 149
Otway, O. 74

Page, D. 43, 45, 53; *see* Arnold, P. *et al*; Greve, J. *et al*
Pahl, J. 125
Park, A. *see* Prescott-Clarke, P. *et al*
Partington, Martin 23
Parton, N. 74
Peach, C. 104
Pearson, G. *see* Sampson, A. *et al*
Penal Affairs Consortium 146
Perez, B. 149
Perry, J. 179
Phillips, D. *see* Sarre, P. *et al*
Pollock, F. 146
Poustie, M. 24-5, 31, 34, 41-2
Prescott-Clarke, P. *et al* 173-4
Preston-Shoot, M. 68
Prichard, M. 146
Prynn, J. 180
Pyatt, J. 152
Pycroft, C. 19, 58

Qureshi, T. 98-9, 113

Randolph, B. 6
Raynsford, Nick 192
Rhodes, D. *see* Bevan, M. *et al*
Riseborough, M. *see* Mullins, D. *et al*
Ritchie, J. *et al* 44
Roberts, B. *see* Hall, S. *et al*
Robson, P. 24-5, 31, 34, 41-2
Rogers, D. 13
Ruddock, J. 24
Rutherford, A. 214
Ryle, S. 7

Sampson, A. *et al* 12, 19
Sanders, A. 138-9
Sandland, R. 148-9
Sarre, P. *et al* 98, 109
Schwehr, B. 67
Seebohm, F. 45
Shelter 192
Sherman, J. 151, 155, 176, 179-80
Simmons, M. 19, 177-9
Skellington, R. *see* Sarre, P. *et al*

Smart, C. *see* Clarke, J. *et al*
Smith, D. 45; *see also* Sampson, A. *et al*
Smith, R. 44, 60
  et al 43
Smith, S. 98, 104
Smithers, R. 202
Solomon, R. 74
Spicker, P. 43
Stewart, A. 6
Stewart, G. and J. 32
Stubbs, P. *see* Sampson, A. *et al*

Taylor, M. *see* Hoyes, L. *et al*
Thistlethwaite, P. *see* Smith, R. *et al*
Thomas, P. 148-9
Thornton, R. 12, 70, 117
Tomas, A. 118
Torode, J. 155
Travis, A. 152, 159
Tunnard, J. 19
Tunstill, J. 69
Vincent-Jones, P. 146-8

Walker, A. 45, 48
Warner, N. 45
Wastell, D. 176
Watchman, P. 21, 42
Watson, S. 118, 142
Weale, S. 150
Webb, A. 10, 12
Whitfield, M. 178
Wikeley, N. *see* Baldwin, J. *et al*; Ogus, A.
  et al
Williams, D. 155
Williams, M. *see* Colton, M. *et al*
Wintour, P. 1, 176-8, 181-2
Wistow, G. 45
Woods, R. 12, 118
Woodward, R. 214
Wright, R. 146
Wynn Davies, P. 176

Young, J. 144
Young, R. *see* Baldwin, J. *et al*